THE MISSED SEMINAR
WORLDMAKING AFTER INTERNATIONALISM

DAS VER-SÄUMTE SEMINAR
WELTERSCHAFFUNG NACH EINEM INTERNATIONALISMUS

2

EDITORIAL NOTE

The *Entangled Internationalisms* research edition includes case studies from India and pan-African geographical regions such as Ghana or Mozambique, while providing a documentary record of the anti-colonial voices that crossed, resonated, and left traces in the German Democratic Republic (GDR). Entanglement here implies a weave of different threads or different directions: at the point where two threads cross over and overlap, one strand always covers the other, concealing it from view depending on which side you look at the fabric from. Yet without interweaving, there would be no surface, no support, no ability to create shapes and forms.

Each edition consists of documents drawn from private, nongovernmental, or national archives, commentaries in the form of essays and oral history interviews, and artistic reflections. The starting point in each case is a historical context in one of the entangled geographies that relates to the GDR and looks beyond it. Here, a film, a photograph, a building, a painting, or a document becomes an archive of its own, out of which images and languages become apparent that can be used to talk about the entanglements inherent in the ambiguities they contain.

The aim of the research edition is to compile an incomplete archive that brings together concepts, names, places, materials, and techniques with the help of which we can reflect on a *geopolitics of memory* celebrating global forms of political friendship. These are located in the structures of state socialism, cultural diplomacy, delegation programs, and communist organizations, while at the same time existing as expanded forms of artistic practice, extending all the way to architecture, that eluded state cooptation and the rhetoric of the Cold War or took advantage of other kinds of independence. They can still be found today as undercurrents in collections, archives, and architecture as well as in families, friendships, and out on the street. The afterlife of these internationalisms affects the archives not only of the global East in Europe but also of global geographies—on the African continent or in Southeast Asia—where the manifestations and traces of this modernity persist. What binds them together are forms of knowledge and practice reflecting an equivocal engagement with modernity in the conflictual zone between decolonization and neocolonialism and between emergent states and community in the global fabric post 1945.

Rather than reconstructing specific forms of cooperation in the context of the global Cold War, the research edition looks at the past in terms of how it has mutated into the present. The idea is to make research visible as a transhistorical process: any time archival material is viewed—no matter how much historiographical rigor is applied—it is invariably actualized and de- and recontextualized. This is caused by the interaction of disparate forms of knowledge and different ways of thinking in academic, museological, institutional, artistic, and curatorial settings.

EDITORISCHE NOTIZ

Die Forschungsedition *Verflochtene Internationalismen* umfasst Fallstudien aus Indien und panafrikanischen Regionen wie Ghana oder Mosambik und sie dokumentiert antikoloniale Stimmen, welche in der Deutschen Demokratischen Republik (DDR) hörbar wurden, Widerhall fanden und dabei ihre Spuren hinterließen. Verflechtung meint hierbei ein Gewebe verschiedener Fäden oder Richtungen: An dem Punkt, an dem sich zwei Fäden kreuzen und verknüpfen, verdeckt – je nachdem, von welcher Seite man auf das Gewebe blickt – immer ein Strang den anderen. Jedoch erst die Verflechtung ergibt Fläche, Halt und Formbarkeit.

Jede Edition besteht aus Dokumenten aus privaten, nichtstaatlichen oder nationalen Archiven, Kommentaren in Form von Essays und Oral-History-Interviews sowie in einigen Fällen künstlerischen Reflexionen. Ausgangspunkt ist jeweils ein historischer Kontext in einer der verflochtenen Geografien – mit Blick auf die DDR und über diese hinaus. Ein Film, eine Fotografie, ein Gebäude, ein Gemälde oder ein Dokument werden dabei jeweils selbst zu einem Archiv, aus dem heraus Bilder und Sprachen offenkundig werden, mit denen sich über die Verflechtungen in ihren Ambiguitäten sprechen lässt.

Das Ziel der Forschungsedition ist die Erarbeitung eines unvollständigen Archives, welches Konzepte, Namen, Orte, Materialien und Techniken zusammenbringt, anhand deren wir über eine *Geopolitik des Erinnerns* an weltumspannende Formen politischer Freundschaft nachdenken können. Diese verorten sich einerseits in Strukturen von Staatssozialismus, Kulturdiplomatie, Delegationsprogrammen und kommunistischen Organisationen. Andererseits existieren sie als Praxisformen der erweiterten Künste bis hin zur Architektur, welche sich einer staatlichen Vereinnahmung und den Rhetoriken des Kalten Kriegs entzogen oder andere Formen der Unabhängigkeit in Anspruch nahmen. Bis heute finden sie sich als archivarische Unterströme in Sammlungen, Archiven und Architektur, aber auch in Familien, Freundschaften oder auf der Straße wieder. Das Nachleben dieser Internationalismen betrifft dabei nicht nur die Archive des globalen Ostens in Europa, sondern insbesondere auch jene in Regionen – auf dem afrikanischen Kontinent, in Südostasien –, welche bis heute die Manifestationen und Spuren dieser Moderne tragen. Was sie verbindet, sind Wissens- und Praxisformen einer ambivalenten Moderne im Spannungsfeld von Dekolonisierung und Neokolonialismus, zwischen Staatswerdung und Gemeinschaft im globalen Gefüge nach 1945.

Anstatt einer historischen Rekonstruktion konkreter Formen der Zusammenarbeit im Kontext des globalen Kalten Krieges betrachtet die Forschungsedition das Historische in seinen Mutationen in der Gegenwart. Dabei geht es darum, Forschung als transhistorischen Prozess sichtbar zu machen: Jede Aufrufung archivarischer Materialien bedeutet – bei aller historiografischen Präzision – ihre Aktualisierung und Dekontextualisierung. Sie ist das Resultat des Zusammenwirkens verschiedener Wissens- und Denkformen in akademischen, musealen, institutionellen, künstlerischen und kuratorischen Umgebungen.

Während ein Teil der wissenschaftlichen Befunde im Kontext des Projektes *Decolonizing Socialism. Entangled Internationalism* (2019–2024) erarbeitet wurde, ist die kuratorische sowie künstlerische

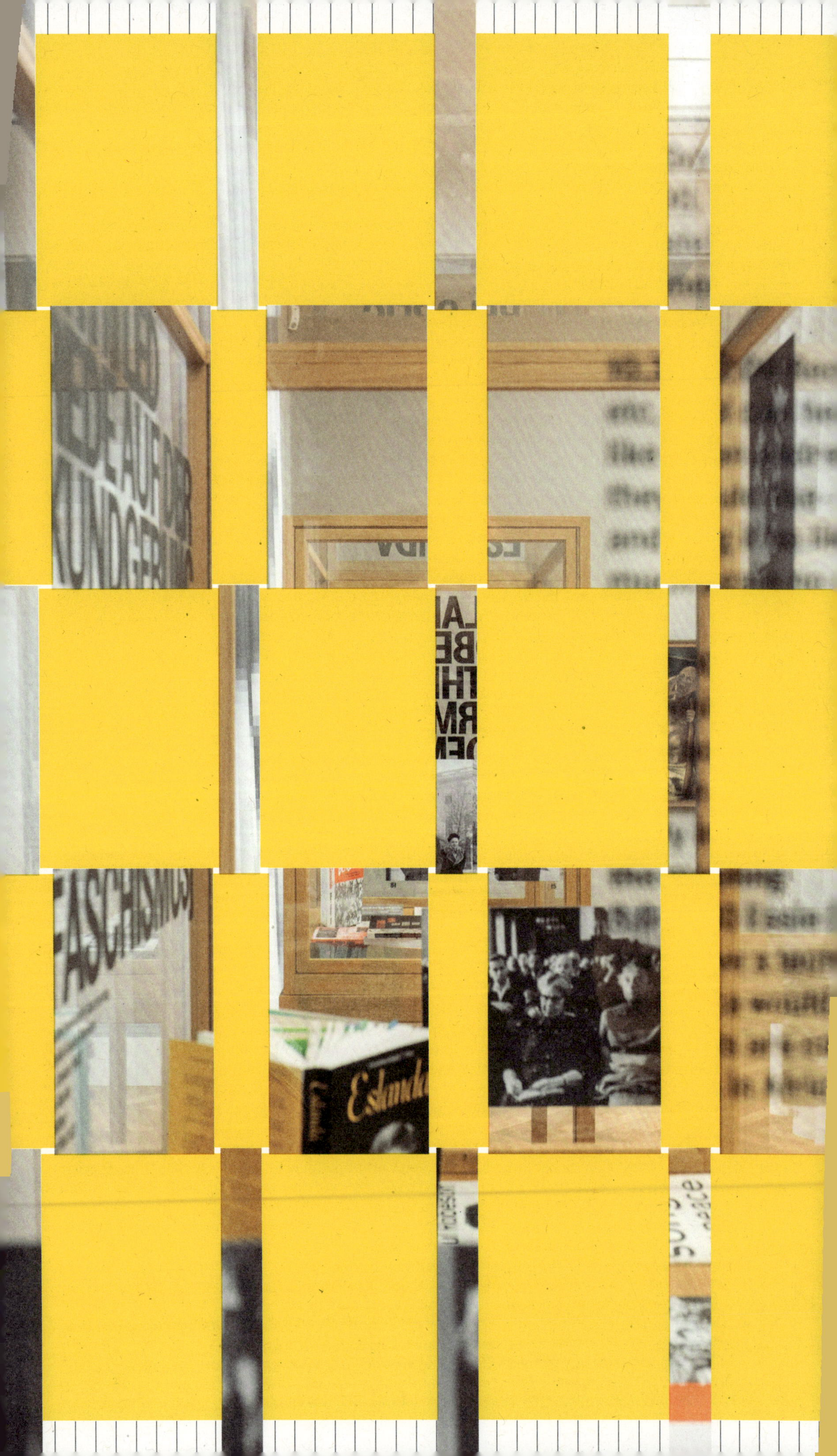

While some of the scholarly findings emerged in the context of the project *Decolonizing Socialism: Entangled Internationalism* (2019–2024), the curatorial and artistic work of processing them has been carried out in partnership with institutions such as Van Abbemuseum Eindhoven (*Deviant Practice*) and Haus der Kulturen der Welt (HKW) in Berlin (*The Whole Life*) and with collectives like blaxTARLINES in Kumasi, Ghana, and the Oralities Research Lab in Jaipur, India.

It was significant that the object-based portion of the research was conducted at the Dresden State Art Collections (Staatliche Kunstsammlungen Dresden, SKD), as this not only fed into the cooperation with the HKW but also helped build correspondences with the exhibition and research project *Revolutionary Romances: Transcultural Art Histories in the GDR*, which ran concurrently at the Albertinum. While *Revolutionary Romances*, with its focus on art history, constitutes a radical reappraisal of a transcultural collection history conducted by the institution itself, *Entangled Internationalisms* engages with the holdings of the SKD, looked at from the perspective of researchers from India, Ghana, Mozambique, and the pan-African movements.

Aufarbeitung in Partnerschaft mit Institutionen wie dem Van Abbemuseum Eindhoven (*Deviant Practice*), dem Haus der Kulturen der Welt (HKW) in Berlin (*The Whole Life*) und mit Kollektiven wie blaxTARLINES in Kumasi (Ghana) oder dem Oralities Research Lab in Jaipur (Indien) entstanden.

Maßgeblich für den objektbasierten Teil der Forschung war die Verortung an den Staatlichen Kunstsammlungen Dresden, die nicht nur die Kooperation mit dem HKW ermöglichte, sondern auch Korrespondenzen mit dem zeitgleich realisierten Ausstellungs- und Forschungsvorhaben *Revolutionary Romances. Transkulturelle Kunstgeschichten in der DDR* im Albertinum. Während *Revolutionary Romances* eine grundlegende kunsthistorische Aufarbeitung einer transkulturellen Sammlungsgeschichte durch die Institution selbst vollzieht, tritt *Verflochtene Internationalismen* aus der Perspektive der Forschenden aus Indien, Ghana, Mosambik und der panafrikanischen Bewegungen in einen Dialog mit den Beständen der Staatlichen Kunstsammlungen Dresden.

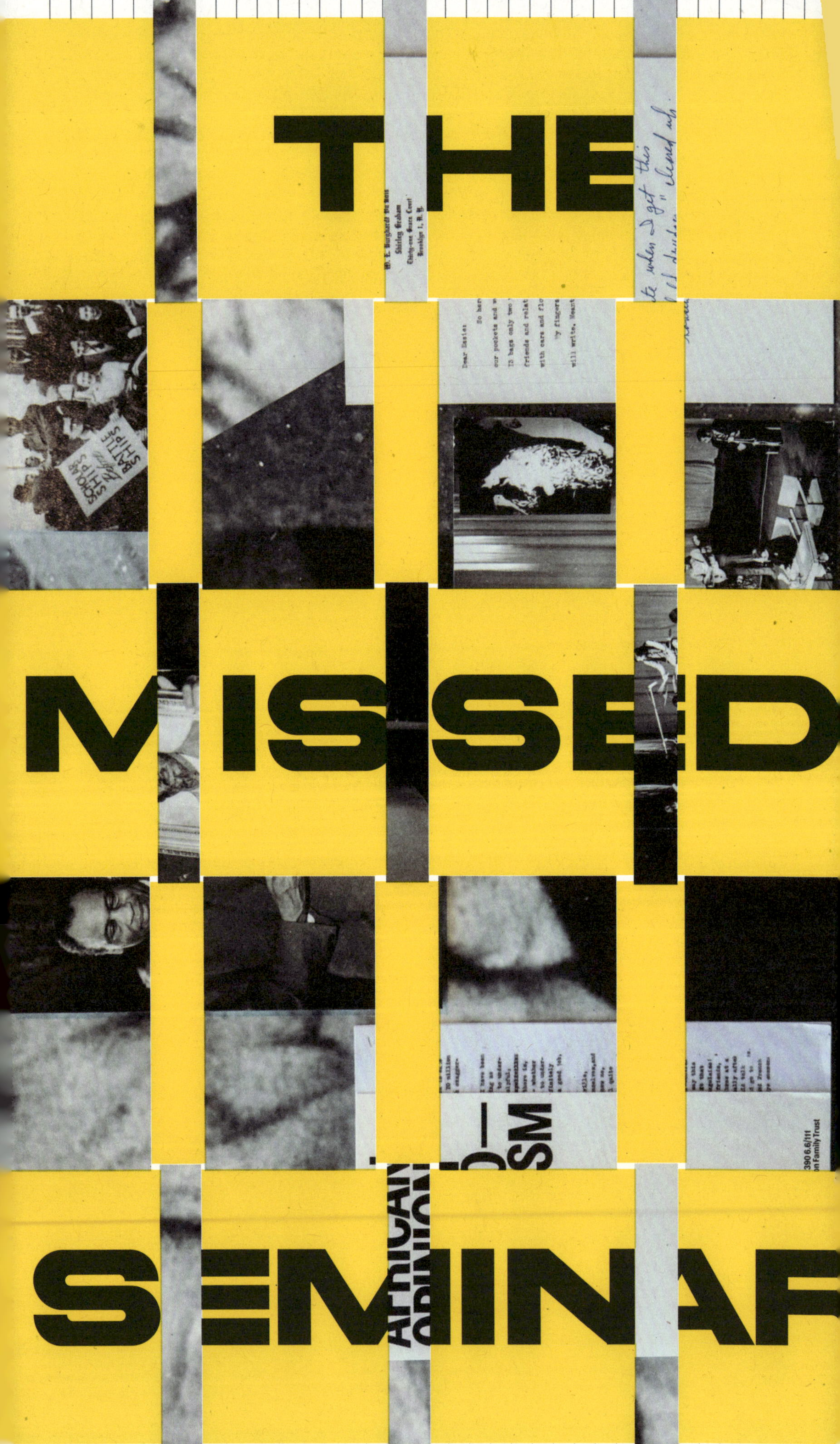
THE
MISSED
SEMINAR

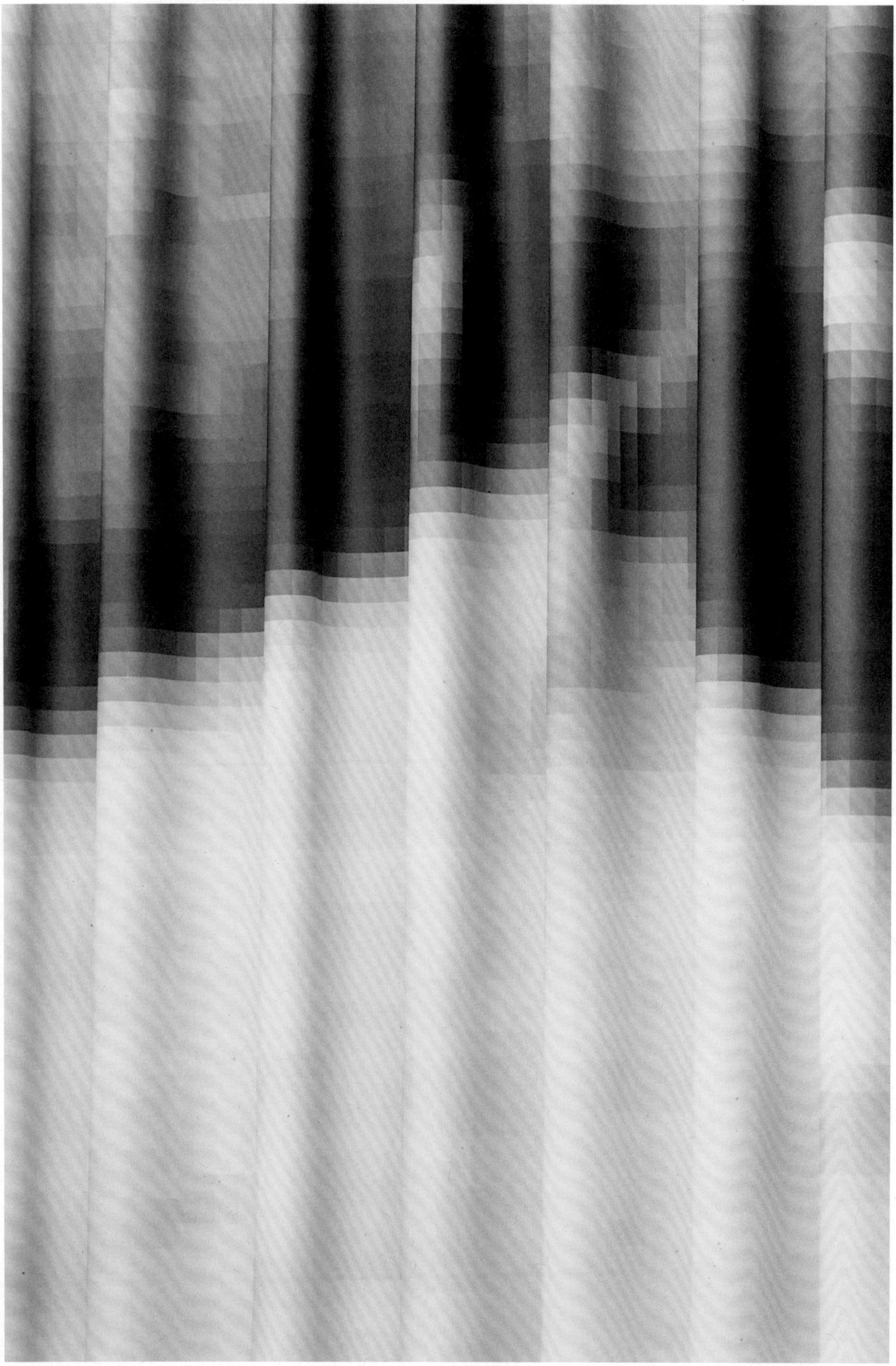

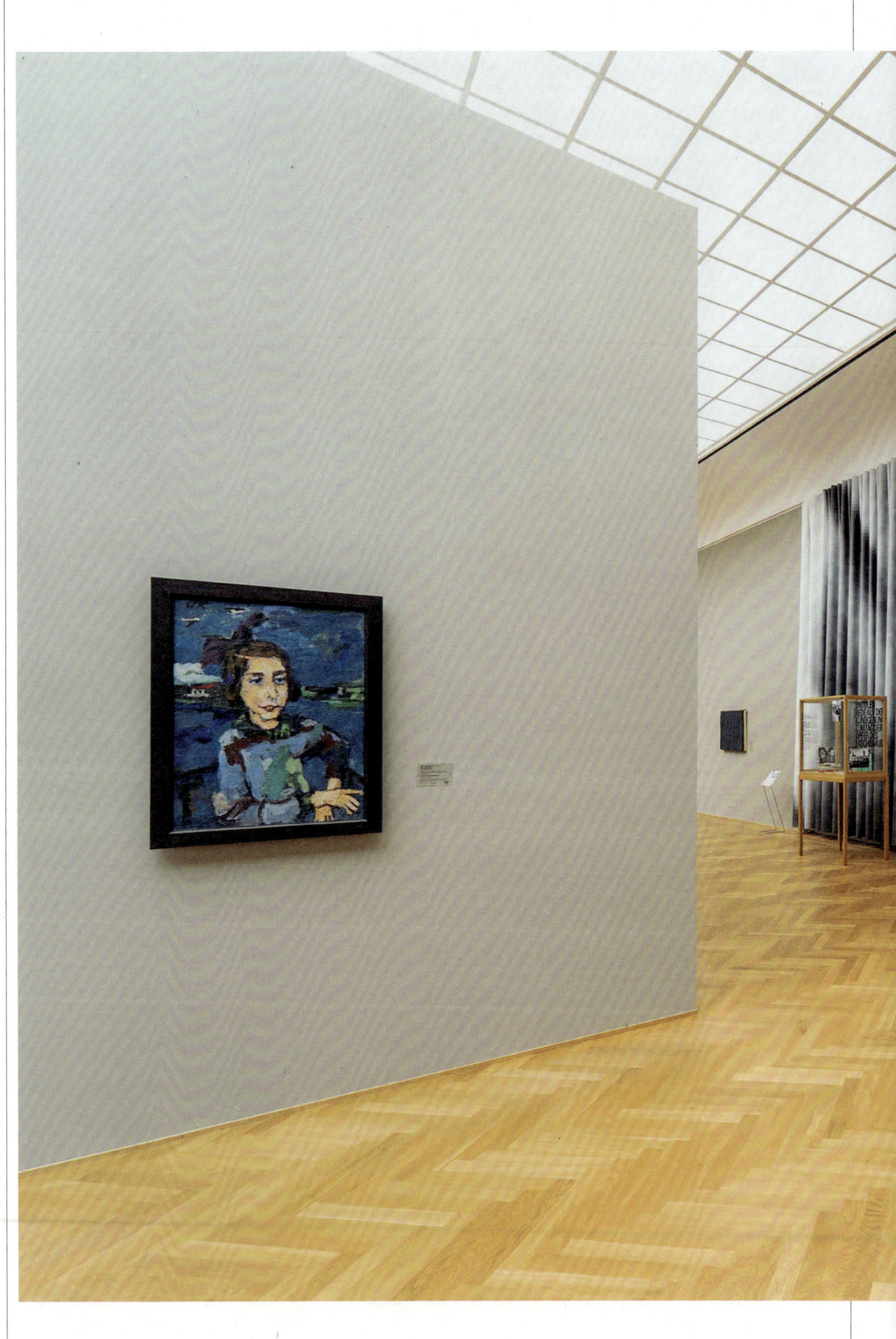

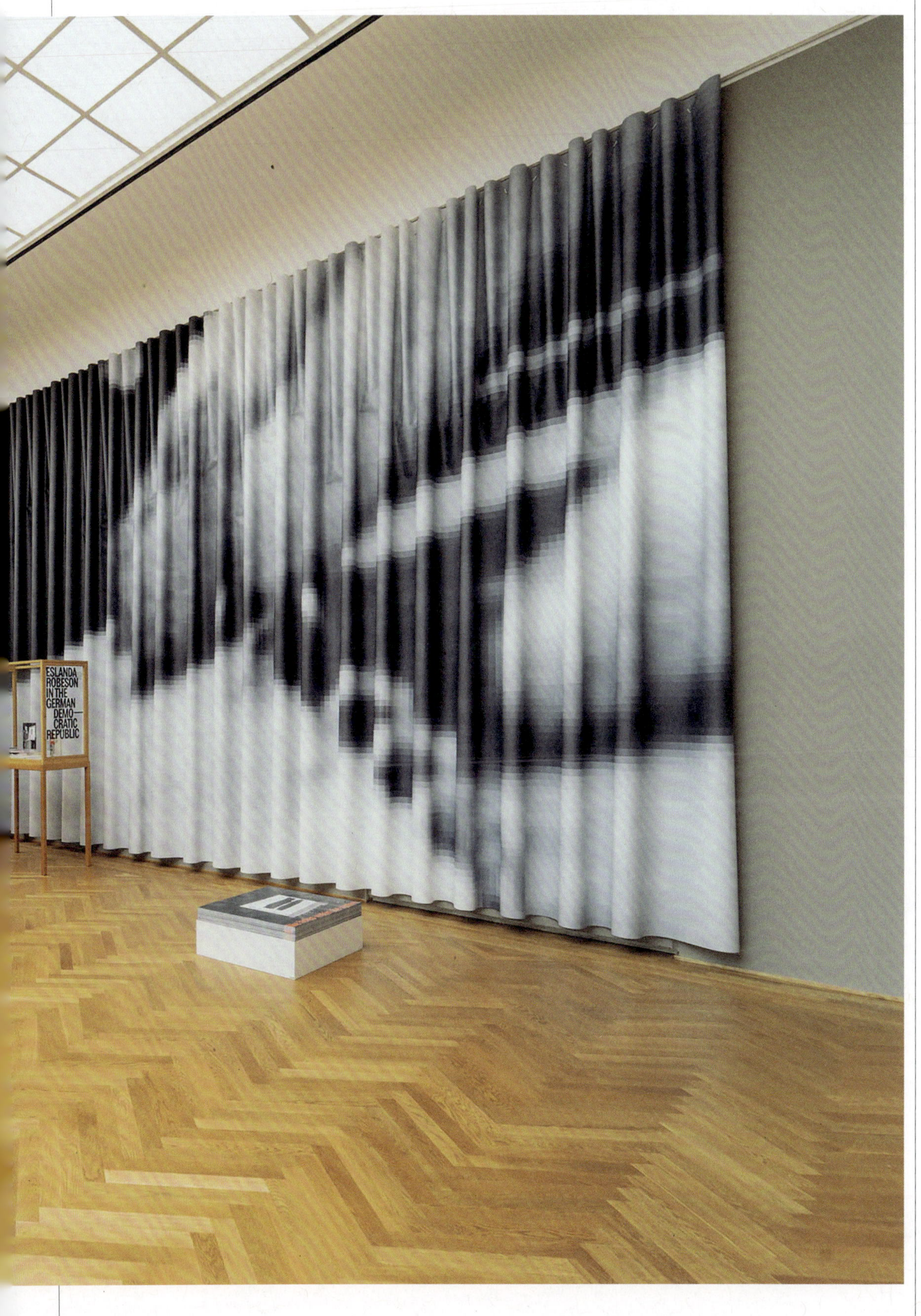

ESLANDA
ROBESON
IN THE
GERMAN
DEMO—
CRATIC
REPUBLIC

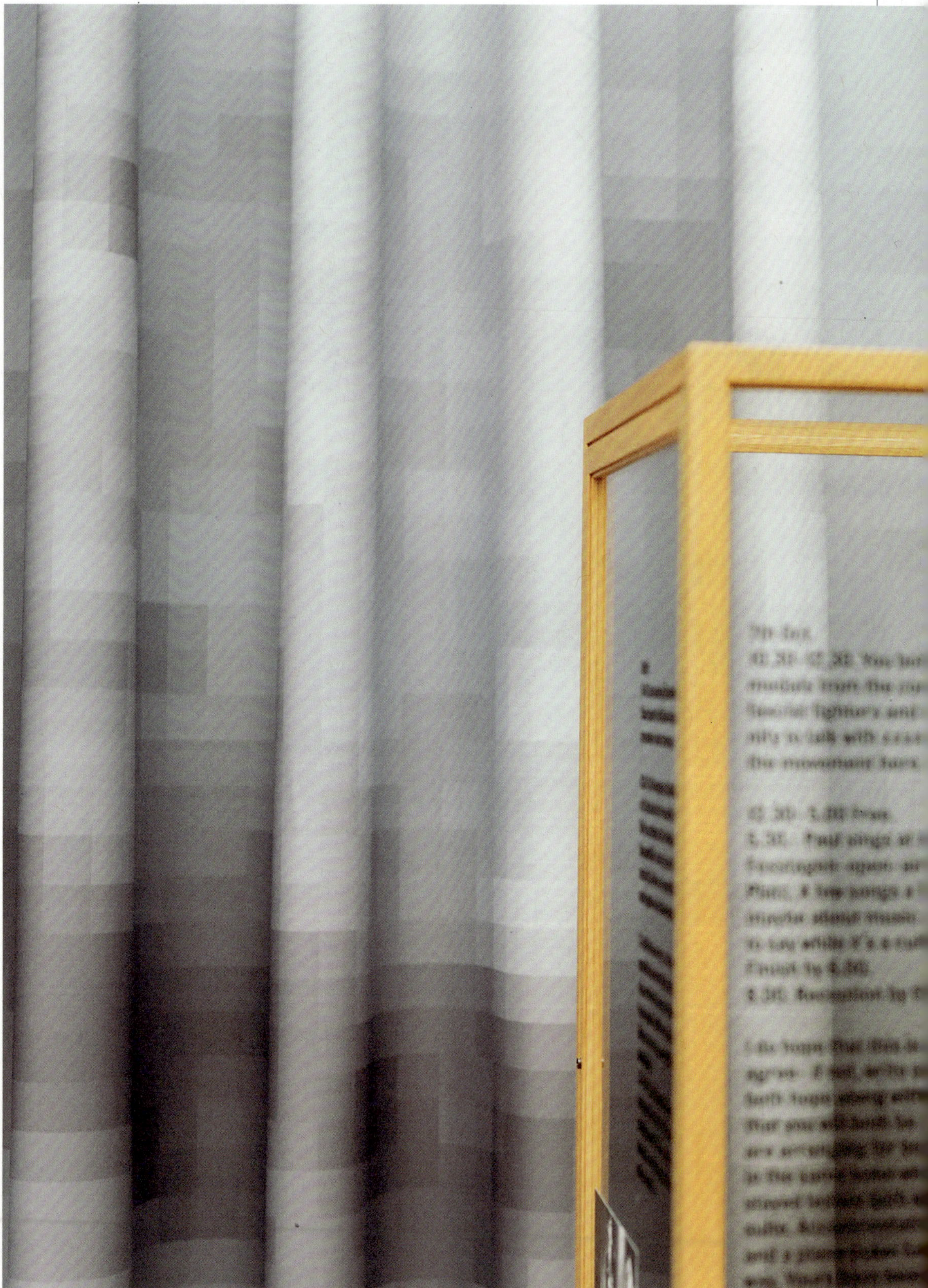

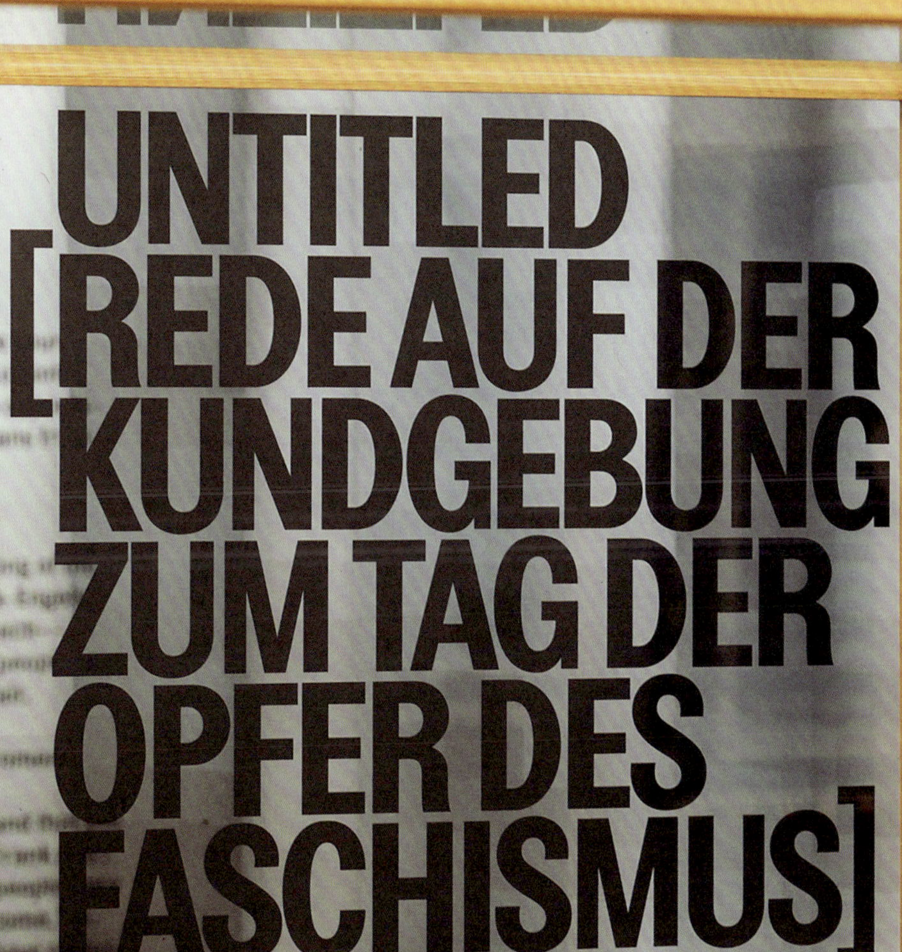
UNTITLED
[REDE AUF DER
KUNDGEBUNG
ZUM TAG DER
OPFER DES
FASCHISMUS]
Maschinenschrift-Durchschlag
Eslanda Goode Robeson
27. Januar 1963
Ost-Berlin
2 Blätter
AdK-RA 343

FOREWORD

Doreen Mende, Avery F. Gordon

VORWORT

The Missed Seminar engages with the presence of the well-known actor and singer Paul Robeson and the anti-colonial feminist, photographer, and anthropologist Eslanda "Essie" Goode Robeson in the GDR in 1963. Both shaped the cultural landscape in East Germany for generations: Eslanda Robeson made the voice of Black feminism audible while Paul Robeson linked the Black civil rights movement with the international labor movement. *The Missed Seminar* makes use of curatorial research and artistic thinking to examine the writings, thoughts, and relationships of the Robesons.

Based on their friendship with German-Jewish Marxist philosopher Franz Loeser and Diana Loeser, the teacher on the GDR television program *English for You*, and on their joint encounters in East Berlin and Leipzig in 1963, *The Missed Seminar* asks: What if their intellectual exchange had formed the framework for a seminar? What can we learn today from the friendship between the Robesons and the Loesers as an expression of solidarity in the struggles against fascism, colonialism, and anti-Semitism?

The Missed Seminar treats this friendship as a dynamic possibility for invoking a *geopolitics of memory*. Invoking this form of memory, in turn, allows us to return to those knowledges—once common, now tacit—that refuse a global racialized capitalism. Conceived of as a reading of transcontinental practices of world making that both reveal and reject the extreme binarisms of the Cold War, *The Missed Seminar* is not a historical construction of the Robesons' legacies in the GDR but a temporally non-linear or chronopolitical metabolization of archival materials: images, manuscripts, documents, and films. These materials speak to the fearlessness, love, and struggle of what Shana L. Redmond calls an "antiphonal life" echoing in the present. In form, then, it is more a study of listening by means of art and research than a documentary. As such, it is an attempt to rehearse methods that interweave Eslanda Robeson's practices of anti-fascism, anti-colonialism, Black feminism, and communism. Photography, film, and media infrastructures operate like methodological interfaces between past and future: they offer a precise portal, like a time machine, accessing a historic moment from the vantage point of today's concerns.

The Missed Seminar befasst sich mit dem Aufenthalt des bekannten Schauspielers und Sängers Paul Robeson und der antikolonialen Feministin, Fotografin und Anthropologin Eslanda „Essie" Goode Robeson in der DDR im Jahr 1963. Beide prägten die kulturelle Landschaft in Ostdeutschland für Generationen: Eslanda Robeson machte die Stimme eines Schwarzen Feminismus hörbar, während Paul Robeson die Schwarze Bürgerrechtsbewegung mit der internationalen Arbeiterbewegung verknüpfte. *The Missed Seminar* bedient sich kuratorischer Forschung und künstlerischem Denken, um die Schriften, das Denken und die Beziehungsnetze der Robesons zu untersuchen.

Unter Rückgriff auf ihre Freundschaft mit dem deutsch-jüdischen marxistischen Philosophen Franz Loeser und der als Lehrerin im DDR-Fernsehprogramm *English For You* auftretenden Diana Loeser und ausgehend von ihren gemeinsamen Begegnungen in Berlin und Leipzig im Jahr 1963 stellt *The Missed Seminar* die Frage: Was, wenn ihr intellektueller Austausch den Rahmen für ein Seminar gebildet hätte? Was können wir heute lernen von der Freundschaft zwischen den Robesons und den Loesers als einem Ausdruck der Solidarität in den Kämpfen gegen Faschismus, Kolonialismus und Antisemitismus?

The Missed Seminar behandelt diese Freundschaft als einen dynamischen Möglichkeitsraum, um eine *Geopolitik der Erinnerung* zu evozieren. Die Aufrufung dieser Form der Erinnerung erlaubt es uns wiederum, zu ihren Erkenntnissen zurückzukehren – einst allgemein bekannt, heute nur noch latent vorhanden – die sich einem globalen rassifizierten Kapitalismus verweigern. Konzipiert als eine Lesart transkontinentaler Praktiken des Welterschaffens [worldmaking], welche die extremen Binaritäten des Kalten Krieges gleichermaßen offenlegen und verwerfen, ist *The Missed Seminar* keine historische Konstruktion des Nachwirkens der Robesons in der DDR, sondern eine zeitlich nicht-lineare bzw. chronopolitische Verstoffwechselung von Archivmaterialien: von Bildern, Manuskripten, Dokumenten und Filmen. Aus ihnen sprechen die Furchtlosigkeit, die Liebe und der Kampf eines „antiphonischen Lebens" (Shana L. Redmond), das in der Gegenwart seinen Widerhall findet. Der Form nach handelt es sich also eher um eine Studie des Zuhörens mit den Mitteln der Kunst und der Forschung und nicht so sehr um eine Dokumentation. Damit ist es ein Versuch, Methoden einzuüben, die Eslanda Robesons Praktiken des Antifaschismus, Antikolonialismus,

The Missed Seminar speculates on a seminar that did not take place, that was missed or of which there is no record, but which students engaged in a globally networked practice of critique, resistance, and imagination in the struggle against fascism, colonialism, and anti-Semitism might have liked to attend. In the form of ongoing conversations, *The Missed Seminar* imagines an intersectional communism by reawakening the geopolitics of memory. This remembering is placed in a present that still suffers from the weight of the aftermath of binary world divisions—including those of colonialism and the global Cold War.

The Missed Seminar is one of the case studies of the larger research project led by Doreen Mende on *Decolonizing Socialism: Entangled Internationalism* (DECOSO, 2019–2024) at HEAD – Genève, part of the University of Applied Sciences and Arts (HES-SO) in Geneva, and funded by the Swiss National Science Foundation (SNFS). The word "decolonizing" in the title invites us, first, to create a condition that will allow the GDR's transcultural network to be de-centered via contemporary collaborations with partners in the project's entangled geographies, including a Black internationalism that has gone through the struggles of popular liberation from colonial rule. Secondly, from a contemporary perspective, decolonizing also musters a vocabulary for de-nationalizing and de-exceptionalizing (GDR) socialism through forms of artistic internationalism without repeating the binarism of categories like "state loyalty" (or "state artist") and "state dissidence" (or "dissident artist"). With this approach, *The Missed Seminar* would like to learn from Eslanda Robeson and her friends how to analyze the continuities of coloniality and fascism in the communist regime and the structures of racism in a "chromatic socialism" (Quinn Slobodian), while also acknowledging the micro-social practices that navigated between protest and protocols in relation to authoritarian regimes. *The Missed Seminar* was further developed in the context of the cooperation project *The Whole Life* (2018–22), which focused on the function and future of the archives of the Haus der Kulturen der Welt (HKW) in Berlin in conjunction with the Dresden State Art Collections (Staatliche Kunstsammlungen Dresden, SKD) as well as the Arsenal – Institute for Film and Video Art e. V. and the Pina Bausch Foundation. The curatorial and

Schwarzen Feminismus und Kommunismus miteinander verflechten. Fotografie, Film und Medieninfrastrukturen operieren wie methodologische Schnittstellen zwischen Vergangenheit und Zukunft: Sie eröffnen ein präzise umrissenes Portal, wie eine Zeitmaschine, das Zugang zu einem historischen Moment verschafft – aus dem Blickwinkel gegenwärtiger Belange.

The Missed Seminar spekuliert also über ein Seminar, das nicht stattgefunden hat, das versäumt wurde, oder von dem keine Aufzeichnungen vorliegen, an dem aber vielleicht gerne Studierende teilgenommen hätten, die sich für eine global vernetzte Praxis von Kritik, Widerstand und Imaginationskraft im Kampf gegen Faschismus, Kolonialismus und Antisemitismus engagieren. In Form von unabgeschlossenen Gesprächen imaginiert *The Missed Seminar* einen intersektionalen Kommunismus, indem die *Geopolitik der Erinnerung* wieder zum Leben erweckt wird. Dieses Erinnern wird in eine Gegenwart gestellt, die immer noch unter dem Gewicht der Nachwirkungen binärer Aufteilungen der Welt leidet – einschließlich jener von Kolonialismus und weltweitem Kalten Krieg.

The Missed Seminar ist eine der Fallstudien des umfassenderen, von Doreen Mende geleiteten Forschungsprojekts *Decolonizing Socialism: Entangled Internationalism* (DECOSO, 2019–2024) am HEAD – Genf, Teil der Universität der angewandten Wissenschaften und Künste (HES-SO) in Genf, gefördert durch den Schweizerischen Nationalfonds (SNFS). Das Wort „decolonizing" im Titel lädt uns erstens dazu ein, die Bedingungen dafür zu schaffen, mittels zeitgenössischer Kollaborationen mit Partnern in den verflochtenen Geografien des Projekts – einschließlich eines Schwarzen Internationalismus, der durch die Kämpfe von Volksbefreiungsbewegungen von kolonialer Herrschaft gegangen ist – eine Dezentrierung des transkulturellen Netzwerks der DDR zu ermöglichen. Zweitens, und aus heutiger Perspektive, stellt der Begriff des „Dekolonisierens" auch ein Vokabular bereit, mit dem der (DDR-)Sozialismus entnationalisiert und seiner vermeintlichen Einzigartigkeit enthoben werden kann. Dazu werden Formen des künstlerischen Internationalismus in Anschlag gebracht, ohne die Binaritäten der Kategorien „Staatstreue" (oder „Staatskünstler") und „Staatsdissident" (oder „dissidenter Künstler") zu wiederholen. Mit diesem Ansatz möchte *The Missed Seminar* von Eslanda Robeson, ihren Freundinnen und Freunden lernen, wie sich die Kontinuitäten von Kolonialität und Faschismus im kommunistischen

artistic realization *of The Missed Seminar* at the HKW and the SKD's Albertinum was designed, in each case, to be context specific.

In presenting *The Missed Seminar: After Eslanda Robeson; In Conversation with Steve McQueen's "End Credits"* at HKW from October 28 to December 30, 2022, the aim was to understand the material substance of the exhibition venue itself as an archive of the global Cold War. The HKW, opened in 1957 as a congress hall, was a gift from the US government to the Federal Republic of Germany and was deliberately placed near the border to East Berlin. It thus contains traces of the violence of a world marked and divided into a liberal-democratic and a communist bloc in which those who subscribed to the communist internationalist or pan-African ideals were persecuted and silenced. The presentation in Berlin was realized in connection with the installation *End Credits* (2012–2022) by filmmaker and artist Steve McQueen. *End Credits* presents a comprehensive portrait of the Robesons, in which it makes the monumental horror of their surveillance audible and visible using digitized FBI files. At the same time, it bears witness to the Robesons' visions, resistance, struggles, and love as a united voice at the site of action, like a manifestation of self-determination against the erected walls of the former Congress Hall. In the context of *The Missed Seminar*, McQueen's *End Credits* was a logical and important extension as a reference for existing artistic reflections on the Robesons' significance, which is explored in greater depth in the conversation with Steve McQueen in this edition. The texts by Avery F. Gordon and Katharina Warda published in this volume were also written for this context, while the conversation between George E. Lewis, Doreen Mende, Matana Roberts, and Kira Thurmann was prepared for the exhibition *Arbeit am Gedächtnis – Transforming Archives* at the Akademie der Künste (AdK) in Berlin in June 2021.

The context-specific nature of the presentation of *The Missed Seminar* at the Albertinum in Dresden from March 30 through November 5, 2023 was the result of the project's resonance with the Dresden State Art Collections. We would particularly like to thank our colleagues from the collaborating collections: Hilke Wagner and Birgit Dalbajewa from the Albertinum, Stephanie Buck and Olaf Simons from the Museum of Prints, Drawings and Photographs

Regime und von Strukturen des Rassismus in einem „chromatischen Sozialismus" (Quinn Slobodian) untersuchen lassen. Zugleich geht es darum, wie mikrosoziale Praktiken gewürdigt werden können, die zwischen Widerständigkeit gegen und Protokolle von einem autoritären Regime navigieren mussten. *The Missed Seminar* wurde weiterentwickelt im Kontext des Kooperationsprojekts *The Whole Life* (2018–22), das der Funktion und Zukunft von Archiven am Haus der Kulturen der Welt (HKW) in Berlin gewidmet war, und in Zusammenarbeit mit den Staatlichen Kunstsammlungen Dresden (SKD) sowie dem Arsenal – Institut für Film und Videokunst e. V., dem Harun Farocki Institut und der Pina-Bausch-Stiftung entstand. Die kuratorische und künstlerische Umsetzung von *The Missed Seminar* am HKW und im Albertinum der SKD war jeweils kontextspezifisch konzipiert.

Die Präsentation von *The Missed Seminar: Nach Eslanda Robeson. Im Dialog mit Steve McQueens „End Credits"* am HKW (28. Oktober bis 30. Dezember 2022) verfolgte das Ziel, die materielle Substanz des Ausstellungsortes selbst als ein Archiv des global geführten Kalten Kriegs zu begreifen. Das Gebäude des HKW, 1957 als Kongresshalle eröffnet, war ein Geschenk der US-Regierung an die Bundesrepublik Deutschland und wurde ganz bewusst in unmittelbarer Nähe der Grenze zu Ost-Berlin errichtet. Somit trägt es in sich die Spuren der Gewalt einer Welt, die in einen liberal-demokratischen und in einen kommunistischen Block geteilt war, und in der diejenigen, die sich kommunistisch-internationalistischen oder panafrikanischen Idealen verschrieben hatten, verfolgt und zum Schweigen gebracht wurden. Die Präsentation in Berlin wurde zusammen mit der Installation *End Credits* (2012–22) des Filmemachers und Künstlers Steve McQueen gezeigt. *End Credits* präsentiert ein umfassendes Porträt der Robesons und macht durch die Verwendung digitalisierter FBI-Akten den unermesslichen Horror ihrer Überwachungsmaßnahmen hör- und sichtbar. Gleichzeitig legt die Arbeit Zeugnis ab von den visionären Vorstellungen der Robesons, von ihrem Widerstand, ihren Kämpfen und ihrer Liebe als einer vereinten Stimme. Und das sozusagen am Ort des Geschehens, gleich einem Akt der Selbstbestimmung, der sich gegen die manifesten Wände der ehemaligen Kongresshalle richtet. Im Kontext von *The Missed Seminar* war McQueens *End Credits* eine logische und wichtige Fortsetzung, ein entscheidendes Beispiel künstlerischer Reflexionen über die Bedeutung der Robesons, was im Gespräch mit Steve McQueen in diesem Band vertieft wird. Ebenso gilt

(Kupferstich-Kabinett) as well as Elisabeth Schmidt and Michael Mäder from the SKD's Research Department. Realized as a "vitrine-intervention," *The Missed Seminar* in the Albertinum's Expressionist Gallery was a commentary on the absence of Black Modernism and the avant-garde of the Harlem Renaissance in the canon of European art and collection history. This iteration of the project speaks directly to the idea of "museums as active sites of democracy" through research, memory work, and art because it recalls the alliances of institutions in the former socialist East such as the art collections in Dresden, the International Leipzig Documentary and Short Film Week (today: International Leipzig Festival for Documentary and Animated Film), the Herder Institute in Leipzig, and the Humboldt University in the GDR with the traditions of the Black civil rights movements. The drawings by the African American artist Charles White, one of which was exhibited in the Albertinum as part of *The Missed Seminar*, were a testimony to these alliances as well, as Kathleen Reinhardt describes in her contribution. *The Missed Seminar* is also given an important contextualization by the contribution of Tiffany N. Florvil, based on her April 2023 Lisa and Heinrich Arnhold Lecture at the SKD in cooperation with the American Academy Berlin.

We would like to express our sincere thanks to Stefan Aue, Lama El-Khatib, and Bernd Scherer (HKW) and Peter Konopatsch, Lina Brion, and Johanna Keller (AdK). Charisse Burden-Stelly, Yulia Gradskova, Charlotte Misselwitz, Barbara Ransby, Zoé Samudzi, and Vanessa E. Thompson made profound and novel research contributions to the public seminar program. We would also like to extend our gratitude to Océane Vé-Réveillac and vinit agarwal (DECOSO), Susanne Grossniklaus (SNFS), Christelle Granite Nobel, Anthony Masure, Lada Umstätter (HEAD Genève), Marion Ackermann, Dirk Burghardt and Cornelia Rabeneck (SKD), and Ana Ramic of the American Academy Berlin. We are also grateful for ongoing conversations with Oluremi Onabanjo of the Museum of Modern Art in New York and Leigh Reiford of the University of California, Berkeley, throughout the research.

Last but not least, we are deeply grateful to Tony Loeser for his trust and support, which have made it possible to reprint parts of his father's story. In this

der Künstlerin Aarti Sunder Aufmerksamkeit, welche der Verstoffwechselung von Archivmaterialien anhand einer Fotografie aus dem Jahr 1963 im Sinne eines historischen Materialismus in Form von Bild, Ton und Poesie nachgeht. Die in diesem Band veröffentlichten Texte von Avery F. Gordon und Katharina Warda wurden ebenfalls in diesem Zusammenhang geschrieben, während das Gespräch zwischen George E. Lewis, Doreen Mende, Matana Roberts und Kira Thurmann im Juni 2021 in Vorbereitung auf die Ausstellung *Arbeit am Gedächtnis – Transforming Archives* an der Akademie der Künste (AdK) in Berlin geführt wurde.

Die kontextspezifische Präsentation von *The Missed Seminar* im Albertinum in Dresden (30. März bis 5. November 2023) war das Ergebnis einer Resonanz des Projekts mit den Staatlichen Kunstsammlungen Dresden. Wir möchten uns insbesondere bei unseren Kolleg·innen von den mit uns kooperierenden Sammlungen bedanken: Hilke Wagner und Birgit Dalbajewa vom Albertinum, Stephanie Buck und Olaf Simons vom Kupferstich-Kabinett wie auch Elisabeth Schmidt und Michael Mäder von der Forschungsabteilung der SKD. Realisiert als eine „Vitrinen-Intervention" in der Expressionisten-Galerie des Albertinums, war *The Missed Seminar* ein Kommentar über die Abwesenheit des Schwarzen Modernismus und der Avantgarde der Harlem Renaissance im Kanon der europäischen Kunst- und Sammlungsgeschichte. Diese Iteration des Projekts befasst sich direkt mit der Idee von „Museen als aktiven Orten der Demokratie" mittels Forschung, Erinnerungsarbeit und Kunst, denn es erinnert an die Allianzen, die Institutionen im ehemals sozialistischen Osten, darunter die Kunstsammlungen in Dresden, die Internationale Leipziger Woche für Dokumentar- und Kurzfilm (heute: Internationales Leipziger Festival für Dokumentar- und Animationsfilm, kurz DOK Leipzig), das Herder-Institut in Leipzig und die Humboldt-Universität, zu Zeiten der DDR mit den Traditionen der Schwarzen Bürgerrechtsbewegung eingegangen sind. Die Zeichnungen des afroamerikanischen Künstlers Charles White, von denen eine als Teil von *The Missed Seminar* im Albertinum ausgestellt wurde, legen ebenfalls Zeugnis ab von diesen Allianzen, wie Kathleen Reinhardt in ihrem Beitrag darlegt. *The Missed Seminar* wird zudem um eine wichtige Kontextualisierung ergänzt durch den Beitrag von Tiffany N. Florvil, der auf ihrer im April 2023 am SKD gehaltenen Lisa and Heinrich Arnhold Lecture in Zusammenarbeit mit der American Academy Berlin beruht.

spirit, we would have liked to have published some of Eslanda Robeson's photographs and unpublished writings, specifically relating to the global East, but permission was not granted. We look forward to the planned publication by the Robeson Family Trust, which will include these items.

We hope that this publication fosters a condition of listening and learning and that it will amplify the voice of Eslanda Robeson as it crosses the east of Germany and invoke her intellectual friendships with thinkers and workers in South Africa, Uganda, Ghana, the United Kingdom, and the United States. It is more urgent than ever that we hear their voices.

We close with a promise and a fact that Robeson made during her speech at the Women's International Democratic Federation (WIDF) congress in Copenhagen in 1953:

"140,000,000 women can't be wrong."

Wir möchten weiteren Personen unseren aufrichtigen Dank aussprechen: Ohne Stefan Aue, Lama El-Khatib und Bernd Scherer (HKW) sowie Peter Konopatsch und Lina Brion (AdK) hätte *The Missed Seminar* in dieser Ausführlichkeit nicht entwickelt werden können. Charisse Burden-Stelly, Yulia Gradskova, Charlotte Misselwitz, Barbara Ransby, Zoé Samudzi und Vanessa E. Thompson haben profunde und neue Forschungsbeiträge zum öffentlichen Seminarprogramm im HKW beigesteuert. Wir möchten uns darüber hinaus bedanken bei Océane Vé-Réveillac und vinit agarwal (DECOSO), Susanne Grossniklaus (SNFS), Christelle Granite Nobel, Anthony Masure und Lada Umstätter (HEAD Genève). Besonderer Dank gilt ebenso Marion Ackermann, Dirk Burghardt und Cornelia Rabeneck (SKD) sowie Ana Ramic von der American Academy Berlin. Wir sind auch dankbar für die über die gesamte Dauer des Forschungsprojekts geführten Gespräche mit Oluremi Onabanjo vom Museum of Modern Art in New York und mit Leigh Reiford von der University of California, Berkeley.

Tony Loeser, dem Sohn von Franz Loeser, sind wir zu großem Dank verpflichtet für sein Vertrauen und seine Unterstützung, durch die es möglich wurde, Teile der Geschichte seines Vaters neu herauszugeben. Im selben Geiste hätten wir gerne einige von Eslanda Robesons Fotografien und unveröffentlichten Schriften publiziert, die sich speziell mit dem globalen Osten befassen, aber die Genehmigung dazu wurde nicht erteilt. Wir freuen uns auf die geplante Publikation des Robeson Family Trust, die diese Beiträge enthalten wird.

Wir hoffen, dass diese Publikation das Zuhören und Lernen befördert, dass sie die Stimme von Eslanda Robeson auf ihrem Weg durch den Osten Deutschlands stärker hervortreten lässt und dass sie ihre intellektuellen Freundschaften mit Denker·innen und Arbeiter·innen in Südafrika, Uganda, Ghana, dem Vereinigten Königreich und den Vereinigten Staaten in Erinnerung ruft. Es ist dringender als je zuvor, ihre Stimmen zu hören.

Wir schließen mit einem Versprechen und einer Tatsache, die Robeson in ihrer Rede auf dem Kongress der Women's International Democratic Federation (WIDF) 1953 in Kopenhagen äußerte:

„140 Millionen Frauen können nicht irren."

A PARTIAL READING LIST FOR A "MISSED SEMINAR" ON ESLANDA ROBESON

Avery F. Gordon

EINE UNVOLLSTÄNDIGE LESELISTE FÜR EIN „MISSED SEMINAR" ZU ESLANDA ROBESON

Eslanda Robeson was in East and West Germany in 1963, and among her various activities she gave a talk at Humboldt University in East Berlin on a panel entitled "The Negro in the United States."[1] Doreen Mende has suggested that there was also a missed seminar in December at the university, led by Eslanda Robeson and Franz Loeser, that "students would have liked to attend."

The missed seminar embodies a certain sensibility or temporality: not only what might have been in the past or what could be in the future but also what was almost or not quite yet or present and at the same time yet to come. The missed seminar takes place in the future conditional or the imperfect past tense, a combination of the past tense and a continuous or repeating aspect, in the realm of what is unfinished. The logic of the missed seminar is expressed well as a question by the Chimurenga Library and Pan African Space Station: "Can a past that the present has not yet caught up with be summoned to haunt the present as an alternative?"[2] I think the answer is yes, if we understand that what lingers from the past are all those aspirations, struggles, and actions—large, small, collective, and individual—for a livable life, a life not ordered by racial capitalism, empire, war, and a police state. These struggles for life are part of the past the present has not yet caught up with. They are present and yet to come. They occupy the utopian margins and constitute an alternative civilization crossing time and place, accumulating a kind of cultural or political surplus that we can engage with and access or possibly present as an alternative.[3]

It turns out that Eslanda Robeson might have been thinking of a missed seminar too, because she left a first-edition copy of James Baldwin's then-new book, *The Fire Next Time*, for the students in Humboldt University's American Studies Department. The inside cover contains a small address label: "Paul Robeson, 45 Connaught Square, London W2." Published by the Dial Press, New York City, on the hundredth anniversary of the Emancipation Proclamation, Baldwin advertised the book with this pithy message: "The country is celebrating one hundred years of freedom one hundred years too soon."[4] There is also a handwritten message in blue ink on the title page, signed with Eslanda Robeson's name: "For the Dept. of American Studies. So your students will know 'what's cooking' in my country with my People."

1. Barbara Ransby, *Eslanda: The Large and Unconventional Life of Mrs. Paul Robeson* (Yale University, 2013), 269–70.

2. See Chimurenga Library and Pan African Space Station, part of *Remembering Silences* curated by Ahmed Al-Nawas (Pan African Space Station, April 13–16, 2022, and Chimurenga Library, April 13 – May 28, 2016), checkpointhelsinki.org/en/works/chimurenga-installation-in-kallio-library, accessed September 10, 2022.

3. Avery F. Gordon, *The Hawthorn Archive: Letters from the Utopian Margins* (Fordham University, 2018).

4. Bill V. Mullen, *James Baldwin: Living in Fire* (Pluto, 2019), 104.

Eslanda Robeson war 1963 sowohl in Ost- als auch Westdeutschland und hielt, neben zahlreichen anderen Aktivitäten, bei einem Panel an der Ost-Berliner Humboldt-Universität einen Vortrag mit dem Titel „The Negro in the United States".[1] Doreen Mende hat den Anstoß zu dem Gedankenspiel gegeben, dass es an der Humboldt-Universität im Dezember desselben Jahres ein Missed Seminar, ein versäumtes Seminar von Eslanda Robeson und Franz Loeser gegeben haben könnte, „an dem Studierende gerne teilgenommen hätten".

Das Missed Seminar ist Ausdruck einer bestimmten Sensibilität oder Zeitlichkeit: nicht nur als etwas, das in der Vergangenheit hätte stattfinden können oder in der Zukunft eintreten könnte, sondern auch als etwas, das fast verwirklicht wurde oder bereits stattgefunden hat und dabei gleichzeitig erst im Entstehen ist. Das Missed Seminar findet unter zukünftigen Bedingungen oder in unvollendeter Vergangenheit statt und verbindet vergangene und widerkehrende Anlässe in einem Modus der Nicht-Abgeschlossenheit. Die Logik des fehlenden Seminars ähnelt folgender Frage der Chimurenga Library und der Pan African Space Station: „Wenn die Gegenwart die Vergangenheit noch nicht eingeholt hat, lässt sich diese heraufbeschwören, um die Gegenwart als Alternative heimzusuchen?"[2] Ich glaube, die Antwort darauf lautet: ja, wenn man in Betracht zieht, was in der Vergangenheit noch alles wartet an großen, kleinen, kollektiven und individuellen Bestrebungen, an Kämpfen und Aktionen für ein lebenswertes Leben. Ein Leben, das nicht dem rassistischen Kapitalismus, Imperialismus, Krieg und Polizeistaat unterworfen ist. Diese Lebenskämpfe gehören einer Vergangenheit an, die die Gegenwart noch nicht eingeholt hat. Sie haben längst stattgefunden und sind gleichzeitig erst im Entstehen. Sie errichten quer durch Zeit und Raum eine alternative Zivilisation an den Rändern der Utopie und akkumulieren eine Art kulturellen oder politischen Mehrwert, auf den wir zugreifen, welchen wir nutzen oder auch als Alternative formulieren können.[3]

Es kann gut sein, dass Eslanda Robeson selbst ein Missed Seminar im Sinn hatte, als sie den Studierenden der Amerikanistik an der Humboldt-Universität eine Erstausgabe von James Baldwins damals neuem Buch *The Fire Next Time* hinterließ. Auf der Innenseite des Umschlags befindet sich ein kleines Adressetikett: „Paul Robeson, 45 Connaught Square, London W2." Bei Dial Press in New York City zum 100. Jahrestag der Emanzipationsproklamation erschienen, bewarb Baldwin das Buch mit der prägnanten Botschaft: „Dieses Land feiert

1. Barbara Ransby, *Eslanda: The Large and Unconventional Life of Mrs. Paul Robeson*, New Haven und London: Yale University Press 2013, S. 269–270.

2. Siehe *Chimurenga Library & Pan African Space Station* im Rahmen des Projekts *Remembering Silences*, kuratiert von Ahmed Al-Nawas (Kallio Library, Helsinki, *Pan African Space Station* 13.–16.4.2016, *Chimurenga Library* 13.4.–28.5.2016), checkpointhelsinki.org/en/works/chimurenga-installation-in-kalliolibrary, letzter Zugriff: 10.9.2022.

3. Avery F. Gordon, *The Hawthorn Archive: Letters from the Utopian Margins*, New York: Fordham University Press 2018.

5. The first Housmans Bookshop was opened in October 1945 on Shaftesbury Avenue in London's theatre district by an elderly Laurence Housman, illustrator, poet, playwright, and founding member of the Men's League for Women's Suffrage and the Peace Pledge Union, with the help of other pacifists. The shop closed after three years, when the rent became too high, and turned into a mail-order bookselling business in Finsbury Park. It reopened

As the Robesons were living in London at the time, I do not know how they acquired a copy of Baldwin's book nor where they bought it (it is likely to have been from Housmans, the radical bookshop in King's Cross) or who brought it to them.[5] Baldwin was a close friend of Paul Robeson and was in London sometime between May and July 1962 to interview him for *Esquire* magazine—and possibly en route for the first time to the African continent, which he visited that July with his sister—but the book was not yet out, with Baldwin finishing its main essay, "Down at the Cross," in late 1962.[6]

This signed copy of *The Fire Next Time* belongs to Melanie Brazzell, a recent PhD graduate from the University of California Santa Barbara who wrote a thesis on transformative justice, around which they are an experienced activist in the US and in Berlin. The book was given to Melanie by a "tattooed, gay Irish poet friend" in 2010 or 2012—they couldn't remember exactly. He got it at a Humboldt

James Baldwin, *The Fire Next Time*, first edition with a dedication by Eslanda Robeson to students at Humboldt Universität Berlin

hundert Jahre Freiheit, aber hundert Jahre zu früh."[4] Auf der Titelseite findet sich, unterzeichnet mit Eslandas Namen, eine handgeschriebene Nachricht in blauer Tinte: „Für das Amerikanistik-Institut. Damit die Studierenden wissen, was in meinem Land und bei meinen Leuten so ‚abgeht'."

Die Robesons lebten damals in London, und ich weiß nicht, wie sie an ein Exemplar von Baldwins Buch kamen, wo sie es hätten kaufen können (vermutlich bei Housmans, einem radikalen Buchladen am King's Cross) oder von wem sie es bekommen haben.[5] Baldwin war zwar eng mit Paul Robeson befreundet und hielt sich irgendwann zwischen Mai und Juli 1962 für ein Interview mit dem *Esquire* in London auf, möglicherweise als Station einer Reise, die ihn im Juli zum ersten Mal, gemeinsam mit seiner Schwester, auf den afrikanischen Kontinent führen sollte. Aber das Buch war zu diesem Zeitpunkt noch nicht erschienen, den langen Essay „Down at the Cross" schloss Baldwin Ende 1962 ab.[6]

Dieses signierte Exemplar von *The Fire Next Time* befindet sich inzwischen im Besitz von Melanie Brazzell. Melanie hat kürzlich an der University of California Santa Barbara eine Dissertation zu transformativer Gerechtigkeit abgeschlossen und verfügt in dem Bereich über viel aktivistische Erfahrung in den USA und Berlin. Das Buch wurde Melanie 2010 oder 2012,

4. Bill V. Mullen, *James Baldwin: Living in Fire*, London: Pluto Press 2019, S. 104.

5. Der erste Housmans Bookshop wurde im Oktober 1945 an der Shaftesbury Avenue im Londoner Theaterviertel eröffnet. Betrieben wurde er von dem bereits älteren Laurence Housman – Illustrator, Dichter, Dramatiker und Gründungsmitglied der Men's League for Women's Suffrage und der Peace Pledge Union – mit der Hilfe weiterer Pazifist·innen. Der Laden schloss nach drei Jahren wegen steigender Miete und wurde zu einer Versandbuchhandlung in Finsbury Park. 1958 folgte

in 1958 at its current location, with the anti-militarists taking the top floors. Perhaps Paul or Eslanda Robeson bought Baldwin's book at Housmans. It would have been known to them and conveniently located close to their home and the places in West London they frequented. New Beacon Books, the first independent Black bookshop in London, serving a related but more Afro-Caribbean radical community, would not open until 1966.

University library fire sale for a couple of euros. As Melanie dryly put it, "The librarians who cleared it out obviously did not notice the inscription at the front of the book." Nor did they seem to appreciate the value of a James Baldwin first edition.

But now we have at least one reading assignment from Eslanda Robeson for the missed seminar, thanks to the librarians who decided, for whatever reason, they no longer wanted the book and delivered it unwittingly into two sets of good hands, one of which passed on the story and the photos of the book to me, as I am now passing them on to you. A dispersal of remnants on the wings of red arrows, as Ernst Bloch might have said.

What was cooking in the US in 1963? A good deal. By 1963, "the fire next time" was already this time as a series of global events converged with a dramatic shift in the long movement for civil rights in the United States. Libya won independence in 1951, Morocco in 1956, and Ghana in 1957; by 1963, with

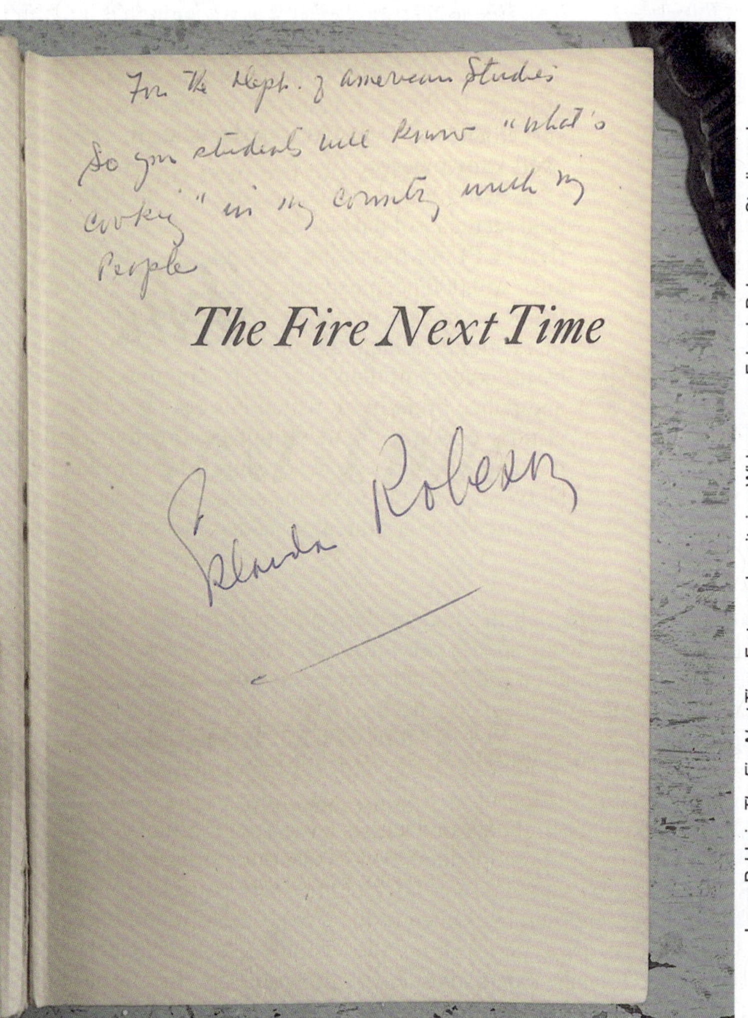

The Fire Next Time

James Baldwin, *The Fire Next Time*, Erstausgabe mit einer Widmung von Eslanda Robeson an Studierende der Humboldt Universität Berlin

das genaue Datum ließ sich nicht eruieren, von einem „tätowierten schwulen irischen Dichterfreund" geschenkt. Dieser wiederum habe es bei einem Verkauf ausgesonderter Bestände der Humboldt-Bibliothek für ein paar Euro erstanden. „Als die Bibliothekar·innen das Buch aussortierten", so Melanie trocken, „haben sie die Widmung im Buch offensichtlich nicht bemerkt." Und den Wert einer Baldwin-Erstausgabe kannten sie, wie es scheint, auch nicht.

Immerhin haben wir nun einen ersten Leseauftrag von Eslanda Robeson für das versäumte Seminar – dank Bibliothekar·innen, die aus unbekannten Gründen entschieden haben, dass das Buch nicht benötigt wird, und es damit unwissentlich in zwei Paar gute Hände gaben. So kamen die Geschichte und die Fotos des Buches zu mir und ich gebe sie an Sie weiter. Wie Ernst Bloch vielleicht gesagt hätte: die Zerstreuung der Überreste auf den Flügeln roter Pfeile.

Was also ging im Jahr 1963 ab in den USA? So einiges. 1963 war das Feuer nach der Flut längst am Lodern, als eine Reihe globaler Ereignisse mit einer dramatischen Wendung in der langen Geschichte der US-amerikanischen Bürgerrechtsbewegung zusammenfiel. Libyen gewann 1951, Marokko 1956, Ghana 1957 seine Unabhängigkeit. Bis 1963 hatte der größte Teil Afrikas, mit Ausnahme der portugiesischen Kolonien und einiger Nachzügler, seine Unabhängigkeit

die Wiedereröffnung am jetzigen Standort, wobei die Antimilitarist·innen die obersten Stockwerke übernahmen. Vielleicht haben Paul oder Eslanda Robeson Baldwins Buch dort gekauft. Housmans wird ihnen bekannt gewesen sein, das Geschäft lag ganz in der Nähe von ihrem Zuhause und von Orten in West-London, die sie häufig besuchten. New Beacon Books, der erste unabhängige Schwarze Buchladen Londons, der eine ähnliche radikale, aber eher afro-karibische Gemeinschaft versorgte, wurde erst 1966 eröffnet.

6. Mullen, *James Baldwin*, S. 99.

6. Mullen, *James Baldwin*, 99.

7. Mullen, *James Baldwin*, 102-3.

8. Cedric Robinson, *Black Movements in America* (Routledge, 1997), 148. His phrase is: "a national spectacle for equality."

9. On abolitionist time, see Martin Luther King, Jr., "Letter from a Birmingham Jail," in *I Have a Dream: Writings and Speeches That Changed the World*, ed. James Melvin Washington (HarperSanFrancisco, 1992), 83–106; see also, Gordon, *The Hawthorn Archive*.

the exception of the Portuguese colonies and a few stragglers, most of Africa had realized independence and now faced a neocolonial order, in which the US became a more prominent player than the British and the French. In 1959, the Cuban Revolution was successful, provoking a boycott of the country by the US and a counterinsurgency campaign that has not yet ended, and also preparing a home for Black Liberation Army fugitive Assata Shakur some twenty years later. By 1960, the year the Student Nonviolent Coordinating Committee (SNCC) was founded, the Nation of Islam's (NOI) membership was 100,000 and growing, thanks to the influence of Malcolm X.

The differences and the tensions between the mass grassroots organizing of the SNCC and the separatist nationalism of the NOI, which Baldwin rejected, was precisely the subject of the long essay in *The Fire Next Time*, "Down at the Cross," in which Baldwin articulated his vision of an "independent African American freedom struggle." It was a vision that led him to align with the SNCC and the Black Panther parties, to take with them—after the war in 1967—a position against Israeli settler colonialism, and to openly assume a radical Black queer position, leading J. Edgar Hoover, the head of the FBI, to justify his long-standing surveillance of Baldwin, at least since the 1940s, on the grounds that he was a "well-known pervert."[7]

On June 12, 1963, one of Baldwin's old friends, Medgar Evans, the skilled field secretary of the National Association for the Advancement of Colored People (NAACP) in Mississippi, was murdered by the Ku Klux Klan. At the end of August, 250,000 people participated in the March on Washington,[8] where Martin Luther King Jr. gave his famous "I Have a Dream" speech. This speech, whose dream of a nation in which his children will "not be judged by the color of their skin but by the content of their character," continues to be shorn of the analysis of poverty and police brutality in which King set it, and shorn of his insistence, rooted in a critique of White "moderation" he forged in a jail cell in Birmingham, that Black freedom would not be held to any other timetable than its own abolitionist time of NOW and would rest on the solidaristic principle of intersectionality that an injustice anywhere is a threat to justice everywhere.[9] Two weeks after the big march on

verwirklicht und fand sich in einer neokolonialen Ordnung wieder, in der die USA eine zentralere Rolle spielten als Großbritannien oder Frankreich. 1959 war die kubanische Revolution erfolgreich, was einen Boykott des Landes durch die USA nach sich zog, außerdem eine nach wie vor laufende Kampagne zur Niederschlagung der Revolution. Gut 20 Jahre später nahm Kuba die flüchtige Assata Shakur von der Black Liberation Army auf. Im Jahr 1960, als das Student Nonviolent Coordinating Committee (SNCC) gegründet wurde, hatte die Nation of Islam (NOI) 100.000 Mitglieder und wuchs unter dem Einfluss von Malcom X.

Die Differenzen und Spannungen zwischen der breiten Basisorganisation des SNCC und dem von Baldwin abgelehnten separatistischen Nationalismus der NOI beschäftigten ihn in „Down at the Cross", dem zentralen Essay in *The Fire Next Time*. Baldwin führte darin seine Vision von einem „unabhängigen afroamerikanischen Freiheitskampf" aus, eine Vision, mit der er sich auf die Seite des SNCC und der Black Panther Party stellte. Nach dem Krieg 1967 lehnte er wie sie den israelischen Siedlerkolonialismus ab und nahm eine offen radikale, Schwarze queere Position ein. Das war Anlass für den FBI-Direktor J. Edgar Hoover, die langjährige, mindestens seit den 1940er Jahren laufende Überwachung Baldwins mit dem Argument zu rechtfertigen, dieser sei ein „allgemein bekannter Perverser".[7]

Am 12. Juni 1963 wurde Medgar Evers, der erfahrene Generalsekretär der National Association for the Advancement of Colored People (NAACP) in Mississippi, ein alter Freund Baldwins, vom Ku-Klux-Klan ermordet. Ende August traten 250.000 Menschen den spektakulären[8] Marsch auf Washington D. C. an, wo Martin Luther King Jr. seine berühmte „I have a dream"-Rede hielt, die Rede vom Traum von einer Nation, in der seine Kinder „nicht nach ihrer Hautfarbe, sondern nach ihrem Charakter beurteilt werden". Nach wie vor wird diese Rede Kings um ihre Anmerkungen zu Armut und Polizeigewalt beschnitten. Übergangen wird auch sein Beharren darauf, dass die Schwarze Freiheit keinem anderen Zeitplan folgt als ihrer eigenen abolitionistischen Zeit des JETZT – das war Teil seiner in einer Birminghamer Gefängniszelle formulierten Kritik einer weißen „Moderation" –, sowie die Überzeugung, dass sie auf dem solidarischen Prinzip der Intersektionalität basiert, also jede einzelne Ungerechtigkeit die Gerechtigkeit im Allgemeinen bedroht.[9] Zwei Wochen nach dem Marsch, am 15. September, wurden in Birmingham bei einem Bombenanschlag auf die Baptist Church in der 16. Straße vier Mädchen

7. Ebd., S. 102-103.

8. Cedric Robinson, *Black Movements in America*, New York und London: Routledge 1997, S. 148. Seine Formulierung lautet: „a national spectacle for equality," ein nationales Spektakel für Gleichberechtigung.

10. Gerald Horne, *Black Revolutionary: William Patterson and the Globalization of the African American Freedom Struggle* (University of Illinois 2013). Patterson was politicized by the accusations of murder against two anarchists, Sacco and Vanzetti, which led him to engage in a career of legal advocacy and to join the Communist Party. He famously helped save the Scottsboro defendants, nine Black youths falsely accused of raping a White woman, and worked as legal counsel later for the Black Panther Party and Angela Y. Davis.

September 15, four girls—Denise McNair, Cynthia Wesley, Carole Robertson, and Addie Mae Collins—were killed when a bomb destroyed the 16th Street Baptist Church in Birmingham, one of the eighteen planted by the Klan in their six-year bombing campaign of Black neighborhoods. By the time Eslanda Robeson was at Humboldt University, even King was describing the situation as a "whirlwind of revolt."

This revolt shifted the class composition and the social base of the main-stream Civil Rights Movement in the United States, shunting the old NAACP with its respectable middle-class ethos from the center of Black struggle to the margins and then taking the struggle well beyond it. The old NAACP was an active accomplice in the post–World War II Red Scare, in which the Robesons, the Trinidadian Communist, journalist, and community leader Claudia Jones, W. E. B. Du Bois, and others were caught up. Eslanda Robeson herself was called to appear before Senator Joseph McCarthy's Senate version of the House Un-American Activities Committee in July of 1953. In 1951, for example, the revolutionary lawyer, Communist, and labor activist William L. Patterson, along with a team of nine others and backed by a host of notable petitioners, including his close friend Paul Robeson, Du Bois, and Mary Church Terrell, had taken their "We Charge Genocide" for historic crimes of government "against the Negro People" to the UN for relief.[10] Rather than support them, the NAACP "bent its efforts to

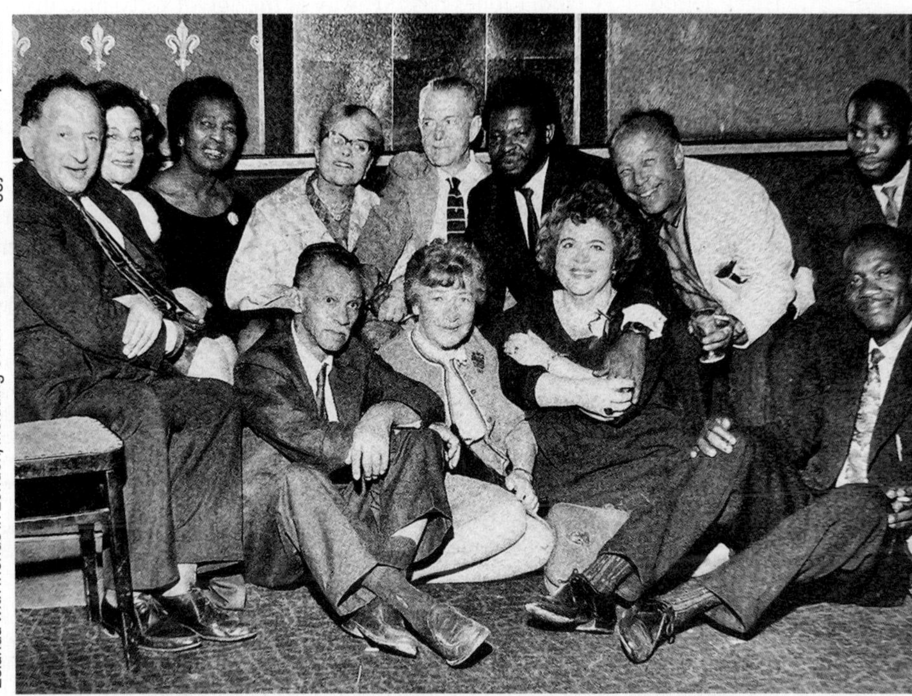

Eslanda with friends in London, including Claudia Jones and Peggy Middleton, ca. 1963

Eslanda mit Freund·innen in London, darunter Claudia Jones und Peggy Middleton, um 1963

getötet – Denise McNair, Cynthia Wesley, Carole Robertson und Addie Mae Collins. 18 solcher Bomben ließ der Klan in einem sechs Jahre andauernden Terror in Schwarzen Nachbarschaften hochgehen. Als Eslanda an der Humboldt-Universität war, bezeichnete selbst King die Situation als „Wirbelsturm einer Revolte".

Diese Revolte führte dazu, dass sich im Mainstream der US-amerikanischen Bürgerrechtsbewegung neue Klassenverhältnisse und eine neue gesellschaftliche Basis zeigten. Sie drängte die alte NAACP und ihr respektables Mittelschichtsethos vom Zentrum an den Rand der Schwarzen Kämpfe, die sich weiter verschärften. Die alte NAACP wurde aktive Komplizin der „Roten Angst" der Nachkriegszeit, die auch die Robesons betraf, die Kommunistin, Journalistin und Community-Aktivistin Claudia Jones aus Trinidad, W. E. B Du Bois und viele andere. Eslanda musste im Juli 1953 vor Senator Joseph McCarthys an den „Ausschuss für unamerikanische Umtriebe" angelehntem Senatsausschuss erscheinen. 1951 richteten sich William L. Patterson – revolutionärer Rechtsanwalt, Kommunist und Aktivist der Arbeiterbewegung – und neun weitere Personen wegen historischer Regierungsverbrechen „an Schwarzen Menschen" mit ihrem „We Charge Genocide" an die Vereinten Nationen. Unter den namhaften Unterzeichner·innen waren auch sein enger Freund Paul Robeson, Du Bois und Mary Church Terrell.[10] Anstatt sie zu unterstützen, „verlagerte" die NAACP „ihre Aktivitäten auf den Aufbau politischer Koalitionen mit liberalen und antikommunistischen Organisationen". Sie ließ Rechtsstreitigkeiten vor US-Bundesgerichten ausfechten, um die internationale Arena der Menschenrechte zu meiden, die diese Kommunist·innen

9. Zur abolitionistischen Zeit siehe Martin Luther King, Jr., „Letter from a Birmingham Jail", in: ders., *I Have a Dream: Writings and Speeches that Changed the World*, hg. von James Melvin Washington, San Francisco: Harper 1992, S. 83–106, und Gordon, *The Hawthorn Archive*.

10. Gerald Horne, *Black Revolutionary: William Patterson and the Globalization of the African American Freedom Struggle*, Champaign: University of Illinois Press 2013. Patterson wurde durch die Mordvorwürfe gegen zwei Anarchisten, Sacco und Vanzetti, politisiert, was zu seiner Laufbahn als Anwalt und zum Beitritt zur Kommunistischen Partei führte. Er half bekanntermaßen dabei, die Angeklagten von

11. William L. Patterson, ed., *We Charge Genocide: The Crime of Government Against the Negro People; A Historic Petition to the United Nations for Relief from a Crime of the United States Government Against the Negro People* (1951; International Publishers, 1970). See Robinson, *Black Movements in America*, 137–38, for the NAACP's response. At the grassroots level, in the American South, the old NAACP was displaced by the brilliant tactics and unstinting efforts of Black women like Ella Baker and Septima Clark and the Highlander Folk School, a socialist anti-racist cooperative, founded in 1932 and still active, which organized unemployed and working people and provided multiracial education and political training. The now-iconic Rosa Parks, for example, was originally trained by Ella Baker in 1944: she also refused to abide by segregated bus rules and became one of Septima Clark's first students when she took over political training there in 1955, a summer marked by the vicious murder and mutilation of Emmet Till

constructing political coalitions with liberal and anti-Communist organizations" and pursuing litigation in the US federal courts, deliberately avoiding the international arena of human rights, which these communists and anti-colonialists sought to radicalize, an arena in which Eslanda Robeson was quite active, having been "an unofficial Council on African Affairs delegate to the founding convention of the United Nations in San Francisco in 1945."[11]

In the articles Eslanda Robeson wrote in 1963 and in 1964, where she is taking the measure of what was "cooking" in the US, such as in "The New Negro Movement," "Long Hot Summer," "Black Revolution and White Backlash," and "The Time is Now," and at a panel hosted by the Committee of Afro-Asian-Caribbean Organizations at Africa Unity House in London the following year (July 1964), she "sided with the increased militancy of the Black freedom movement" and advocated "building up the idea of Resistance and Self-Defense," including "taking the streets in a massive general strike."[12] But she would not live to see it through and find out what came of it. Her generation of Black radicals—and her friends—were dispersed or exiled and were not key participants in this stage of the Black Freedom Struggle in the US. The Robesons returned there in 1963, and Eslanda died in 1965, Paul remaining quite ill and somewhat reclusive until his death in 1976. Several of Eslanda Robeson's close women friends and political comrades died prematurely around the same time, a roster of important Black feminists. Claudia Jones passed away at the age of forty-nine in 1966, and the Tobagonian actress and classically trained singer Pearl Prescod, at the age of forty-six in 1966. The radical Black lesbian playwright Lorraine Hansberry was the youngest, passing away in January 1965 at the age of thirty-four in Harlem, her eulogy given by Paul Robeson. Amy Ashwood Garvey moved between London, Liberia, and Jamaica, unable to settle until she passed away in 1969.

Their absence would be felt.

Eslanda Robeson was part of a remarkable cohort of highly educated elite Black intellectuals and cultural workers raised up in the US and the Caribbean who came of age politically in the 1930s and 1940s. Out of both their intimacy with and their alienation from European and American power, culture, and society,

---

und Antikolonialist·innen gerade zu radikalisieren versuchten. Eslanda Robeson war in dieser Arena ziemlich aktiv, etwa als „inoffizielle Delegierte des Rates für afrikanische Angelegenheiten bei der Gründungsversammlung der Vereinten Nationen in San Francisco im Jahr 1945".[11]

In den Artikeln, in denen Eslanda Robeson 1963 und 1964 beschrieb, was in den USA „abging" – „The New Negro Movement", „Long Hot Summer", „Black Revolution and White Backlash" und „The Time is Now" – sowie auf einem Panel des Committee of Afro-Asian-Caribbean Organizations im Londoner Africa Unity House im Juli 1964 stellte sie sich „auf die Seite der zunehmenden Militanz der Schwarzen Freiheitsbewegung" und einer „Stärkung der Idee des Widerstands und der Selbstverteidigung", sie forderte dazu auf, „auf die Straße zu gehen für einen massiven Generalstreik".[12] Sie hat es selbst nicht mehr erlebt und konnte nicht mehr beobachten, wohin dieser Weg führte. Die radikalen Schwarzen ihrer Generation – ihre Freund·innen – wurden auseinandergetrieben oder gingen ins Exil, sie wurden nicht zu Schlüsselfiguren dieser Phase des Schwarzen Freiheitskampfes in den USA. Paul und Eslanda Robeson kehrten 1963 zurück. Eslanda starb 1965, Paul lebte ziemlich krank und zurückgezogen bis zu seinem Tod im Jahr 1976. Mehrere ihrer engen Freundinnen und politischen Weggefährtinnen, eine Reihe wichtiger Schwarzer Feministinnen, verstarben etwa zur gleichen Zeit frühzeitig. Claudia Jones im Alter von 49 im Jahr 1966, die Schauspielerin und klassische Sängerin Pearl Prescod ebenfalls 1966 im Alter von 46. Die radikale Schwarze lesbische Dramatikerin Lorraine Hansberry starb als Jüngste im Januar 1965 im Alter von 34 Jahren in Harlem. Paul hielt ihre Grabrede. Amy Ashwood Garvey konnte keine Ruhe finden und lebte bis zu ihrem Tod 1969 zwischen London, Liberia und Jamaika.

Ihre Abwesenheit war deutlich zu spüren.

Eslanda Robeson gehörte zu einer bemerkenswerten Gruppe hochgebildeter Schwarzer Intellektueller und Kulturschaffender, die in den USA und der Karibik aufgewachsen waren und in den 1930er und 1940er Jahren politisch erwachsen wurden. Ihre Nähe und gleichzeitige Distanz zu europäischer und US-amerikanischer Macht, Kultur und Gesellschaft ließ sie eine konsequente Schwarze internationalistische Politik entwickeln. Die wesentliche Forderung war eine radikale Neugestaltung der Gesellschaft auf den Grundlagen von

Scottsboro zu entlasten, neun Schwarze Jugendliche, die fälschlicherweise beschuldigt wurden, eine weiße Frau vergewaltigt zu haben, und arbeitete später als Rechtsberater für die Black Panther Party und Angela Y. Davis.

11. William L. Patterson (Hg.), *We Charge Genocide: The Crime of Government Against the Negro People. A Historic Petition to the United Nations for Relief from a Crime of the United States Government Against the Negro People*, New York: International Publishers [1951] 1970. Siehe Robinson, *Black Movements in America*, S. 137–138, zur Antwort der NAACP. An der Basis im Süden der USA wurde die alte NAACP verdrängt durch das brillante Vorgehen und die unermüdlichen Bemühungen Schwarzer Frauen, darunter etwa Ella Baker und Septima Clark, und durch die Arbeit der Highlander Folk School, einer sozialistischen, antirassistischen Kooperative, die 1932 gegründet wurde und immer noch aktiv ist. Als Organisation für Arbeitslose und Werktätige bot sie multiethnische Bildung und politische Trainings an. Die längst zur Ikone gewordene

in August. On Robeson and the UN, see Ransby, *Eslanda*, 4–5, 80, 145–47.

12. Ransby, *Eslanda*, 270–71.

13. Cedric Robinson, *Black Marxism: The Making of the Black Radical Tradition* (1983; University of North Carolina, 2000), 177–78.

they forged an enduring Black internationalist politics grounded in a demand for a radical reconstruction of society based in socialism, anti-colonialism, feminism, and Pan-Africanism. For the Americans especially, their extensive travels—free and forced—enabled them to escape the narrow confines of US culture and to develop a capacious form of internationalism. In the US and the Caribbean, as Cedric Robinson put it, "Black peoples were no longer conveniently lodged in or organized by slave systems"; being enslaved was not the salient experiential or historical category, as people "assumed more diverse and diffuse positions in the changing economic order."[13] In the encounter with African and Caribbean intellectuals, artists, and political activists whose lives were bound up with the reshaping of European colonialism in which they were an agency, the Americans found a larger purpose. That purpose was honed further in their fight against Fascism in Europe (the Robesons went to Spain in the winter of 1937) and in the punishing fight against anti-Communism in the US, one of whose main purposes was to suppress the revolutionary anti-racism that linked racism, capitalism, Fascism, and imperialism. They were able to connect their understanding of racialized and gendered labor exploitation to authoritarianism and the racial state in a way that tied them politically to ordinary Black people in the US and elsewhere, rather than to the narrow interests of their own class strata or to the interests of a reformed nation-state. In 1963, now almost at the end of her life, Eslanda Robeson

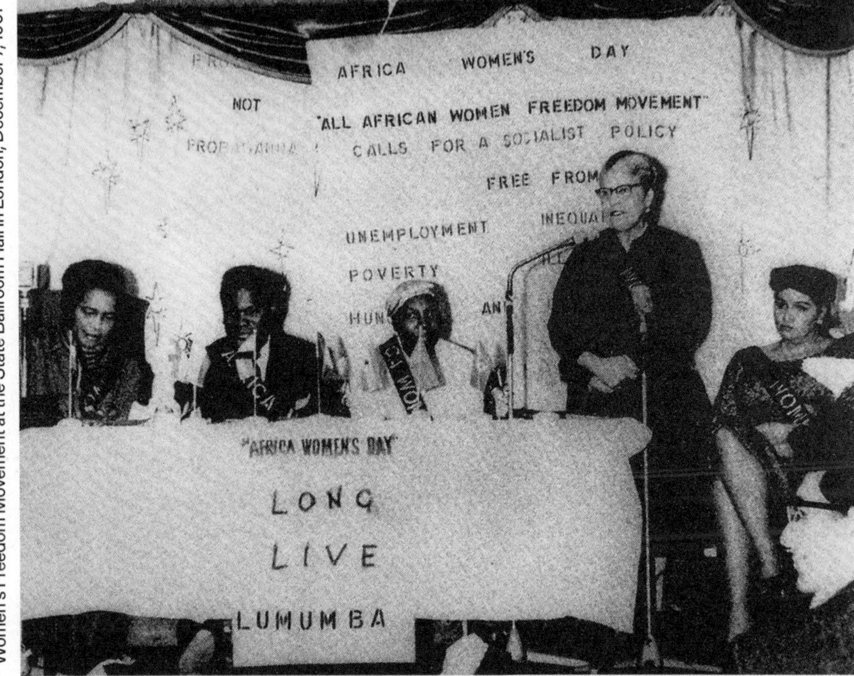

Eslanda Robeson speaking at "Africa Women's Day" as part of the All-African Women's Freedom Movement at the State Ballroom Hall in London, December 7, 1961

Eslanda spricht auf dem „Africa Women's Day" im Rahmen der gesamtafrikanischen Frauenbewegung in der State Ballroom Hall in London, 7. Dezember 1961

Sozialismus, Antikolonialismus, Feminismus und Panafrikanismus. Vor allem die US-Amerikaner·innen unter ihnen entkamen durch ausgedehnte – freiwillige wie erzwungene – Reisen den engen Grenzen der US-amerikanischen Kultur und konnten eine umfassende Form des Internationalismus entwickeln. In den USA und der Karibik waren, mit den Worten Cedric Robinsons, „Schwarze Menschen nicht mehr problemlos in Systemen der Sklaverei untergebracht oder organisiert"; versklavt zu sein war nicht mehr die zentrale Kategorie der Erfahrung und Geschichte, da die Menschen „in der sich verändernden Wirtschaftsordnung unterschiedlichere und vielfältigere Positionen einnahmen".[13] Ein übergreifendes Ziel fanden die US-Amerikaner·innen im Kontakt mit afrikanischen oder karibischen Intellektuellen, Künstler·innen und politischen Aktivist·innen, deren Leben und Wirken im Zeichen der Neuordnung des europäischen Kolonialismus standen. Dieses Ziel verschärfte sich sowohl im Kampf gegen den europäischen Faschismus (Eslanda und Paul Robeson gingen im Winter 1937 nach Spanien) als auch im strapaziösen Widerstand gegen den US-amerikanischen Antikommunismus. Dessen Hauptziel war die Unterdrückung eines revolutionären Antirassismus, der Rassismus, Kapitalismus, Faschismus und Imperialismus in ihren Verbindungen begriff. Sie wendeten ihr Verständnis von rassifizierter und gegenderter Arbeitsausbeutung auf den Autoritarismus des rassistischen Staats an, womit sie politisch den meisten Schwarzen Menschen in den USA und anderswo näherstanden als den eingeschränkten Interessen ihrer eigenen Klasse oder den Vorstellungen von einem reformierten Nationalstaat. 1963, gegen Ende ihres Lebens, rief Eslanda

Rosa Parks etwa wurde 1944, als sie sich bereits weigerte, die Regeln für getrennte Busse einzuhalten, zunächst von Ella Baker ausgebildet und war später eine der ersten Schülerinnen von Septima Clark, als diese im Jahr 1955 das politische Training dort übernahm. Dieser Sommer war von dem brutalen Mord und der Verstümmelung von Emmett Till im August gezeichnet. Zu Robeson und den UN siehe Ransby, *Eslanda*, S. 4–5, 80, 145–147.

12. Ransby, *Eslanda*, S. 270–271.

13. Cedric Robinson, *Black Marxism: The Making of the Black Radical Tradition* (1983), Chapel Hill und London: University of North Carolina Press 2000, S. 177–178.

14. Ransby, *Eslanda*, 272.

called for "Resistance and Self-Defense," a call she made from the heart of Black Unofficial America. In the last speech she gave in Germany, she explained: "Ever since I can remember, from my childhood as an American Negro, I have worked and fought against and resisted fascism in all its forms, including the fight against exploitation and lynching … and I will continue to fight fascism in all its forms."[14] This is a struggle we would do well to remember today as we recover the history of the Robesons.

A missed seminar is always here and yet to come, a past the present hasn't caught up with yet, a work and a struggle to commit to now, if you haven't already.

Robeson zu „Widerstand und Selbstverteidigung" auf, ein Aufruf aus dem Herzen von Black Unofficial America. In ihrer letzten Rede in Deutschland erklärte sie: „Seit ich denken kann, seit meiner Kindheit als amerikanische Schwarze habe ich gegen Faschismus in all seinen Formen gearbeitet, gekämpft und Widerstand geleistet, auch gegen Ausbeutung und Lynchjustiz … Und ich werde auch weiter gegen Faschismus in all seinen Formen kämpfen."[14] Wenn wir heute die Geschichte der Robesons wiederentdecken, tun wir gut daran, diesen Kampf nicht zu vergessen.

Ein Missed Seminar ist immer schon da und dennoch gerade im Entstehen, als eine Vergangenheit, mit der die Gegenwart noch nicht mithält, als Arbeit und als Kampf, für den es sich jetzt einzusetzen gilt, falls Sie das noch nicht tun.

14. Ransby, Eslanda, S. 272.

THE ADVENTURES OF AN EMIGRANT: MEMOIRS (EXCERPT)

Franz Loeser

DAS VERSÄUMTE SEMINAR

DIE ABENTEUER EINES EMIGRANTEN. ERINNERUNGEN (AUSZUG)

The first time Franz Loeser and Eslanda Robeson met was in September 1949. It was a few days after Paul Robeson had been attacked by white supremacists during his concert in Peekskill in upstate New York, while the police looked on. Loeser had originally come to study political science with Forrest O. Wiggins at the University of Minnesota, where he also became an active member of the Communist student movement, which organized Robeson's personal protection during the so-called Peekskill Riots. Loeser, who was slightly injured in the attempted lynching, was one of the students who directly protected him at close quarters. Robeson survived unharmed.

Throughout his life, Loeser, a Jewish Marxist philosopher, endured various forms of persecution. As a child, he fled to Great Britain to escape Nazi Germany, where part of his family was killed in the Buchenwald concentration camp during the Holocaust. Following his emigration to the US, in the late 1940s he was subjected to so much duress by the anti-Communist McCarthy regime that he was eventually compelled to leave the country. After returning to Britain from the US, he went to Manchester and London, where Loeser and his wife, English teacher Diana Loeser, applied for East German citizenship. However, Jewish re-immigration to Communist Germany after the war was not allowed for years and only became possible in 1957.

Shortly before Loeser departed for the GDR, he and his friends Cedric Belfrage and Peggy Middleton organized the first transatlantic "telephone concert" in Manchester, which was broadcast at St. Pancras Town Hall on May 26, 1957, and came to be known by the slogan "Let Paul Robeson Sing." The following excerpt from the 1980 East German version of Loeser's autobiography describes the organization of the telephone concert and shows the connection of technology, geography, sound, and politics with the struggle against "Fascism in all its forms." (A West German version titled *Sag nie, du gehst den letzten Weg: Ein deutsches Leben*, was published in 1986, three years after Loeser had failed to return to the GDR from a US lecture tour because he refused to accept state control of his publishing practices in the *Deutsche Zeitschrift für Philosophie*.)

Franz Loeser und Eslanda Robeson sind sich erstmals im September 1949 begegnet. Nur wenige Tage zuvor war Paul Robeson während seines Konzerts in Peekskill, im Norden des US-Bundesstaates New York, unter den Augen der Polizei von weißen Rassisten angegriffen worden. Ursprünglich war Loeser in die Vereinigten Staaten gekommen, um bei Forrest O. Wiggins an der University of Minnesota Politikwissenschaften zu studieren, wo er auch ein aktives Mitglied der kommunistischen Studentenbewegung wurde, die den Personenschutz von Paul Robeson während der sogenannten Peekskill Riots organisierte. Loeser, der bei dem versuchten Lynchmord leicht verletzt wurde, war einer der Studierenden, die Paul Robeson unmittelbar aus nächster Nähe schützten. Paul Robeson überlebte den Angriff unverletzt.

Im Laufe seines Lebens musste der jüdisch-marxistische Philosoph Franz Loeser verschiedene Formen der Verfolgung erfahren. In seiner Kindheit floh er aus Nazi-Deutschland, wo ein Teil seiner Familie im Konzentrationslager Buchenwald ermordet wurde, nach Großbritannien. Nach seiner Emigration in die USA wurde er Ende der 1940er Jahre während der antikommunistischen McCarthy-Ära so unter Druck gesetzt, dass er das Land verlassen musste. Nach seiner Rückkehr nach Manchester und London beantragte Loeser mit seiner Frau, der Englischlehrerin Diana Loeser, die Einbürgerung in die Deutsche Demokratische Republik. Die jüdische Wiedereinwanderung in das kommunistische Deutschland nach dem Krieg wurde jedoch jahrelang, bis 1957, nicht gewährt.

Kurz vor seiner Ausreise in die DDR organisierte Loeser in Manchester zusammen mit seinen Freund·innen Cedric Belfrage und Peggy Middleton das erste transatlantische „Telefonkonzert", das am 26. Mai 1957 in der St. Pancras Town Hall übertragen wurde und unter dem Slogan „Let Paul Robeson sing" berühmt werden sollte. Der folgende Auszug aus der DDR-Ausgabe von Franz Loesers Autobiografie aus dem Jahr 1980 beschreibt die Organisation des Telefonkonzerts und zeigt die Verbindung von Technik, Geografie, Klang und Politik mit dem Kampf gegen den „Faschismus in all seinen Formen". (Eine westdeutsche Ausgabe des Buchs wurde unter dem Titel *Sag nie, du gehst den letzten Weg. Ein deutsches Leben* 1986 veröffentlicht; drei Jahre nachdem Loeser von einer US-Vortragsreise nicht in die DDR zurückgekehrt war, weil er sich weigerte, die staatliche Kontrolle seiner Publikationspraxis in der *Deutschen Zeitschrift für Philosophie* zu akzeptieren.)

Franz and Diana's engagement could also relate to the reflections of W. E. B. DuBois in "The Negro and the Warsaw Ghetto" (1949), where DuBois writes:

> In the first place, the problem of slavery, emancipation, and caste in the United States was no longer in my mind a separate and unique thing as I had so long conceived it. It was not even solely a matter of color and physical and racial characteristics, which was particularly a hard thing for me to learn, since for a lifetime the color line had been a real and efficient cause of misery. It was not merely a matter of religion. I had seen religions of many kinds—I had sat in the Shinto temples of Japan, in the Baptist churches of Georgia, in the Catholic cathedral of Cologne and in Westminster Abbey. No, the race problem in which I was interested cut across lines of color and physique and belief and status and was a matter of cultural patterns, perverted teaching and human hate and prejudice, which reached all sorts of people and caused endless evil to all men.

The excerpt is included here to suggest that the lifelong friendship between the Robesons and the Loesers was one of various iterations of alliances across race, gender, age, geography, and culture. In this constellation, Fascism, racism, and anti-Semitism appear as intertwined struggles in which the technologies and infrastructures of telecasting are key tools.

Doreen Mende

Franz und Diana Loesers Engagement kann auch mit den Überlegungen von W.E. B. DuBois in *The Negro and the Warsaw Ghetto* (1949) verbunden werden. DuBois schreibt:

> „In erster Linie waren Sklaverei, Emanzipation und Klasse in den Vereinigten Staaten in meinen Augen keine isolierten und singulären Probleme mehr, wie ich sie so lange aufgefasst hatte. Es war nicht einmal mehr nur eine Frage der Hautfarbe und der körperlichen und rassischen Merkmale, was für mich besonders schwer zu begreifen war, denn mein Leben lang war die color line eine reale und wirksame Ursache des Elends gewesen. Es war nicht nur eine Frage der Religion. Ich hatte schon viele Religionen gesehen – ich hatte in den Shinto-Tempeln Japans gesessen, in den Baptistenkirchen Georgias, im katholischen Kölner Dom und in der Westminster Abbey. Nein, das Race-Problem, für das ich mich interessierte, ging über die Grenzen von Hautfarbe, Körperbau, Glaube und Status hinaus und war eine Angelegenheit kultureller Muster, pervertierter Lehren und menschlichen Hasses und Vorurteils, die alle Arten von Menschen erreichten und allen Menschen unendliches Leid zufügten."

Der Auszug wird in diesen Materialabschnitt aufgenommen, um auf die lebenslange Freundschaft zwischen den Robesons und den Loesers hinzuweisen – eine Allianz über Race, Geschlecht, Alter, Geografie und Kultur hinweg. In dieser Konstellation werden die Kämpfe gegen Faschismus, Rassismus und Antisemitismus als verflochtene Kämpfe geführt, bei denen Technologien und Infrastrukturen der Teleübertragung entscheidende Werkzeuge sind.

Doreen Mende

On May 27 [1956], the first conference of the National Robeson Committee was to meet, with a wide variety of local committees planning to form a national organization. Johnny Williamson would come to Manchester from London as a representative of the party leadership. He was someone I could talk to. He would remember me from our time in the United States. We had a similar fate. Like me, Johnny had been expelled to England after his five-year penitentiary sentence as a member of the National Committee of the US Communist Party. Johnny would help me!

The provisional National Paul Robeson Committee was constituted at the conference held in the Millgate Hotel in Manchester. Cedric Belfrage was elected chairman and Frank Loeser, secretary. The position of treasurer went to Barry Lawson. The task of the Provisional National Committee was to prepare a national Paul Robeson Conference on the broadest possible basis by the end of the year.

After the conference, I first talked with Johnny about the tactical line of the National Paul Robeson Committee. Johnny was able to give me valuable advice. Then I got down to my personal business.

"You have no reason to be despondent, Frank. There've been many injustices to comrades in our international movement. But that will be corrected. We'll take care of you and your family. I'll speak with Harry Pollitt as soon as I get to London. You'll hear from me through Syd Abbott, the party secretary here in Manchester."

…

The main burden for the preparation of the Paul Robeson conference lay on my shoulders. It was a matter not only of attracting the most influential and representative delegates possible from all parts of Great Britain but also of mobilizing the support of public world opinion.

…

Gradually, the tide began to turn. Registrations began to come in. At first sporadic and sparse, a mere trickle. But then the letters arriving at 8 Cliff Crescent began to multiply. By the end of November [1956], just before the conference, it had become a glut of letters. All our expectations were far exceeded. Besides the trade unions and political parties, leading artists, and other figures, numerous local Paul Robeson committees that had been newly constituted registered their delegates

Am 27. Mai [1956] sollte die erste Konferenz des Nationalen Robeson-Komitees tagen, auf der die verschiedensten örtlichen Komitees sich zu einer nationalen Organisation zusammenschließen wollten. Johnny Williamson würde als Vertreter der Parteiführung aus London nach Manchester kommen. Mit ihm konnte ich reden. Er würde sich an mich erinnern aus der Zeit in den USA. Wir hatten ein ähnliches Schicksal. Johnny Williamson war nach seiner fünfjährigen Zuchthausstrafe als Mitglied des Nationalkomitees der KP der USA wie ich nach England ausgewiesen worden. Johnny würde mir helfen!

Auf der Konferenz im Millgate-Hotel von Manchester konstituierte sich das provisorische Nationale Paul-Robeson-Komitee. Zum Vorsitzenden wählte man Cederic Belfrage, zum Sekretär Frank Loeser. Die Funktion des Schatzmeisters erhielt Barry Lawson. Der Auftrag an das provisorische Nationale Komitee lautete, bis zum Ende des Jahres eine nationale Paul-Robeson-Konferenz auf breitester Basis vorzubereiten.

Nach der Konferenz sprach ich mit Johnny zunächst über die taktische Linie des Nationalen Paul-Robeson-Komitees. Johnny konnte mir wertvolle Hinweise geben. Dann kann ich auf mein Persönliches zu sprechen.

„Du hast keinen Grund, verzweifelt zu sein, Frank. Es hat in unserer internationalen Bewegung zahlreiche Ungerechtigkeiten gegenüber Genossen gegeben. Aber das wird korrigiert. Um dich und deine Familie werden wir uns kümmern. Ich spreche mit Harry Pollitt, sobald ich in London bin. Du hörst von mir über Syd Abbott, den Sekretär der Partei hier in Manchester.“

[…]

Die Hauptlast für die Vorbereitung der Paul-Robeson-Konferenz lag auf meinen Schultern. Es kam nicht nur darauf an, möglichst einflußreiche und repräsentative Delegierte aus allen Teilen Großbritanniens zu gewinnen, sondern auch die Unterstützung der Weltöffentlichkeit zu mobilisieren.

[…]

Allmählich begann sich das Blatt zu wenden. Anmeldungen gingen ein. Zuerst vereinzelt und spärlich, beinahe zaghaft und schüchtern. Aber dann mehrten sich die Briefe, die in der 8 Cliff Crescent eintrafen. Ende November [1956], kurz vor der Konferenz, war es eine Fülle von Zuschriften geworden. Alle Erwartungen wurden bei weitem übertroffen. Neben den Gewerkschaften und den

for the Manchester conference. The most influential was the London Paul Robeson Committee, which included the well-known journalist Tom Driberg as chairman and prominent members of the Labour Party, with Peggy Middleton as secretary and the driving force behind it. I estimated that the total number of people who showed solidarity with the goals of the National Paul Robeson Committee amounted to several million. In addition, the Committee received greetings from the USSR, the US, Australia, Sweden, Canada, France, Holland, the Polish People's Republic, Czechoslovakia, and the Hungarian People's Republic. India's Prime Minister Nehru wished the conference every success.

I also received numerous messages of solidarity from the GDR: from Herbert Warnke on behalf of the Federal Executive Committee of the Free Federation of German Trade Unions, from Max Zimmering on behalf of the Writers' Association, from the Akademie der Künste, the director of the Hans Otto Theater, and the president of the Kulturbund, to name just a few. The Deputy Minister of Culture, Professor [Hans] Pischner, sent the following telegram: "I most warmly welcome the national conference for Paul Robeson's freedom called for December 2, 1956, by your National Paul Robeson Committee. . . . May your efforts and the worldwide movement, which can also be assured of our support, soon lead to success."

As usual at this time of year in Manchester, December 2 was a damp, cold, foggy day. The weather added a gloomy touch to an already gloomy cityscape. But the delegates did not allow this to affect them. The mood could not have been better.

Will Griffith opened the conference, and Mr. [Roland] Casasola, President of the Foundry Workers Union, gave the introductory address. Then I delivered the committee's report. This was followed by the contributions of the delegates to the discussion—not exceeding three minutes each. Shortly before four o'clock, the leadership of the committee was elected. To rapturous applause, the delegates voted for Will Griffith as president, Arnold Gregory as chairman, Frank Loeser as general secretary, and Barry Lawson as treasurer.

I breathed a sigh of relief. The conference had been a great success. A strong movement for Paul Robeson's civil rights had been created. Now it was a matter of using that strength properly to be able to realize the goals of the committee.

politischen Parteien, führenden Künstlern und anderen Persönlichkeiten meldeten zahlreiche örtliche Paul-Robeson-Komitees, die sich neu konstituiert hatten, ihre Delegierten für die Manchester-Konferenz. Das einflußreichste war das Londoner Paul-Robeson-Komitee mit dem bekannten Publizisten Tom Driberg als Vorsitzenden und prominenten Mitgliedern der Labour Party, mit Peggy Middleton als Sekretärin und treibendem Motor. Ich schätzte, daß die Zahl der Menschen, die sich mit den Zielen des Nationalen Paul-Robeson-Komitees solidarisiert hatten, insgesamt mehrere Millionen betrug. Darüber hinaus erreichten das Komitee Grußbotschaften aus der UdSSR, den USA, aus Australien, Schweden, Kanada, Frankreich, Holland, aus der Volksrepublik Polen, der ČSR und der Ungarischen Volksrepublik. Indiens Premierminister Nehru wünschte der Konferenz einen vollen Erfolg.

Auch aus der DDR erhielt ich zahlreiche Solidaritätssendungen: von Herbert Warnke für den Bundesvorstand des FDGB, von Max Zimmering im Namen des Schriftstellerverbandes, von der Akademie der Künste, dem Intendanten des Hans-Otto-Theaters, dem Präsidenten des Kulturbundes, um nur einige zu nennen. Der Stellvertreter des Ministers für Kultur, Professor Pischner übersandte folgendes Telegramm:

„Ich begrüße die für den 2. Dezember 1956 von Ihrem Nationalen Paul-Robeson-Komitee einberufene nationale Konferenz für die Freiheit Paul Robesons auf das wärmste … Mögen Ihre Bemühungen und die weltweite Bewegung, die auch unserer Unterstützung gewiß sein kann, zum baldigen Erfolg führen."

Wie üblich zu dieser Jahreszeit in Manchester, war der 2. Dezember ein feuchtkalter, nebliger Tag. Das Wetter gab dem ohnehin düsteren Stadtbild einen noch trübseligeren Anstrich. Doch die Delegierten ließen sich dadurch nicht beeindrucken. Die Stimmung hätte nicht besser sein können.

Will Griffith eröffnete die Konferenz, und Mr. Cassasola, der Präsident der Gewerkschaft der Gießereiarbeiter, hielt das einleitende Referat. Dann gab ich den Bericht des Komitees. Es folgten die Diskussionsbeiträge der Delegierten – jeweils nicht länger als drei Minuten. Kurz vor sechzehn Uhr wurde die Leitung des Komitees gewählt. Unter stürmischem Beifall stimmten die Delegierten für Will Griffith als Präsidenten, Arnold Gregory als Vorsitzenden, Frank Loeser als Generalsekretär und Barry Lawson als Schatzmeister.

Gradually I began to recover from the exertions of the conference. Then it came back to me: the threatening letter! I had forgotten about it. Obviously, the Fascists had not dared to disrupt the conference or attack me personally. The stewards, organized by Aubrey, had been watching like hawks, and three or four sturdy trade unionists had always been in my immediate vicinity.

A concert was planned for the evening. I was not sure if it would be as successful. The press had tried to hush it up. The committee had used the last of its funds to have fifty large posters made, but the local authority had had every one of them pasted up in out-of-the-way streets.

A fiasco? Some would have liked to see it that way. I stood in the lobby. People were streaming toward the ticket windows. The crowd was getting bigger. It wasn't long before the ticket windows had to close.

"All sold out!"

People were pushing and shoving in the hope of still being able to grab a ticket. I was pulled into a tangle of people. I felt a strong hand on my back. Now it was squeezing my shoulder tightly, very tightly. The threatening letter flashed through my mind.

"Frank, hello, Frank!"

Somewhere I had heard this voice before. But where? I turned around with difficulty.

"Bob, Bob Hutchinson," I called out. "Gee, boy, it's great to see you again."

"Get your knees brown." Bob laughed and hugged me. "Had to come and support your Paul Robeson event."

It had been over fourteen years since we had met in North Africa and fought in the Battle of Al-Alamein. Bob was still living in his "two up and two down" in the same Manchester slum as then. But he now had a decent job and wasn't earning badly.

I heard him saying, "I belong to the left wing of the Labour Party, and I also read the *Daily Worker*," then I was pushed away by the crowd.

In the hall the concert began. The opening was the showing of the film *The Proud Valley*. Paul Robeson played a miner in the 1930s who shared the hard lot

Ich atmete erleichtert auf. Die Konferenz war ein großer Erfolg. Eine starke Bewegung für die Bürgerrechte Paul Robesons war geschaffen worden. Jetzt ging es darum, diese Kraft richtig einzusetzen, um die Ziele des Komitees realisieren zu können.

Allmählich begann ich mich von den Anstrengungen der Konferenz zu erholen. Da fiel es mir wieder ein. Der Drohbrief! Ich hatte ihn vergessen. Offensichtlich hatten die Faschisten nicht gewagt, die Konferenz zu stören oder mich persönlich anzugreifen. Die Ordner, von Aubrey organisiert, hatten wie Schießhunde aufgepaßt, und drei, vier kräftige Gewerkschafter hatten sich immer unmittelbar in meiner Nähe aufgehalten.

Für den Abend war ein Konzert geplant. Ich war mir nicht sicher, ob es auch so erfolgreich sein würde. Die Presse hatte versucht, das Konzert totzuschweigen. Mit seinen letzten finanziellen Mitteln hatte das Komitee fünfzig große Plakate anfertigen lassen, aber die zuständige städtische Behörde hatte sie ausnahmslos in abgelegenen Straßen aufkleben lassen.

Ein Fiasko? So hätten es einige allzu gern gesehen. Ich stellte mich in das Foyer. Die Menschen strömten auf die Kassen zu. Der Andrang wurde stärker. Es dauerte nicht lange, und die Kassen mußten schließen.

„Alles ausverkauft!"

Die Menschen drängten und schubsten, um vielleicht doch noch eine Karte ergattern zu können. Ich wurde in ein Menschenknäuel hineingezogen. Ich fühlte eine kräftige Hand auf meinem Rücken. Jetzt drückte sie meine Schulter fest, sehr fest. Der Drohbrief, blitzte es durch meinen Kopf.

„Frank, hallo, Frank!"

Irgendwo hatte ich diese Stimme schon einmal gehört. Aber wo? Ich drehte mich mühsam um.

„Bob, Bob Hutchinson", rief ich. „Mann, Junge, ist das toll, dich wiederzusehen."

„Get your knees brown." Bob lachte und umarmte mich.

„Mußte doch unbedingt kommen und deine Paul-Robeson-Veranstaltung unterstützen."

Über vierzehn Jahre waren es her, seit wir uns in Nord-Afrika kennengelernt und die Schlacht von Al-Alamein mitgemacht hatten. Bob lebte immer noch in

of unemployment with his fellow miners and took part in the struggle for better working conditions.

After the film, lights went on in the hall; on the stage was a sixty-strong male miners' choir from South Wales. Among them were the sons of the miners who had appeared with Robeson in the film. Then came the highlight: a greeting from Paul Robeson and the song "Ol' Man River," as only Robeson could sing it.

I jumped up enthusiastically from my seat, singing along with the many others who got to hear Paul Robeson's voice that night: "We shall not be moved, just like a tree that's standing by the water, we shall not be moved."

. . .

Peggy Middleton, Cedric Belfrage and I were sitting in the living room of Peggy's apartment at 19 Kidbrooke Park Road in London. The room was, as in so many English households, incredibly cluttered. I could hardly have found my way around the muddle, but Peggy's clutter had a system. She found everything the three of us were looking for in preparation for the London Paul Robeson conference.

"We must come up with something new this time. The London conference must be the final and decisive battle." My voice sounded forceful and determined.

"But what?" asked Cedric.

Peggy searched frantically for a good idea.

"The tape method was successful, but this time we need a new feature."

"I've got it!" I suddenly cried out. I was so excited about my idea that I jumped up and ran up and down excitedly.

Peggy and Cedric looked at me expectantly.

"I've got it," I shouted again, clapping my hands together, "it's a stunner."

"Come on, don't keep us in suspense," Cedric demanded.

I spoke so fast that Cedric and Peggy could hardly follow.

"You know that a new transatlantic telephone cable has recently been laid between the United States and England. It's said to have excellent sound quality. We are going to ask Paul to sing over the telephone from a studio in New York directly into London's St. Pancras Hall. This will make a fool of the American government in front of the whole world."

seinem „two up and two down" in demselben Elendsviertel von Manchester wie damals. Aber er hatte jetzt eine anständige Arbeit und verdiente nicht schlecht.

„Ich gehöre zum linken Flügel der Labour Party, und den ‚Daily Worker' lese ich auch …", konnte ich noch hören, dann wurde ich von der Menschenmenge weggedrängt.

Im Saal begann das Konzert. Den Auftakt bildete die Vorführung des Films „Das stolze Tal". Paul Robeson spielte einen Bergarbeiter in den dreißiger Jahren, der das schwere Schicksal der Arbeitslosigkeit und den Kampf für bessere Arbeitsbedingungen mit seinen Kumpeln teilte.

Nach dem Film gingen Lichter im Saal an, auf der Bühne stand ein sechzig Mann starker Bergarbeiterchor aus Südwales. Unter ihnen Söhne der Kumpel, die mit Robeson in dem Film aufgetreten waren. Dann der Höhepunkt: eine Grußadresse von Paul Robeson und das Lied „Ol' Man River", wie cs eben nur Robeson singen konnte.

Ich sprang vor Begeisterung vom Sitz auf. Zusammen mit den vielen anderen, die an diesem Abend Paul Robesons Stimme zu hören bekamen, sang ich:

„We shall not be moved, just like a tree that's standing by the water, we shall not not be moved …"

[…]

Peggy Middleton, Cedric Belfrage und ich saßen im Wohnzimmer von Peggys Wohnung in der 19 Kidbrooke Park Road in London. Das Zimmer war, wie in so vielen englischen Haushalten, erstaunlich unordentlich. Ich hätte mich kaum in dem Durcheinander zurechtfinden können, aber Peggys Unordnung besaß System. Sie fand alles, was wir drei suchten, um die Londoner Paul-Robeson-Konferenz vorzubereiten.

„Wir müssen uns dieses Mal etwas Neues ausdenken. Die Londoner Konferenz muß die letzte und entscheidende Schlacht sein." Meine Stimme klang eindringlich und bestimmt. „Aber was?" fragte Cedric.

Peggy suchte krampfhaft nach einer guten Idee.

„Die Tonbandmethode war ja erfolgreich, aber dieses Mal brauchen wir eine neue Qualität."

„Ich hab's!" schrie ich auf einmal auf. Ich war so begeistert von meiner Idee, daß ich aufsprang und aufgeregt auf und ab lief.

"A great idea." Peggy was impressed.

"Will Griffith needs to talk to the Postmaster General. There will be a struggle until we get permission for the telephone concert, but if we get it, our victory is all but assured."

"Let's figure out how to implement Frank's proposal, because it's not going to be quite as simple as he's expounded it here."

Cedric's warnings were apposite. When the American Embassy in London got wind of the venture, it used every means at its disposal to try to stop the telephone concert from happening and to put pressure on the British government, especially the Postmaster General. But the Robeson Committee had a strong group of MPs in the House of Commons who opposed any interference by a foreign power. They invoked postal secrecy, which was guaranteed to every citizen under the law. A tug of war between opponents began, and no one could know how it would end.

On May 26, 1957, St. Pancras Hall in the heart of London was filled to capacity. I felt the almost unbearable tension hanging over the hall. Would the telephone concert go ahead, or would the American government succeed in jamming the connection? Neither I nor anyone else in the hall knew the answer.

On the stage hung an oversized portrait of Paul Robeson. In front of it was a small table with the telephone. At the table sat the well-known English emcee Alfie Bass.

The telephone rang. Everyone in the room held their breath.

Alfie Bass excitedly picked up the phone and shouted:

"Hello, Paul, hello, Paul!"

But no one answered.

Then he exclaimed again, "Paul, hello, Paul! Can you hear me?"

No answer. Clearly, Paul Robeson in New York could not hear him. The telephone line had been deliberately disrupted. A murmur went through the hall.

The telephone concert had not come off. The superiority of the American government had once again won the day. My heart began to pound, my fists clenched. I could have screamed out loud with rage.

Peggy und Cedric schauten mich erwartungsvoll an.

„Ich hab's", rief ich noch einmal und klatschte mit den Händen, „das ist eine Wucht."

„Na los, spann uns nicht auf die Folter", forderte Cedric.

Ich sprach so schnell, daß Cedric und Peggy kaum folgen konnten.

„Ihr wißt, daß vor kurzem ein neues transatlantisches Telefonkabel von den USA nach England gelegt worden ist. Es soll eine hervorragende Tonqualität haben. Wir werden Paul bitten, über das Kabel aus einem Studio in New York direkt in die Londoner St. Pancras Hall zu singen. Damit werden wir die amerikanische Regierung vor aller Welt lächerlich machen."

„Eine tolle Idee." Peggy war beeindruckt.

„Will Griffith muß mit dem Minister für Postwesen sprechen. Es wird einen Kampf geben, bis wir die Erlaubnis für das Telefonkonzert erhalten, aber wenn wir sie bekommen, ist unser Sieg so gut wie sicher."

„Laßt uns überlegen, wie wir Franks Vorschlag realisieren können, denn ganz so einfach, wie er das hier entwickelt hat, wird es nicht sein."

Cedrics Warnungen waren angebracht. Als die amerikanische Botschaft in London von dem Unternehmen Wind bekam, suchte sie mit allen Mitteln, das Telefonkonzert zu unterbinden und Druck auf die britische Regierung, insbesondere den Minister für Postwesen, auszuüben. Doch das Robeson-Komitee besaß eine starke Gruppe von Abgeordneten im Unterhaus, die sich gegen jegliche Einmischung einer bestimmten ausländischen Macht zur Wehr setzten. Dabei beriefen sie sich auf das Postgeheimnis, das laut Gesetz jedem Bürger garantiert war. Es begann ein Tauziehen zwischen Kontrahenten, und niemand konnte wissen, wie es ausgehen würde.

Am 26. Mai 1957 war die St. Pancras Hall im Herzen von London bis auf den letzten Platz gefüllt. Ich fühlte die fast unerträgliche Spannung, die über dem Saal lag. Würde das Telefonkonzert zustande kommen, oder würde es der amerikanischen Regierung gelingen, die Telefonverbindung zu stören? Weder ich noch irgendein anderer im Saal wußten eine Antwort darauf.

Auf der Bühne hing ein überdimensionales Porträt von Paul Robeson. Davor stand ein kleiner Tisch mit dem Telefon. Am Tisch saß der bekannte englische Conférencier Alfie Bass.

Why did we have to accept these defeats again and again? Back in Minneapolis in the Wiggins case, in the movement for Ethel and Julius Rosenberg, now again in the campaign for Paul Robeson. It was always the same. The powerful were too powerful. Tears of disappointment welled up in my eyes. We had done everything, yet it had been in vain.

But then, suddenly and unexpectedly, the unmistakable deep, warm voice of Paul Robeson sounded from the telephone!

He was singing the song of Daniel in the lion's den. The sound quality was excellent. It seemed as if Paul was not thousands of miles away but was on stage in person here in London's St. Pancras Hall. The concert lasted a total of twenty-three minutes. I calculated feverishly. It cost the committee the round sum of ninety-one pounds. I shuddered to think of it. How would we be able to raise so much money?

The audience called for "Ol' Man River."

Cedric Belfrage took the stage. "Paul is going to sing 'Ol' Man River,'" he announced to the audience, "but then we have to raise money for the phone fees."

The money was thrown on stage—more than enough. "Paul, sing 'Ol' Man River,'" echoed through the large auditorium. And Paul in New York sang "Ol' Man River" through the telephone, to his friends in London. Not the old version he had sung in the 1928 musical *Show Boat*:

"Git a little drunk
An' you land in jail.
Ah gits weary
An' sick of tryin'
Ah'm tired of livin'
An' skeered of dyin'."

Instead, Paul sang:

"You show a little grit
An' you lands in jail.
But I keeps laffin'
Instead of cryin'

Das Telefon klingelte. Alle im Saal hielten den Atem an.

Alfie Bass hob aufgeregt den Telefonhörer ab und schrie:

„Hallo, Paul, hallo, Paul!"

Aber niemand antwortete.

Dann schrie er noch einmal: „Paul, hallo, Paul! Kannst du mich hören?"

Keine Antwort. Ganz offensichtlich konnte ihn Paul Robeson in New York nicht hören. Die Telefonleitung war vorsätzlich gestört worden. Ein Raunen ging durch den Saal.

Das Telefonkonzert war nicht zustande gekommen. Die Übermacht der amerikanischen Regierung hatte wieder einmal den Sieg davongetragen. Mein Herz begann zu pochen, meine Fäuste ballten sich. Ich hätte vor Wut laut schreien können.

Warum mußten wir immer wieder diese Niederlagen hinnehmen? Damals in Minneapolis bei dem Wiggins-Fall, bei der Bewegung für Ethel und Julius Rosenberg, jetzt wieder in der Kampagne für Paul Robeson. Es war immer dasselbe. Die Mächtigen waren zu mächtig. Tränen der Enttäuschung stiegen mir in die Augen. Alles hatten wir getan, dennoch, es war umsonst gewesen.

Doch da, plötzlich und unerwartet, tönte die unverkennbare tiefe, warme Stimme Paul Robesons aus dem Telefon!

Er sang das Lied von Daniel im Löwenkäfig. Die Tonqualität war hervorragend. Es schien, als ob Paul Robeson nicht Tausende Kilometer entfernt wäre, sondern höchstpersönlich hier in der Londoner St. Pancras Hall auf der Bühne stände. Das Konzert dauerte insgesamt dreiundzwanzig Minuten. Ich rechnete fieberhaft. Das kostete dem Komitee die runde Summe von einundneunzig Pfund. Ich schauderte, wenn ich daran dachte. Wie würden wir soviel Geld aufbringen können?

Die Zuschauer forderten „Ol' Man River".

Cedric Belfrage betrat die Bühne. „Paul wird ‚Ol' Man River' singen" rief er dem Publikum zu, „aber dann müssen wir Geld für die Telefongebühren sammeln."

Das Geld wurde auf die Bühne geworfen – mehr als genug.

„Paul, sing ‚Ol' Man River'", so hallte es durch den großen Saal. Und Paul in New York sang „Ol' Man River" durch das Telefon, für seine Freunde in London. Nicht die alte Version, die er 1928 in dem Musical „Show Boat" gesungen hatte:

I must keep fightin'
Until I'm dyin'."

"I must keep fightin' until I'm dyin'"—that's what was going through my mind as I headed back to Manchester in the evening.

The next day, the influential *Manchester Guardian* newspaper wrote: "American Telephone and Telegraph, in New York, and the General Post Office, in London, last night between them helped to make the United States Department of State look rather silly." It went on to say that the telephone concert at London's St. Pancras Hall proved that Paul Robeson could now give concerts anywhere in the world, even without his passport and asked if it wouldn't be wiser, tactically speaking, to lift Paul Robeson's travel ban.

Di[ana] and I had said goodbye to comrades, relatives, friends, and acquaintances. Now we were sitting all by ourselves in the restaurant at Manchester Airport, waiting for our flight to Tempelhof. From there, we would cross the border into the GDR.

"I hope we can fly in this fog," Di sighed.

"They take off in all kinds of weather. They can't afford any interruptions in service. Besides, they have a good radar system here."

I was right. It was announced over the loudspeaker that the plane to Tempelhof would take off in a few minutes.

From Franz Loeser, *Die Abenteuer eines Emigranten: Erinnerungen* (Neues Leben, 1980), 326–43

„Wenn du ein wenig betrunken bist, landest du im Gefängnis.
Ich bin des Versuches müde,
Ich möchte nicht mehr leben,
doch ich fürchte mich vor dem Sterben …",
sondern Paul sang:
„Du zeigt etwas Mut
und landest im Gefängnis,
doch ich lache weiter,
anstatt zu weinen,
ich muß weiterkämpfen, bis ich sterbe."

„Ich muß weiterkämpfen, bis ich sterbe", so ging es mir durch den Kopf, als ich abends nach Manchester zurückfuhr.

Am nächsten Tag schrieb die einflußreiche Zeitung „Manchester Guardian":

„Die amerikanische Telefongesellschaft und die britische Post haben Paul Robeson gestern Abend geholfen, die amerikanische Regierung als recht lächerlich hinzustellen. Das Telefonkonzert in der Londoner St. Pancras Hall hat bewiesen, daß Paul Robeson auch ohne seinen Paß jetzt überall in der Welt Konzerte geben kann. Wäre es nicht taktisch klüger, Paul Robesons Reiseverbot aufzuheben?"

Di[ana] und ich hatten uns von den Genossen, Verwandten, Freunden und Bekannten verabschiedet. Jetzt saßen wir ganz für uns im Restaurant des Flughafens von Manchester und warteten auf unseren Abflug nach Tempelhof. Von dort würden wir die Grenze in die DDR überschreiten.

„Hoffentlich können wir bei diesem Nebel fliegen." Di seufzte.

„Die starten bei jedem Wetter. Sie können es sich gar nicht leisten zu pausieren. Außerdem verfügen sie hier über ein gutes Radarsystem."

Ich hatte recht. Über den Lautsprecher wurde bekanntgegeben, daß das Flugzeug nach Tempelhof in wenigen Minuten starten würde.

Aus: Franz Loeser, *Abenteuer eines Emigranten*, Berlin: Verlag Neues Leben 1980, S. 326–343.

Steve McQueen and Doreen Mende in conversation

ON END CREDITS

ÜBER END CREDITS

Steve McQueen und Doreen Mende im Gespräch

1. See Barbara Ransby, *The Large and Unconventional Life of Mrs. Paul Robeson* (Yale University Press, 2013).

2. Eslanda Robeson, *African Journey* (Victor Gollancz, 1946).

Steve McQueen's audiovisual installation *End Credits* (2012–22) displays thousands of digitized FBI files scrolling slowly up a large-scale screen for twelve hours and fifty-four minutes. The material includes file numbers, dates, and registration codes, some heavily redacted or blacked out. Voice recordings, with a duration of sixty-seven hours, four minutes, and forty-three seconds, render the FBI informants' reports audible asynchronously to the images. The artwork is a haunting monument to the state surveillance and smear campaigns orchestrated by the US government against the writer, photographer, Pan-Africanist, feminist, and anthropologist Eslanda Robeson (1895–1965). Robeson also managed the media communication of her husband, the world-renowned singer, actor, lawyer, and social activist Paul Robeson (1898–1976), who was also under attack by the FBI for his civil rights work, support of trade unions, and sympathy with Soviet-Communist ideas. Eslanda wrote a biography of Paul as well.

Although often overshadowed by her husband, Eslanda Goode Cardozo Robeson was an outstanding intellectual. She studied with anthropologist Bronisław Malinowski at the London School of Economics in the 1930s. She was a brilliant photographer and developed an anti-colonial feminism in and beyond the discipline.[1] Her politics shaped her photographic practice during her journeys to the Belgian Congo, Uganda, and South Africa;[2] the scholar Leigh Raiford has described her perspective as a "pan-African gaze." Paul Robeson connected the Black civil rights movement and the workers' movement to an interracial, anti-colonial internationalism through the sonic traditions of East African music, European chorales, and Negro spirituals. Both Robesons made significant contributions to the Black avant-garde of the Harlem Renaissance, and they continue to influence generations of Black diasporic imaginaries. Their work also circulated in the mainstream media of smaller socialist countries, such as the German Democratic Republic (GDR) and the Czech Republic.

They were banned from travel and work outside the US between 1950 and 1958 and were interrogated by the notorious House Un-American Activities Committee. However, they were supported and honored by intellectuals, students, anti-Fascist activists, and governmental representatives in Communist and nonaligned countries

Steve McQueens audiovisuelle Installation *End Credits* (2012–22) zeigt Tausende digitalisierte FBI-Akten, die langsam auf einer großen Leinwand entlangrollen, über eine Dauer von zwölf Stunden und vierundfünfzig Minuten. Das Material enthält Aktenzeichen, Daten und Registrierungscodes, einige davon stark zensiert oder geschwärzt. Stimmenaufnahmen mit einer Gesamtddauer von siebenundsechzig Stunden, vier Minuten und dreiundvierzig Sekunden geben die Berichte der FBI-Informanten auf der Tonspur wieder, asynchron zu den Bildern. Das Kunstwerk ist ein eindringliches Mahnmal der von der US-Regierung orchestrierten staatlichen Überwachung und der Schmutzkampagnen gegen die Schriftstellerin, Fotografin, Panafrikanistin, Feministin und Anthropologin Eslanda Robeson (1895–1965). Robeson kümmerte sich zudem um die Medienauftritte ihres Ehemanns, des weltberühmten Sängers, Schauspielers, Anwalts und Sozialaktivisten Paul Robeson (1898–1976), der aufgrund seines Einsatzes für die Bürgerrechte, seiner Unterstützung von Gewerkschaften und seiner Sympathie für sowjetisch-kommunistische Ideen ebenfalls ins Visier des FBI geriet. Eslanda schrieb auch eine Biografie über Paul.

Auch wenn sie oft im Schatten ihres Ehemannes stand, war Eslanda Goode Cardozo Robeson eine herausragende Intellektuelle. In den 1930er Jahren studierte sie bei dem Anthropologen Bronisław Malinowski an der London School of Economics. Sie war eine brillante Fotografin und entwickelte einen anti-kolonialen Feminismus innerhalb und außerhalb der Grenzen dieses Mediums.[1] Ihre politischen Haltungen prägten ihre fotografische Praxis während ihrer Reisen nach Belgisch-Kongo, Uganda und Südafrika;[2] die Professorin für African American Studies Leigh Raiford beschrieb ihre Perspektive als einen „panafrikanischen Blick".[3] Paul Robeson verschmolz unter Rückgriff auf die Klangtraditionen ostafrikanischer Musik, europäische Choräle und Schwarze Spirituals, die Schwarze Bürgerrechtsbewegung und die Arbeiterbewegung zu einem vielfältigen, anti-kolonialen Internationalismus. Beide Robesons leisteten einen bedeutenden Beitrag zur Schwarzen Avantgarde der Harlem Renaissance und inspirieren nach wie vor Generationen Schwarzer Diaspora-Vorstellungen. Ihr Schaffen zirkulierte auch in den etablierten Medien kleinerer sozialistischer Länder wie der Deutschen Demokratischen Republik (DDR) und der Tschechoslowakei.

Zwischen 1950 und 1958 wurden sie mit einem Reise- und Arbeitsverbot außerhalb der USA belegt und vom berüchtigten House Un-American Activities

1. Siehe Barbara Ransby, *The Large and Unconventional Life of Mrs. Paul Robeson*, New Haven, CT: Yale University Press 2013.

2. Eslanda Robeson, *African Journey*, London: Victor Gollancz 1946.

3. Leigh Bradford, „The Here and Now of Eslanda Robeson's African Journey", in: *Journal of Transnational American Studies*, 8(1) 2017, S. 149.

3. Franz Loeser, *Die Abenteuer eines Emigranten: Erinnerungen* (Neues Leben, 1980).

4. Katharina Warda, "Ostdeutsche of Color," Rise, November 2, 2021, https://rise-jugend-kultur.de/artikel/ostdeutsche-of-color/.

5. "Pan-Africanism, Communism, Anti-Fascism: A Radical Provocation," panel discussion with Charisse Burden-Stelly, Doreen Mende, Charlotte Misselwitz, and Zoé Samudzi, moderated by Avery F. Gordon, October 29, 2022, "The Missed Seminar," Haus der Kulturen der Welt, Berlin.

around the world. Among their supporters was the Jewish German philosopher Franz Loeser and his wife, Diana Loeser, an "English for you" teacher on GDR television. In the East German version of his autobiography, Loeser writes that as a student at the University of Minnesota, he guarded Paul Robeson against a mob of White supremacists during the Peekskill riots in 1949.[3] Shortly after that attack, Loeser himself became subject to anti-Communist policy in the US and was obliged to leave the country. After a stay in Manchester for a few years, he moved to East Berlin in 1957, where he contributed significantly to the building of the Paul Robeson Archive at the Akademie der Künste in East Berlin, of which Paul Robeson became a corresponding member in 1963. His membership was canceled around 1994 when the Akademie der Künste (East) was "reunited" with the Akademie der Künste (West).

In other words, the aftermath of the global Cold War not only disregarded the archives and silenced the histories of Communist and anti-Fascist lives in Europe, it also erased the presence in these geographies of Black radical histories and their transcontinental networks. In the context of East Germany, this double erasure, which the sociologist Katharina Warda has described as a "double invisibilization" by white patriarchal liberal power, created the conditions for the ethno-nationalism and neofascism that we face today.[4] Or, as Charisse Burden Stelly has argued, being Black and Communist is what Fascists fear most.[5]

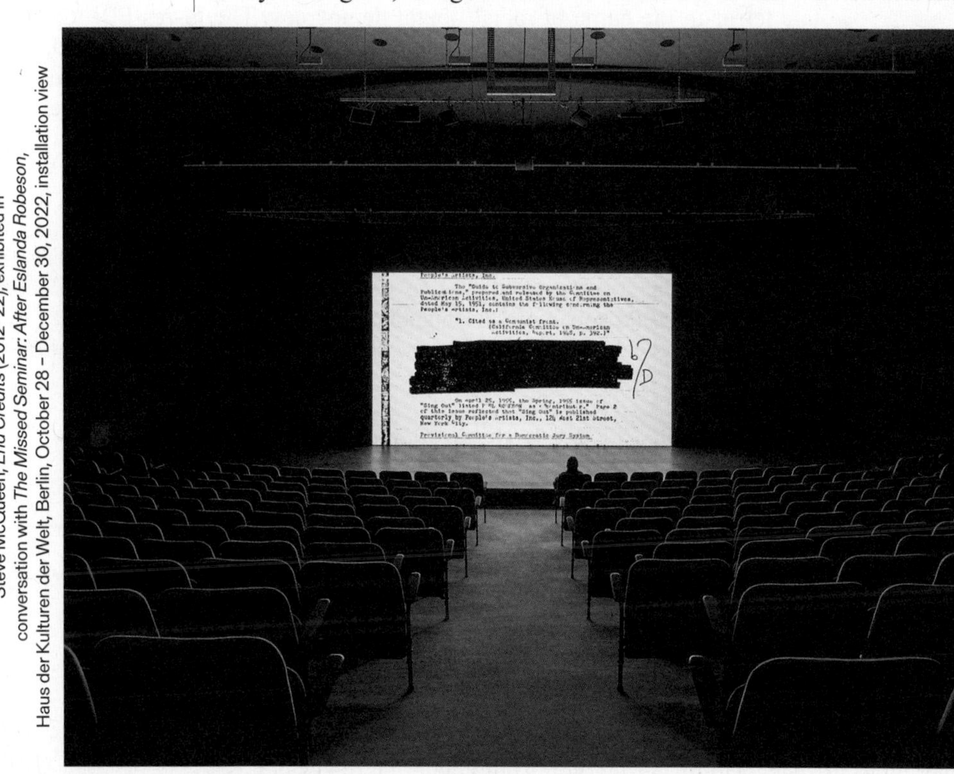

Steve McQueen, *End Credits* (2012–22), exhibited in conversation with *The Missed Seminar: After Eslanda Robeson,* Haus der Kulturen der Welt, Berlin, October 28 – December 30, 2022, installation view

Steve McQueen, *End Credits* (2012–2022), ausgestellt im Gespräch mit *The Missed Seminar: After Eslanda Robeson,* Haus der Kulturen der Welt, Berlin, 28. Oktober – 30. Dezember 2022, Installationsansicht

Committee verhört. Dennoch wurden sie von Intellektuellen, Studierenden, antifaschistischen Aktivist·innen und Regierungsvertreter*innen in kommunistischen und blockfreien Ländern in aller Welt unterstützt und verehrt. Zu ihren Unterstützer·innen zählten auch der jüdisch-deutsche Philosoph Franz Loeser und dessen Frau, Diana Loeser, die im Fernsehen der DDR als Lehrerin in der Sendung „English for you" wirkte. In der ostdeutschen Ausgabe seiner Autobiografie schreibt Loeser, dass er als Student an der University of Minnesota Paul Robeson während der Peekskill Riots 1949 vor einem Mob weißer Rassisten beschützt habe.[4] Kurz nach diesem Angriff wurde Loeser selbst zur Zielscheibe der antikommunistischen Politik in den USA und war gezwungen, das Land zu verlassen. Nach einem mehrjährigen Aufenthalt in Manchester übersiedelte er 1957 nach Ost-Berlin, wo er wesentlich zum Aufbau des Paul-Robeson-Archivs an der Akademie der Künste in Ost-Berlin beitrug, der Paul Robeson seit 1963 als korrespondierendes Mitglied angehörte. Seine Mitgliedschaft wurde ca. 1994 widerrufen, als die Akademie der Künste (Ost) mit der Akademie der Künste (West) „wiedervereinigt" wurde.

Anders gesagt, die Nachwehen des globalen Kalten Krieges ignorierten nicht nur die Archive und machten die Geschichten kommunistischer und antifaschistischer Biografien mundtot, sie führten auch zur Auslöschung der in diesen Geografien präsenten Schwarzen radikalen Geschichten und ihrer transkontinentalen Netzwerke. Im Kontext Ostdeutschlands schuf diese doppelte

4. Franz Loeser, *Die Abenteuer eines Emigranten: Erinnerungen,* Berlin: Neues Leben 1980.

The ongoing instrumentalization of memory politics, particularly with regard to the fights against racism and anti-Semitism, makes it urgent to engage with unfinished conversations between friends and movements that created intersectional solidarity between the struggles of the East and South. In *End Credits*, McQueen invokes these geopolitical entanglements through an artistic mobilization of archival material, which enables viewers to link racism with colonialism, anti-Semitism, and Fascism. The following conversation about *End Credits* took place on October 25, 2022, during the lead-up to the first full-length exhibition of the work, at the Haus der Kulturen der Welt in Berlin, and is presented in poster form as part of the vitrine intervention at the Albertinum in 2023 in the context of the multipart curatorial project "The Missed Seminar."

Doreen Mende

DM: *End Credits* exhibits an aesthetics of bureaucracy and a pathology of administration as methods of anti-Communist horror during the postwar McCarthyite regime in the name of US law. The FBI files documenting the surveillance of Eslanda and Paul Robeson span the period between 1941 and 1978. The excessive number of files and registration codes indicates the quality and quantity of surveillance and reveals the building blocks of state terror in the name of racial liberal democracy. The hi-res FBI material used in *End Credits* is accessible today, but it used to be classified, top secret, and FBI coded. How does this expose the surveillance system while invisibilizing the Robesons? What remains indiscernible despite the high-resolution exposure?

SM: What was fascinating to me when I first saw the documents was the erasure of certain information within them. There was a structure. Things which were revealed were sealed. It was done in such an orderly fashion because, of course, these things were classified. Now they're unclassified, but they're still classified in a way because we don't see all the evidence or facts that had apparently been gathered. It's decorative to a certain extent: what is revealed and what is unrevealed, what is fact and what is fiction. So

---

Ausradierung, die die Soziologin Katharina Warda als ein „doppelt unsichtbar"-Machen seitens der patriarchalen liberalen Macht beschreibt, die Bedingungen für den Ethnonationalismus und den Neofaschismus, dem wir heute gegenübertreten.[5] Oder, wie Charisse Burden Stelly dargelegt hat, Schwarz und Kommunist zu sein, ist, was die Faschisten am meisten fürchten.[6]

Die fortwährende Instrumentalisierung der Erinnerungspolitik, insbesondere im Hinblick auf den Kampf gegen Rassismus und Antisemitismus, macht die Auseinandersetzung mit nicht zuende geführten Gesprächen zwischen Freunden und Bewegungen, die intersektionale Solidaritäten zwischen den Kämpfen des Ostens und des Südens herstellten, zu einer vordringlichen Aufgabe. In *End Credits* evoziert McQueen diese geopolitischen Verflechtungen mithilfe einer künstlerischen Mobilisierung von Archivmaterial, die es den Betrachter·innen ermöglicht, Rassismus mit Kolonialismus, Antisemitismus und Faschismus in Verbindung zu setzen. Das folgende Gespräch über *End Credits* fand am 25. Oktober 2022 im Vorfeld der ersten Präsentation des Werks in voller Länge im Haus der Kulturen der Welt in Berlin statt und wurde als Teil der Vitrinenintervention im Albertinum 2023 im Rahmen des mehrteiligen kuratorischen Projekts „The Missed Seminar" als Poster präsentiert.

Doreen Mende

DM: *End Credits* zeigt eine Ästhetik der Bürokratie und eine Pathologie der Verwaltung als Methoden des antikommunistischen Schreckens der Nachkriegszeit, der vom Regime des McCarthyismus im Namen des amerikanischen Rechts begangen wurde. Die FBI-Akten, in denen die Überwachung von Eslanda und Paul Robeson dokumentiert ist, umfassen den Zeitraum zwischen 1941 und 1978. Die exzessive Zahl der Akten und der Erfassungscodes geben einen Hinweis auf die Qualität und Quantität der Überwachung und enthüllen die Bausteine des Staatsterrors im Namen einer rassischen liberalen Demokratie. Das in *End Credits* verwendete hochaufgelöste FBI-Material ist heute zugänglich, unterlag aber der Geheimhaltung, war teils ‚top secret' und vom FBI klassifiziert. Wie wird hierdurch das Überwachungssystem entlarvt, während die Robesons unsichtbar gemacht werden? Was bleibt trotz der hochauflösenden Darstellung unsichtbar?

5. Katharina Warda, „Ostdeutsche of Color", in: *Rise*, 2. November 2021, https://rise-jugend-kultur.de/artikel/ostdeutsche-of-color/.

6. „Pan-Africanism, Communism, Anti-Fascism: A Radical Provocation", Podiumsdiskussion mit Charisse Burden-Stelly, Doreen Mende, Charlotte Misselwitz und Zoé Samudzi, moderiert von Avery F. Gordon, 29. Oktober 2022, „The Missed Seminar", Haus der Kulturen der Welt, Berlin.

then it's about what the spectator projects onto those files. The blackness was almost like holes within the system. Those holes tell you a lot about the failures of state surveillance and, more than anything, about the triumphs of the Robesons.

DM: Imagining the erasures in the files as blackness, or as holes in the system, creates such a beautiful optics. It immediately turns the spectator's perspective toward the unboundedness of human existence and, specifically, the Robesons' unconventional lives. It suggests the possibility of futurity, or as you put it, it blurs the lines between fact and fiction. At the same time, there is still a great deal of intimate information accessible. You've also just said that *End Credits* invites the audience to make something out of what they imagine. How do you cope with the exposure of intimate information about the Robesons—their illnesses, struggles, relationship problems, love affairs, friendships, mental problems, and health issues? The first audience for the files were secret service operatives. What does shifting the material of the FBI files into an art space allow? How do you deal with the intimacy?

SM: If anything, it makes them more heroic. Their vulnerabilities were their strengths. These were as important to document as their political activism. This tells you how scared the FBI were of them. In just an emotional sense, for me, it makes them more endearing as characters, because they were real people who were intimidated to the point of madness. And also a lot of those things—their health and the trouble in their relationship—were instigated, were activated, by the FBI themselves.

DM: The files are also evidence of their resistance and the fearlessness of their love.

SM: I would say so.

DM: The complete *End Credits* contains about twelve hours of video and sixty-seven hours of audio. There is also an asynchronous relationship

SM: Was mich faszinierte, als ich die Dokumente das erste Mal zu Gesicht bekam, war die Ausradierung bestimmter darin enthaltener Informationen. Das hatte eine Struktur. Dinge, die offengelegt wurden, wurden versiegelt. Das geschah auf penible Weise, denn diese Dinge waren natürlich unter Verschluss. Jetzt sind sie freigegeben, aber in gewisser Weise sind sie immer noch unter Verschluss, denn wir bekommen nicht alle Beweise oder Fakten zu sehen, die allem Anschein nach gesammelt worden waren. In gewissem Maße ist das dekorativ: Was enthüllt ist und was nicht, was Fakt ist, was Fiktion. Es geht also darum, was der Betrachter auf diese Akten projiziert. Die Schwärze glich beinahe Löchern im System. Diese Löcher verraten viel über das Versagen der staatlichen Überwachung und vor allem über die Triumphe der Robesons.

DM: Wenn man sich die Löschungen in den Akten als Schwärze oder als Löcher im System vorstellt, entsteht eine so schöne Optik. Sie lenkt den Blick des Betrachters sofort auf die Unbegrenztheit der menschlichen Existenz und insbesondere auf das unkonventionelle Leben der Robesons. Sie suggeriert die Möglichkeit von Zukunft, oder wie Sie es ausdrücken, sie verwischt die Grenzen zwischen Fakt und Fiktion. Gleichzeitig sind aber immer noch viele intime Informationen zugänglich. Sie sagten gerade, dass *End Credits* das Publikum dazu einlädt, etwas aus dem zu machen, was es sich vorstellt. Wie werden Sie der Enthüllung intimer Informationen über die Robesons gerecht – ihren Krankheiten, Mühen, Beziehungsproblemen, Liebesaffären, Freundschaften, mentalen Problemen und gesundheitlichen Problemen? Das erste Publikum für die Akten waren Geheimagenten. Was ermöglicht die Verschiebung des Materials der FBI-Akten in einen Kunstort? Wie gehen Sie mit der Intimität um?

SM: Wenn überhaupt, dann macht es sie noch heldenhafter. Ihre Verletzlichkeit war ihre Stärke. Sie zu dokumentieren, war ebenso wichtig wie die Dokumentation ihres politischen Aktivismus. Daran erkennt man, wie viel Angst das FBI vor ihnen hatte. Aus emotionaler Sicht macht es sie für mich als Charaktere noch liebenswerter, weil sie echte Menschen waren, die so stark unter Druck gesetzt wurden, dass sie beinahe dem Wahnsinn

between the audio and video. It's obviously a profoundly different time concept from your film production work. In your film productions, you are tied to the feature length of the film. How do you mobilize duration as a methodology in *End Credits* differently from in your film productions?

SM: It's very different. It's about duration and meditation. I'm not asking the audience to sit through sixty-seven hours straight, it's about what you take and what you bring. It's about the fact that once you leave the space, you know that it's still going on. It's like a painting. It doesn't just survive on the wall, it's an aspect of something. It brings you to a point and you grow and work with it. And that's why you can keep going back to the same image. *End Credits* tracks the constant surveillance of the Robesons until two years after Paul's death in 1976. We have to have this journey into his surveillance because it is about surveillance over an elongated period of time. Either you are in the room or you are not, but you carry it with you.

DM: As a spectator?

SM: Of course, yes. You can imagine how this was going on for such a long period of time. It was relentless. The whole idea of *End Credits* was of a film with this sort of scroll of information that just goes on and on and on. That's what I wanted to represent within the context of an artwork in order to replicate or visualize this, to carry the weight in some way.

DM: *End Credits* exposes the paratext of a plot, of a narrative, of a life. We might say that the duration is an indicator of the surveillance apparatus. On the other hand, could we say that this surveillance did not define the life of Eslanda and Paul Robeson?

SM: Absolutely.

DM: *End Credits* was presented at the Haus der Kulturen der Welt (HKW) in Berlin for the first time in complete form. It was shown in the context of the "The Missed Seminar," which is a multipart curatorial research project

verfielen. Und viele dieser Dinge – ihre Gesundheit und die Probleme in ihrer Beziehung – wurden vom FBI selbst angezettelt, ausgelöst.

DM: Die Akten sind auch Beweis ihres Widerstands und der Furchtlosigkeit ihrer Liebe.

SM: Ich würde sagen, ja.

DM: Die vollständige Fassung von *End Credits* umfasst ungefähr zwölf Stunden Video- und siebenundsechzig Stunden Audiomaterial. Audio und Video stehen in einem asynchronen Verhältnis zueinander. Das ist natürlich ein völlig anderes Zeitkonzept als bei Ihren Arbeiten mit Filmproduktionen. Bei Ihren Filmproduktionen sind Sie an die üblichen Spielfilmlängen gebunden. Wie setzen Sie die Laufzeit als Methode in *End Credits* anders ein als in Ihren Filmproduktionen?

SM: Das ist etwas ganz anderes. Es geht um Dauer und Meditation. Ich verlange vom Publikum nicht, dass es siebenundsechzig Stunden am Stück durchhält, sondern es geht darum, was man mitnimmt und was man mitbringt. Es geht darum, zu wissen, dass es immer noch weitergeht, auch wenn man den Saal verlässt. Es ist wie ein Gemälde. Es überlebt nicht nur an der Wand, es ist ein Aspekt von etwas. Es bringt einen an einen Punkt, an dem man wächst und mit ihm arbeitet. Und deshalb kann man immer wieder zu demselben Bild zurückkehren. *End Credits* verfolgt die ständige Überwachung der Robesons bis zwei Jahre nach Pauls Tod im Jahr 1976. Wir müssen diese Reise in seine Überwachung machen, denn es geht um Überwachung über einen längeren Zeitraum. Entweder man ist im Saal oder nicht, aber man trägt es mit sich.

DM: Als Zuschauer?

SM: Ja, natürlich. Man kann sich vorstellen, wie das für einen solch langen Zeitraum vonstattenging. Es war unerbittlich. Die ganze Idee von *End Credits* war es, einen Film als laufenden Abspann von Informationen zu machen, der einfach immer und immer weiterläuft. Das wollte ich im Rahmen eines Kunstwerks darstellen, um dies zu replizieren oder zu visualisieren, um diese Bürde in irgendeiner Weise kenntlich zu machen.

that seeks to metabolize archival material documenting the presence of the Robesons in the context of the Communist geographies of Europe, specifically in the German Democratic Republic, in light of Eslanda's journeys to the continent. HKW was built in 1957 as a congress venue in West Berlin; it is an articulation of Cold War architecture par excellence. As a gesture of opposition to the people of East Berlin, quite literally at their border, the Congress Hall was designed to promote anti-Communism as a condition for de-Nazification and "freedom." Thus, your installation in Berlin denounces, both in curatorial and juridical terms, the promises of liberal democracy as an instrument of war. What are your thoughts regarding the presentation of *End Credits* at HKW, a building that was originally gifted by the same US government that banned the Robesons from traveling? What are your thoughts about presenting *End Credits* in the belly of the beast, so to speak, in architecture that was built from the same political violence that surveilled them?

SM: In some ways it's bringing it back home, which is kind of interesting to witness. This is how the situation always ends up. But at the same time, I don't know what that means. We now have the advantage of time. And time allows this kind of orchestration where we can put a project about surveillance in a place of surveillance. I don't know if that's a victory or an irony—I have no idea. It's something to witness and I'm looking forward

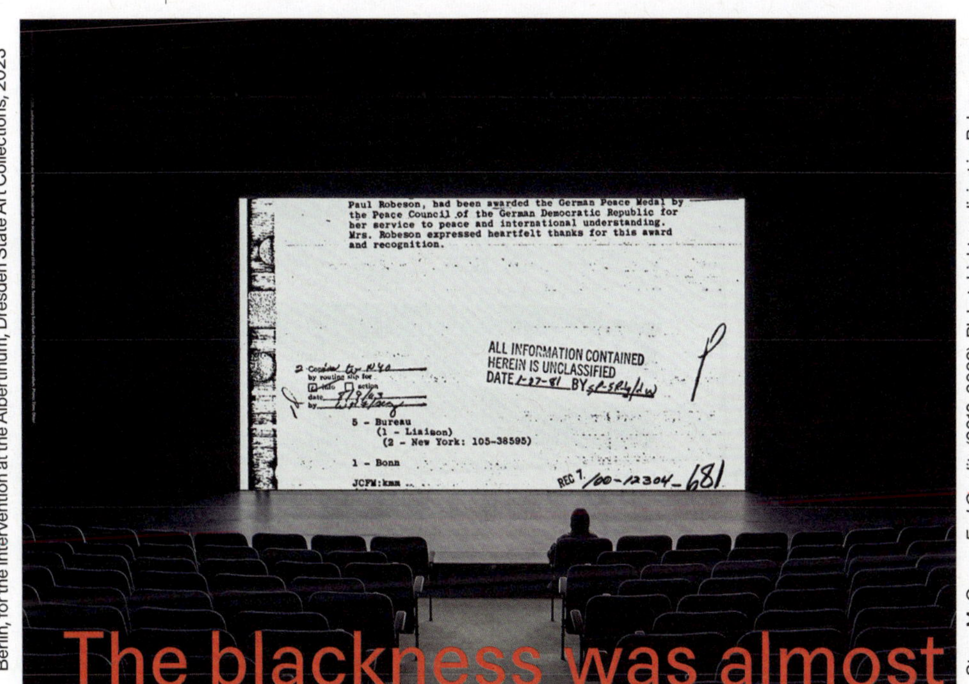

Steve McQueen, *End Credits* (2012–22), poster object, realized in the context of *The Missed Seminar* at Haus der Kulturen der Welt, Berlin, for the intervention at the Albertinum, Dresden State Art Collections, 2023

Steve McQueen, *End Credits* (2012–2022), Plakatobjekt, realisiert im Rahmen von *The Missed Seminar* im Haus der Kulturen der Welt, Berlin, für die Intervention im Albertinum, Staatliche Kunstsammlungen Dresden, 2023

DM: *End Credits* legt den Paratext eines Plots, einer Erzählung, eines Lebens offen. Wir könnten sagen, dass die Dauer ein Indikator des Überwachungsapparats ist. Könnten wir andererseits sagen, dass diese Überwachung das Leben von Eslanda und Paul Robeson nicht bestimmt hat?

SM: Auf jeden Fall.

DM: *End Credits* wurde am Haus der Kulturen der Welt (HKW) in Berlin zum ersten Mal in ganzer Länge präsentiert. Die Arbeit wurde gezeigt im Kontext von „The Missed Seminar", einem mehrteiligen kuratorischen Forschungsprojekt, das Archivmaterial, welches die Präsenz der Robesons im Kontext der kommunistischen Geografien Europas, insbesondere der Deutschen Demokratischen Republik, dokumentiert, im Lichte von Eslandas Reisen auf den Kontinent auszuwerten versucht. Das HKW wurde 1957 als Kongresshalle in West-Berlin errichtet und ist ein Ausdruck der Architektur des Kalten Krieges par excellence. Als Geste der Opposition gegenüber der Bevölkerung Ost-Berlins, buchstäblich an ihrer Grenze, wurde die Kongresshalle entworfen, um den Antikommunismus als Voraussetzung für Entnazifizierung und „Freiheit" zu propagieren. So brandmarkt Ihre Installation in Berlin, sowohl in kuratorischer als auch in juristischer Hinsicht, die Versprechen der liberalen Demokratie als ein Instrument des Krieges. Wie denken Sie über die Präsentation von *End Credits* im HKW, einem Gebäude, das ursprünglich von derselben US-Regierung gestiftet wurde, die

to seeing it in that space and seeing what happens. I can only really answer that question once I have seen it in the space.

DM: HKW is not a neutral venue—not that there is ever a neutral exhibition space. Perhaps it's a victory to exhibit *End Credits* at HKW, because projecting the surveillance files into the space of the main auditorium confronts the venue itself as a material manifestation of the violence of Cold War politics.

SM: I don't know if it's a victory. Many people have been lost along the way. Many people didn't survive to see this. It's the long game. And I don't know what it is. Is it a triumph? Or is it a defeat?

DM: It's a past in the present, it's a *longue durée*.
SM: It's not celebratory at all.

DM: I agree.
SM: At the same time, I don't know if it's a defeat. But I can witness it.

DM: Would you say that it's a form of manifestation?
SM: No. You're the one putting it there, not me. I don't know if it's a demonstration or superfluous. These things are gone, and other things are

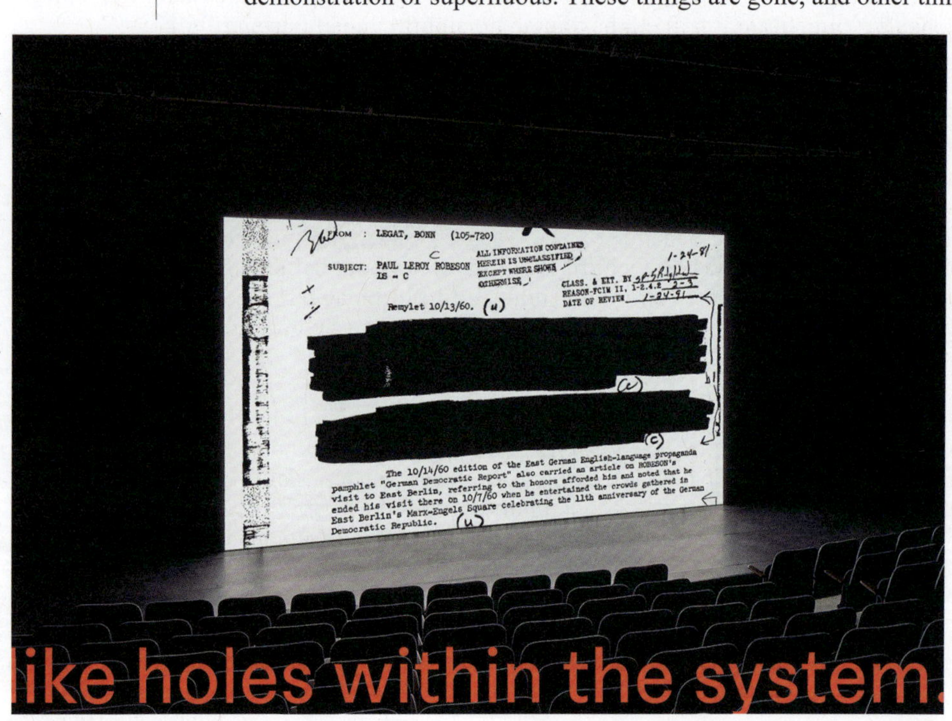

Steve McQueen, *End Credits* (2012–22), poster object, realized in the context of *The Missed Seminar* at Haus der Kulturen der Welt, Berlin, for the intervention at the Albertinum, Dresden State Art Collections, 2023

Steve McQueen, *End Credits* (2012–2022), Plakatobjekt, realisiert im Rahmen von *The Missed Seminar* im Haus der Kulturen der Welt, Berlin, für die Intervention im Albertinum, Staatliche Kunstsammlungen Dresden, 2023

den Robesons ein Reiseverbot erteilt hat? Was halten Sie davon, *End Credits* sozusagen im Bauch der Bestie zu präsentieren, in einer Architektur, die aus derselben politischen Gewalt entstanden ist, die die beiden überwacht hat?

SM: In gewisser Weise ist es eine Art Heimkehr, und es ist interessant, das zu beobachten. So endet es immer. Zugleich weiß ich nicht, was das bedeuten soll. Wir haben jetzt den Vorteil der Zeit. Und die Zeit ermöglicht solch eine Art der Orchestrierung, wo wir ein Projekt über Überwachung an einem Ort der Überwachung zeigen können. Ich weiß nicht, ob das ein Sieg ist oder eine Ironie – ich habe wirklich keine Ahnung. Es ist ein wichtiges Erlebnis und ich bin schon sehr gespannt, die Arbeit in diesem Raum anzusehen und zu beobachten, was passieren wird. Ich kann diese Frage erst dann wirklich beantworten, wenn ich es in diesem Raum gesehen habe.

DM: Das HKW ist kein neutraler Ort – nicht, dass es jemals einen neutralen Ausstellungsraum gäbe. Vielleicht ist es ein Sieg, *End Credits* im HKW auszustellen, weil die Projektion der Überwachungsakten im Raum des großen Auditoriums den Ort mit sich selbst in seiner Materialität als wichtigen Ausdruck der Gewalt der Politik des Kalten Krieges konfrontiert.

SM: Ich weiß nicht, ob es ein Sieg ist. Viele Menschen haben auf dem Weg dorthin verloren. Viele Menschen haben nicht überlebt und können das jetzt nicht mehr erfahren. Es ist ein Spiel, das auf lange Sicht angelegt ist. Und ich weiß nicht, was es ist. Ist das ein Triumph? Oder eine Niederlage?

happening already. New surveillance and new kinds of observations are happening as we speak on this call, wherever. It just goes on in different forms. I don't know who the victors are, but it is what it is.

DM: The post-1990 political depression still resonating in the present was one motivation for me to engage with the narratives, lives, and struggles of the Robesons. What kind of space do you think reconnecting with their legacies opens up? What do we learn from thinking about the legacies of the anti-Communist witch hunts and Communist alliances across race and geographies from a contemporary perspective?

SM: What you learn from it is what you're willing to surrender for a sense of liberty. And not a lot of people are willing. As we all know now, we've all surrendered to it to a certain extent with our phones and our computers. We know that there is surveillance, we know that we're being monitored. And we surrender to it. Because in some ways what has happened is that we've been put in a position where we can't function without it. And that's it. We're put in a position . . . What are you willing to give up? What are you willing to sacrifice? It's very difficult. The structures of power and authority have made it, I don't want to say impossible, but at least very difficult to not be in their pocket one way or the other. Freedom is just whatever that is, I'm not too sure.

DM: Absolutely. It brings us back to the exhibition venue's history. It was built on the premise of liberal democracy and the idea of freedom. Yet, freedom here is an instrument of war. And that's what I think becomes pertinent and palpable when we engage and reconnect with the Robesons through *End Credits*. Maybe, to put the question differently, Why *End Credits* today?

SM: Interesting. Why *End Credits* today? It's an interesting topic when you think of all these whistleblowers and what's going on around the world. What I wanted to do in one way, shape, or form was to be very direct, because I think these FBI files are quite formal. It's literally black and

---

DM: Es ist eine Vergangenheit in der Gegenwart, es ist eine *longue durée*.
SM: Es hat überhaupt nichts von einer Siegesfeier.

DM: Da stimme ich zu.
SM: Zugleich weiß ich nicht, ob es eine Niederlage ist. Aber ich kann es beobachten.

DM: Würden Sie sagen, dass es eine Form der Offenbarung ist?
SM: Nein. Sie stellen es dort aus, nicht ich. Ich weiß nicht, ob es etwas beweist oder ob es überflüssig ist. Diese Dinge sind vorbei und andere Dinge geschehen bereits. Neue Überwachungsoperationen und neue Formen der Observierung sind im Gange, während wir hier miteinander telefonieren. Es geht einfach immer weiter, auf verschiedene Arten und Weisen. Ich weiß nicht, wer die Sieger sind, aber es ist, wie es ist.

DM: Die nach 1990 einsetzende politische Depression, die bis zum heutigen Tag nachklingt, war für mich einer der Beweggründe, mich mit den Geschichten, dem Leben und den Kämpfen der Robesons auseinanderzusetzen. Welche Art von Raum eröffnet sich Ihrer Meinung nach durch das Wiederaufnehmen einer Verbindung zu ihrem Wirken? Was können wir lernen, wenn wir aus einer heutigen Perspektive über die Nachwirkungen der antikommunistischen Hexenjagden und über die ethnische und geografische Grenzen überschreitenden kommunistischen Allianzen nachdenken?

SM: Man kann davon lernen, was man bereit ist, für ein Gefühl der Freiheit aufzugeben. Und dazu sind nicht besonders viele Menschen bereit. Wir alle sind uns heute darüber im Klaren, dass wir uns mit unseren Mobiltelefonen und Computern diesem System bis zu einem gewissen Grad unterworfen haben. Wir wissen, dass es Überwachung gibt, wir wissen, dass unsere Daten und Bewegungen erfasst werden. Und wir kapitulieren davor. Denn es ist inzwischen in gewisser Weise so, dass wir in eine Position gedrängt worden sind, wo wir ohne dieses System nicht mehr funktionieren. Und das war's. Das ist die Situation, in der wir uns befinden … Was ist man bereit aufzugeben? Was ist man bereit zu opfern? Es ist sehr schwierig. Die

42

6. Steve McQueen in conversation with Donna De Salvo, April 29, 2016, in the context of Steve McQueen's exhibition *Open Plan*, Whitney Museum of American Art, 2016

white. There is a tactility to it that makes it possible to engage with people in a very direct manner. Why now? Because you can see these things in a very direct fashion: the narrative of people being surveilled for over thirty years and the toll that it takes and how it chips away at this couple—Paul, in particular. The mental health issues and so forth. And therefore I had hoped that seeing these documents in this narrative form would prompt people to reflect upon their own individual situations and how we live today. This is basically all one can do, to reflect on the past. And to reflect on the past in the present.

DM: What kind of thinking do you hope *End Credits* produces? Is it trans-generational thinking? Communist thinking? Pan-African thinking? Politics-of-friendship thinking?

SM: I wouldn't want to say. That's not for me. I'm not here to direct people's thoughts. It's the exact opposite. It's about reflecting on the present within the past, or the past in the present. Otherwise, I have no idea. The fact that people can view it is as much as I could hope for.

DM: Let's speak about the Transatlantic Telephone Concert, which transmitted the voice of Paul Robeson live—for the first time across the Atlantic—to St. Pancras Town Hall in London on May 26, 1957. I remember you talking enthusiastically with the curator Donna DeSalvo about it in 2016.[6] The concert was organized by the German Jewish Marxist philosopher Franz Loeser, a friend of Paul's. The Transatlantic Telephone Concert was an incredibly important act of solidarity against the US governmental travel ban that had prevented Robeson from performing in Europe. It was also an important moment of friendship between Robeson and Loeser. Later that year, Loeser immigrated to East Berlin, where he mobilized a state-approved initiative to support Robeson, demanding the end of the anti-Communist travel ban. Robeson is as famous for a generation born after the 1940s in East Germany as Angela Davis is for a generation born

---

Strukturen der Macht und der Obrigkeit haben es – ich will nicht sagen unmöglich –, aber doch zumindest äußerst schwierig gemacht, nicht in der einen oder anderen Weise in deren Tasche zu stecken. Das bestimmt, was Freiheit noch ist, ich bin mir da nicht besonders sicher.

DM: Absolut. Das bringt uns zurück zur Geschichte des Ausstellungsorts. Er wurde gebaut unter den Prämissen von liberaler Demokratie und der Idee der Freiheit. Freiheit ist hier allerdings ein Mittel des Krieges. Und ich denke, wenn wir uns über *End Credits* mit den Robesons auseinandersetzen und an sie anknüpfen, dann wird das relevant und greifbar. Vielleicht, um die Frage anders zu stellen: Warum *End Credits* gerade heute?

SM: Ein interessanter Punkt. Warum gerade heute *End Credits*? Das ist ein wichtiges Thema, gerade wenn man an all die Whistleblower denkt und was auf der ganzen Welt los ist. Ich wollte in irgendeiner Form sehr direkt sein, denn ich denke, dass diese FBI-Akten sehr formal sind. Sie sind buchstäblich schwarz und weiß. Das hat eine Taktilität, die es ermöglicht, sich auf eine sehr direkte Weise mit Leuten auseinanderzusetzen. Warum heute? Weil man diese Dinge auf eine äußerst direkte Art beobachten kann: Die Geschichte von Leuten, die über einen Zeitraum von mehr als dreißig Jahren überwacht werden, welchen Tribut das gefordert hat und wie es an diesem Paar nagt – vor allem an Paul. Die Probleme mit der psychischen Gesundheit und so weiter. Deshalb hegte ich die Hoffnung, dass die Leute durch das Ansehen dieser Dokumente in solch einer narrativen Form dazu angeregt würden, über ihre eigene individuelle Situation nachzudenken und darüber, wie wir heute leben. Das ist im Grunde genommen alles, was man tun kann, über die Vergangenheit nachzudenken. Und über die Vergangenheit in der Gegenwart nachzudenken.

DM: Welche Art von Denken erhoffen Sie sich von *End Credits*? Ist es ein generationenübergreifendes Denken? Kommunistisches Denken? Pan-afrikanisches Denken? Eine Politik der Freundschaft?

SM: Da würde ich mich nicht festlegen wollen. Das ist nicht meine Sache. Ich bin nicht hier, um die Gedanken der Menschen zu lenken. Es geht um das genaue Gegenteil. Es geht darum, die Gegenwart in der

7. Eslanda Goode Robeson, "'Kidnapped!' A True Story," Paul Robeson Archive, Akademie der Künste Berlin.

after the 1960s. This friendship—and the concert—has also been a main interest of "The Missed Seminar." What fascinates you about the Transatlantic Telephone Concert? What does it allow us to imagine?

SM: I think breaking the lines. The fact that where there's a will, there's a way. And that's what art can do. Art has always been a tool, has always been a thing that can transform and transcend a situation. And I think that's a great example of that. The whole idea that a voice can actually generate that amount of enthusiasm and love. And you can echo that with *End Credits* in terms of voices; those voices can actually reverberate and communicate.

DM: On August 27, 1963, a few days after their arrival in East Berlin, Eslanda wrote a kind of report called "'Kidnapped!' A True Story," documenting their escape from the media harassment they had experienced in London.[7] Both she and Paul had moved to London between 1958 and 1963, shortly after the travel ban was ended. Journalists besieged their house at Connaught Square in London, hunting for any sort of information on the Robesons, specifically on Paul's health. In "'Kidnapped!' A True Story," Eslanda describes in detail their tricks to fool the waiting journalists: boarding a Polish Airlines plane to East Berlin, meeting Loeser at the airport, and the welcome by the Peace Council in East Berlin, which had invited them. Eslanda writes in a diaristic form. Hers is a kind of autotheory writing, taking lived experience as a foundation for analyzing political realities. It situates her approach in the tradition of Black diaristic writing—Zora Neale Hurston, Nella Larsen, and authors around *The Crisis*, a journal founded by W. E. B. DuBois, in which literature intersects with memoir and journalistic reports. Eslanda's many writings, which remain as yet unpublished as an anthology, evidence Black life as well as her commitment to a Pan-African feminism. "'Kidnapped!' A True Story" was published in three parts in *The Afro-American* newspaper in November 1963.

SM: Which newspaper?

Vergangenheit zu reflektieren, oder die Vergangenheit in der Gegenwart. Ansonsten habe ich keine Ahnung. Die Tatsache, dass die Leute es sehen können, ist alles, was ich mir erhoffen konnte.

DM: Lassen Sie uns über das Transatlantische Telefonkonzert sprechen, bei dem am 26. Mai 1957 die Stimme von Paul Robeson live – und zum ersten Mal über den Atlantik – in die St. Pancras Town Hall in London übertragen wurde. Ich erinnere mich, wie sie sich 2016 im Gespräch mit der Kuratorin Donna DeSalvo ganz begeistert darüber geäußert haben.[7] Das Konzert war von dem deutsch-jüdischen marxistischen Philosophen Franz Loeser, einem Freund von Paul, organisiert worden. Das Transatlantische Telefonkonzert war ein unglaublich wichtiger Akt der Solidarität gegen das von der US-Regierung verhängte Reiseverbot, das Robeson daran gehindert hatte, in Europa aufzutreten. Es war darüber hinaus ein wichtiger Moment der Freundschaft zwischen Robeson und Loeser. Später im selben Jahr emigrierte er nach Ost-Berlin, wo er mit staatlicher Zustimmung eine Unterstützungsinitiative für Robeson mobilisierte, die ein Ende des antikommunistischen Reiseverbots forderte. Robeson ist für die Generation der nach 1940 Geborenen genauso wichtig wie Angela Davis für die Generation der nach 1960 Geborenen. Diese Freundschaft – und das Konzert – standen auch im Mittelpunkt des Interesses von „The Missed Seminar". Was fasziniert Sie am Transatlantischen Telefonkonzert? Was können wir uns dabei erträumen?

SM: Ich glaube, es geht um die Vorstellung, die Dinge durchbrechen zu können. Die Tatsache, dass wo ein Wille ist, auch ein Weg ist. Das ist es, wozu Kunst in der Lage ist. Kunst war immer ein Werkzeug, sie war schon immer etwas, mit dem sich eine Situation verändern und überwinden lässt. Und ich denke, das hier ist ein großartiges Beispiel dafür. Die ganze Idee, dass eine Stimme tatsächlich so viel Enthusiasmus und Liebe hervorrufen kann. Und das findet hinsichtlich der Stimmen ein Echo in *End Credits*; diese Stimmen sind tatsächlich in der Lage, nachzuhallen und in einen Austausch zu treten.

DM: Am 27. August, wenige Tage nach ihrer Ankunft in Ost-Berlin, verfasste Eslanda eine Art Bericht mit dem Titel „'Kidnapped!' A True

7. Steve McQueen im Gespräch mit Donna De Salvo, 29. April 2016, im Rahmen der Ausstellung *Open Plan: Steve McQueen*, Whitney Museum of American Art, 2016.

DM: It's called *The Afro-American*. To my knowledge, it was founded in 1892 in Baltimore, starting as a daily newspaper and later becoming a weekly, with nine national editions published in several major cities across the US around the time Eslanda was publishing with them. The first part of "Kidnapped!" was titled "Why He 'Sneaked' to East Germany," and was published on November 2, 1963. The second part, published a week later, was titled "'Escape' Reads Like Movie Thriller," and the third part is "'Only Trying to Give Paul a Rest,'" published on November 16, 1963. The reason I share this with you is to ask: Why do you think there hasn't been a feature film on Paul and Eslanda Robeson yet?

SM: More than ten years ago, I tried to do something on the subject, but it proved very difficult to deal with the estate and the family. It's understandable. There's a lot going on with their legacy.

DM: Eslanda's writings, as well as all the material in archives not only at the Akademie der Künste in Berlin but also in the FBI files, operate like a script for a film that imagines their lives.

SM: No, it's not about imagining. It's a fact. It's actuality. It's fact and it's fiction. And there it is, and in the length of *End Credits*. This is my picture, my film, on the Robesons. It couldn't have been anything else. This was it. Sometimes you're looking at something and you think you should go a certain way and actually it's right in front of you. And I discovered that this was the ultimate picture that I could make of the Robesons, of Paul. I think biographical films are very tricky. I haven't really made one. They're particularly tricky with historical characters. With these files I made my narrative. It's a document, it's documentary, it's factual, it's all those things. All the things I would have ever wanted are in *End Credits*.

DM: I wasn't thinking so much of a biographical film on Paul and Eslanda but rather about the fabric, the relations, the friendships, the infrastructure they were part of.

Story" ('Entführt!' Eine wahre Geschichte), der ihre Flucht vor der andauernden Belästigung durch die Medien, die ihnen in London widerfahren war, dokumentiert.[8] Sie und Paul waren zwischen 1958 und 1963 nach London gezogen, kurz nach Beendigung des Reiseverbots. Journalisten belagerten ihr Haus am Connaught Square in London und jagten jeder kleinsten Information über die Robesons hinterher, insbesondere über Pauls Gesundheitszustand. In „,Kidnapped! A True Story" beschreibt Eslanda in tagebuchartigen Aufzeichnungen detailliert die Tricks, mit denen sie die wartenden Journalisten täuschten; wie sie ein Flugzeug der polnischen Luftfahrtgesellschaft LOT nach Ost-Berlin bestiegen, dort am Flughafen von Loeser begrüßt wurden und vom Empfang, den ihnen der Friedensrat in Ost-Berlin bereitete, dessen Einladung sie gefolgt waren. Sie praktiziert eine Art autotheoretisches Schreiben, dass die gelebte Erfahrung zur Grundlage für die Analyse politischer Realitäten nimmt. Das verortet ihren Ansatz in der Tradition Schwarzer Tagebuchliteratur –wie Zora Neale Hurston, Nella Larsen und die Autor·innen aus dem Zirkel um *The Crisis*, einer von W. E. B. DuBois gegründeten Zeitschrift –, in der sich Literarisches, Memoiren und journalistische Reportagen überschneiden. Eslandas zahlreiche Schriften, die bis heute nicht gesammelt veröffentlicht worden sind, bezeugen Schwarzes Leben wie auch ihr Engagement für einen panafrikanischen Feminismus. „,Kidnapped!' A True Story" wurde im November 1963 in drei Teilen in der Zeitung *The Afro-American* veröffentlicht.

SM: Welche Zeitung ist das?

DM: Sie hieß *The Afro-American*. Meines Wissens wurde sie 1892 in Baltimore gegründet, fing als Tageszeitung an und erschien später wöchentlich, mit neun nationalen Ausgaben in verschiedenen großen Städten in den USA zu der Zeit, als Eslanda dort publizierte. Der erste Teil von „,Kidnapped!'" trug den Titel „Why He ,Sneaked' to East Germany" (Warum er sich nach Ostdeutschland ,fortgeschlichen' hat) und erschien am 2. November 1963. Der eine Woche darauf veröffentlichte zweite Teil war übertitelt „,Escape' Reads Like Movie Thriller" (,Flucht' liest sich

8. Eslanda Goode Robeson, „Kidnapped!' A True Story", Paul Robeson Archiv, Akademie der Künste Berlin.

SM: Whatever you do, there is an element of the biographical. You can't escape that. It is what it is. And I didn't want to go down that road. In the end, this is it. *End Credits* couldn't have been a better demonstration of that.

DM: I wanted to mention another film reference—an unmade, unrealized film. In 1934, Paul received a letter from Sergei Eisenstein suggesting a film on the Haitian Revolution, with Paul as Toussaint Louverture. This anecdote was related by Paul Robeson Jr. in the documentary *Paul Robeson: Here I Stand*, directed by St. Clair Bourne, which came out in 1999. Paul Sr. also went to Moscow to speak with Eisenstein. What do you think would be needed to realize the Eisenstein film today, ninety years later?

SM: I can't really answer that. I don't know. I wish that it had been made. That's about all that I can say. I wish that it had been made, but it wasn't.

DM: I'm also asking because *End Credits* engages with the image as a tool of speaking, as politics. It goes beyond illustration. *End Credits* is not an illustration, yet it is an audiovisual portrait by other means, a film of extreme duration on the lives and struggles of the Robesons, as you put it so beautifully earlier.

SM: Yes, *End Credits* is not an interpretation. It's documenting a document. It's not a reinterpretation.

DM: The files contain an excess of documents, but through the erasures and the visibility of the infrastructure, this project goes beyond the document. Am I understanding you correctly? Are we returning to the holes in the system, the redactions and erasures in the documents?

SM: It doesn't go beyond the document. A document remains a document. These files were released in the seventies or eighties, so there is a distance. The first documents are from the mid-thirties. Now we are in 2022. They're almost like relics now, if anything. What can we learn from these relics, from bringing them into our everyday life today? I don't know.

---

wie ein Filmthriller), und der dritte Teil hieß „,Only Trying to Give Paul a Rest'" (‚Ich versuche bloß, Paul ein wenig Ruhe zu verschaffen'), veröffentlicht am 16. November 1963. Der Grund, warum ich Ihnen das erzähle, ist die Frage: Warum hat es Ihrer Ansicht nach bislang noch keinen Spielfilm über Paul und Eslanda Robeson gegeben?

SM: Vor mehr als zehn Jahren habe ich versucht, etwas zu dem Thema zu machen, aber der Umgang mit dem Nachlass und der Familie erwies sich als sehr schwierig. Was verständlich ist. Es passiert viel mit ihrem Erbe.

DM: Die Schriften von Eslanda wie auch das ganze Material in Archiven wie dem der Akademie der Künste in Berlin, aber auch in den Akten des FBI funktionieren wie ein Skript für einen Film, der sich ihr Leben vorstellt.

SM: Nein, es geht nicht ums Vorstellen. Es sind Fakten. Es ist die Wirklichkeit. Es ist Fakt und es ist Fiktion. Und das ist alles da, und es ist in der Dauer von *End Credits*. Das ist mein Bild, mein Film über die Robesons. Es hätte gar nichts anderes sein können. Das war es. Manchmal schaut man auf etwas und denkt, man sollte in eine bestimmte Richtung gehen, dabei liegt es einem tatsächlich direkt vor Augen. Und ich entdeckte, dass dies der ultimative Film ist, den ich über die Robesons, über Paul, machen konnte. Ich halte biografische Filme für äußerst heikel. Ich habe noch nie wirklich einen gemacht. Besonders heikel sind sie, wenn es um historische Figuren geht. Aus diesen Akten habe ich meine Geschichte gebaut. Es ist ein Dokument, es ist dokumentarisch, es ist faktisch, es ist all das. Alle Dinge, die mir jemals wichtig waren, sind in *End Credits* enthalten.

DM: Ich dachte gar nicht so sehr an einen biografischen Film über Paul und Eslanda, sondern über das Gewebe, die Beziehungen, die Freundschaften, die Infrastruktur, an der sie teilhatten.

SM: Egal, was du machst, es gibt darin immer ein Element des Biografischen. Dem kannst du nicht entkommen. So ist das nun mal. Und diesen Weg wollte ich nicht einschlagen. Und darum geht es letztendlich. *End Credits* hätte gar keinen besseren Beweis dafür darstellen können.

DM: It makes me think of Okwui Enwezor's exhibition *Archive Fever: Uses of the Document in Contemporary Art*, which was shown at the ICP in New York in 2008. The curatorial essay starts with a reflection on the archive in relation to the document and Foucault's "law of what can be said" as evidence. *End Credits* exposes the whole infrastructure of surveillance. Documenting a document, as you put it, makes it possible to honor the practice of resistance that we witness in the documents, while at the same time analyzing the violence from a distance. Documenting a document activates an estrangement effect, perhaps.

SM: There you go. An interpretation of an event in the past, which could be put into the present. What did that mean *then* to do a movie about Toussaint Louverture with Paul Robeson and Sergei Eisenstein? What was the intent?

Originally published in *e-flux journal* 136, May 2023

Steve McQueen, *End Credits* (2012–22), exhibited in conversation with *The Missed Seminar: After Eslanda Robeson*, Haus der Kulturen der Welt, Berlin, October 28 – December 30, 2022, installation view

Steve McQueen, *End Credits* (2012–2022), ausgestellt im Gespräch mit *The Missed Seminar: After Eslanda Robeson*, Haus der Kulturen der Welt, Berlin, 28. Oktober – 30. Dezember 2022, Installationsansicht

DM: Ich möchte noch eine weitere Filmreferenz erwähnen – einen liegengebliebenen, nicht realisierten Film. 1934 erhielt Paul einen Brief von Sergei Eisenstein, der einen Film über die Haitianische Revolution vorschlug, mit Paul als Toussaint Louverture. Diese Anekdote erzählt Paul Robeson Jr. im Dokumentarfilm *Paul Robeson: Here I Stand*, der unter der Regie von St. Clair Bourne entstand und 1999 herauskam. Paul Sr. ging sogar nach Moskau, um mit Eisenstein zu sprechen. Was glauben Sie, wäre nötig, um diesen Eisenstein-Film heute, neunzig Jahre später, zu realisieren?

SM: Das kann ich nicht wirklich beantworten, Ich weiß es nicht. Ich wünschte, der Film wäre gedreht worden. Das ist ungefähr alles, was ich dazu sagen kann. Ich wünschte, er wäre gemacht worden, aber das ist nicht passiert.

DM: Ich frage auch danach, weil *End Credits* sich mit dem Bild als einem Werkzeug des Sprechens auseinandersetzt, mit dem Bild als Politik. Der Film geht über die Illustration hinaus. *End Credits* ist keine Illustration, und doch ist es ein audiovisuelles Porträt mit anderen Mitteln, ein Film mit einer extremen Dauer über das Leben und die Kämpfe der Robesons, wie Sie es vorhin so schön gesagt haben.

SM: Ja, *End Credits* ist keine Interpretation. Er dokumentiert ein Dokument. Es ist keine Neuinterpretation.

DM: Die Akten enthalten einen Exzess an Dokumenten, aber durch die Ausradierungen und die Sichtbarkeit der Infrastruktur geht das Projekt über das Dokument hinaus. Verstehe ich Sie richtig? Kehren wir zu den Löchern im System zurück, den Schwärzungen und Auslassungen in den Dokumenten.

SM: Er geht nicht über das Dokument hinaus. Ein Dokument bleibt ein Dokument. Diese Akten wurden in den 1970er oder 1980er Jahren freigegeben, also gibt es da eine Distanz. Die ersten Dokumente stammen aus der Mitte der 1930er Jahre. Jetzt haben wir 2022. Sie sind beinahe so etwas wie Relikte, wenn überhaupt irgendetwas. Was können wir von diesen Relikten lernen, was können wir davon lernen, wenn wir sie in unser heutiges Alltagsleben einschleusen? Ich weiß es nicht.

DM: Es lässt mich an Okwui Enwezors Ausstellung *Archive Fever: Uses of the Document in Contemporary Art* denken, die am ICP in New York 2008 gezeigt wurde. Der kuratorische Essay beginnt mit einer Reflexion über das Archiv in Bezug auf das Dokument und Foucaults „Gesetz dessen, was gesagt werden kann" als Evidenz. *End Credits* legt die gesamte Infrastruktur der Überwachung offen. Ein Dokument zu dokumentieren, wie Sie es nennen, ermöglicht es, die Praxis des Widerstands zu würdigen, die wir in den Dokumenten antreffen, und zugleich die Gewalt aus einer gewissen Distanz zu analysieren. Ein Dokument zu dokumentieren, aktiviert möglicherweise einen Verfremdungseffekt.

SM: Da haben wir's. Eine Interpretation eines Ereignisses in der Vergangenheit, das in die Gegenwart versetzt werden kann. Was bedeutete es *damals*, einen Film über Toussaint Louverture mit Paul Robeson und Sergei Eisenstein zu machen? Was war die Absicht?

Zuerst veröffentlicht in *e-flux journal* 136, Mai 2023

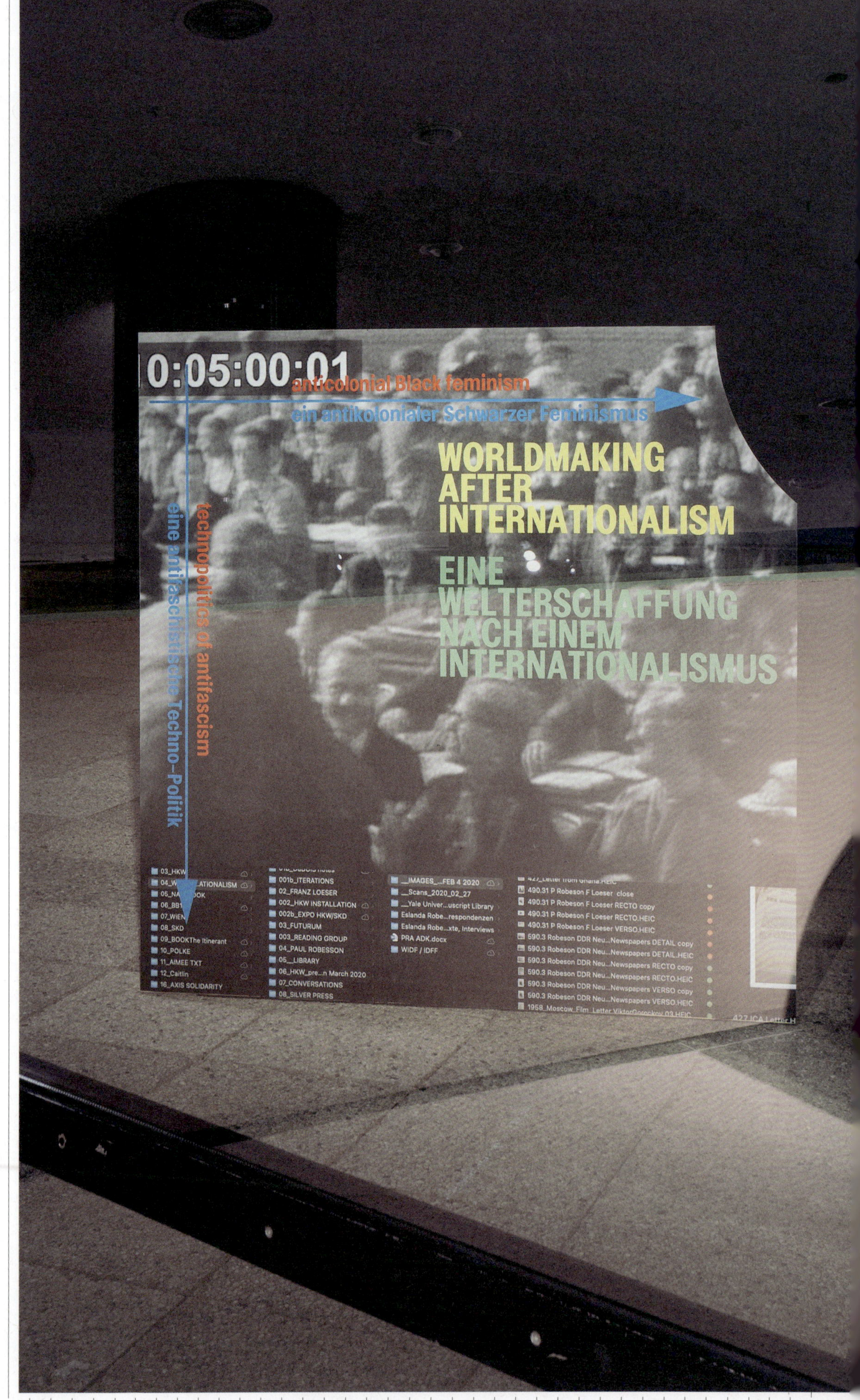
0:05:00:01
anticolonial Black feminism
ein antikolonialer Schwarzer Feminismus
technopolitics of antifascism
eine antifaschistische Techno-Politik
WORLDMAKING
AFTER
INTERNATIONALISM
EINE
WELTERSCHAFFUNG
NACH EINEM
INTERNATIONALISMUS
03_HKW
04_W...RNATIONALISM
06_NA...OK
06_BB1
07_WIEN
08_SKD
09_BOOKThe Itinerant
10_POLKE
11_AIMEE TXT
12_Caitlin
16_AXIS SOLIDARITY
001b_ITERATIONS
02_FRANZ LOESER
002_HKW INSTALLATION
002b_EXPO HKW/SKD
03_FUTURUM
003_READING GROUP
04_PAUL ROBESSON
05__LIBRARY
06_HKW_pre...n March 2020
07_CONVERSATIONS
08_SILVER PRESS
IMAGES...FEB 4 2020
_Scans_2020_02_27
_Yale Univer...uscript Library
Eslanda Robe...respondenzen
Eslanda Robe...xte, Interviews
PRA ADK.docx
WIDF / IDFF
427_Letter from Ghana.HEIC
490.31 P Robeson F Loeser close
490.31 P Robeson F Loeser RECTO.HEIC
490.31 P Robeson F Loeser RECTO copy
490.31 P Robeson F Loeser VERSO.HEIC
590.3 Robeson DDR Neu...Newspapers DETAIL copy
590.3 Robeson DDR Neu...Newspapers DETAIL.HEIC
590.3 Robeson DDR Neu...Newspapers RECTO copy
590.3 Robeson DDR Neu...Newspapers RECTO.HEIC
590.3 Robeson DDR Neu...Newspapers VERSO copy
590.3 Robeson DDR Neu...Newspapers VERSO.HEIC
1958_Moscow_Film_Letter ViktorGoonckow 03.HEIC
427 ICA Letter H

THE MISSED SEMINAR: AFTER ESLANDA ROBESON

A diagrammatic image creating a viewing axis to John-Foster-Dulles Allee, which *The Missed Seminar* imagines as Eslanda-Robeson-Allee. The coordinates "anti-colonial Black feminism" and "technopolitics of anti-fascism" emerge from the archival presence of Eslanda Robeson and Franz Loeser attending the first day (July 8, 1963) of the trial in the Supreme Court of the GDR of a case brought in absentia against the Nazi-era lawyer and then West German state secretary Hans Globke: a mediatized state spectacle, produced by Intervision / Интервидение, that both loudly protests the state's anti-fascism and obscures the continuity of fascist ideology under state socialism in the GDR. Pulsing beneath the surface is a research infrastructure that invokes tentacles of memory entwining fact, fiction, and the unfolding of the future.

THE MISSED SEMINAR: NACH ESLANDA ROBESON

Ein Diagramm-Bild bildet eine Blickachse zur John-Foster-Dulles Allee, die *The Missed Seminar* als Eslanda-Robeson-Allee imaginiert. Die Koordinaten „anti-kolonialer Schwarzer Feminismus" und „Technopolitik des Antifaschismus" ergeben sich aus der archivarischen Gegenwart von Eslanda Robeson und Franz Loeser. Am 8. Juli 1963, dem ersten Tag des Prozesses vor dem Obersten Gericht der DDR gegen den Verwaltungsjuristen des NS-Regimes und damaligen westdeutschen Staatssekretär Hans Globke in Abwesenheit sind die beiden vor Ort: ein mediales Staats-Spektakel, produziert von Intervision / Интервидение, das einerseits einen staatlichen Antifaschismus-Anspruch erhebt, aber andererseits auch die Kontinuität der faschistischen Ideologie im Staatssozialismus der DDR verschleiert. Darunter pulsiert eine Forschungsinfrastruktur, die Tentakel des Erinnerns zwischen Fakt, Fiktion und Futurum erscheinen lässt.

A split-image attempting to look at the architecture of Haus der Kulturen der Welt (HKW) as an exhibit, both curatorially and juridically: on the one hand, the viewing axis evokes the lifelong fearlessness, love, and friendship of Eslanda and Paul Robeson as they resisted the structural racial violence they were forced to endure, evident in the thousands of FBI files. On the other hand, the violence can also be found in the architecture of the HKW. Constructed in 1957 as a congress hall, it was a gift from the US

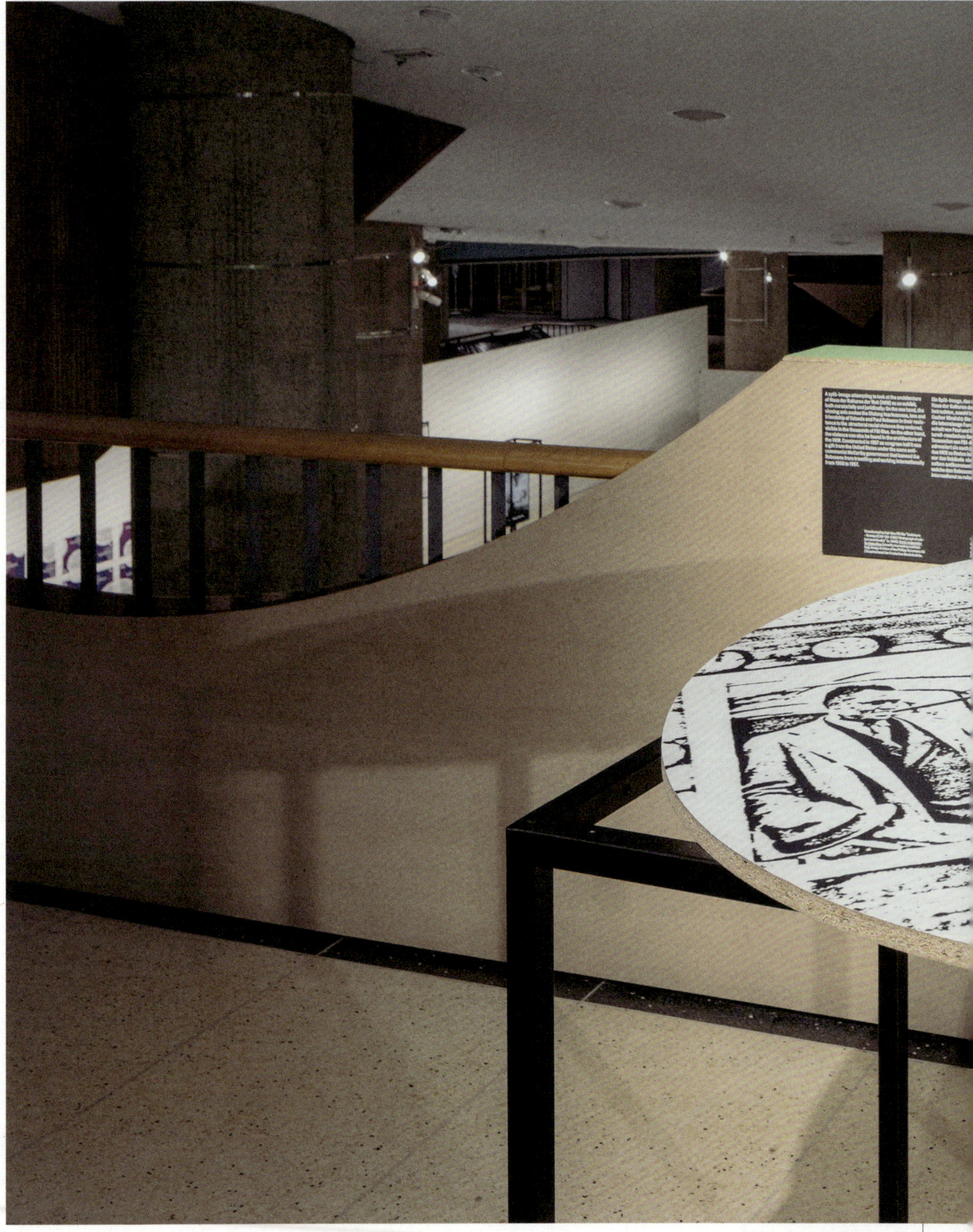

Ein geteiltes Bild, das versucht, die Architektur des Hauses der Kulturen der Welt (HKW) als *exhibit* zu betrachten, kuratorisch als Ausstellungs-, juristisch als Beweisstück: Die Blickachse evoziert einerseits die lebenslange Furchtlosigkeit, Liebe und Freundschaft von Paul und Eslanda Robeson, die der strukturell-rassischen Gewalt entgegentritt, wie sie in Tausenden von FBI-Akten sichtbar wird. Andererseits adressiert sie auch jene Gewalt, die in der Architektur des HKW zu finden ist. 1957 als Kongresshalle erbaut,

under the same anti-communist McCarthy-era government that banned the Robesons from traveling and working internationally from 1950 to 1957.

Transformative fair use of the FBI file "Enclosure – Bureau (1) NY 100-25857 Photograph of subject and his wife" (ca. 1945) and *stetig steigender Gerüstaufbau* (Steadily Mounting Scaffolding) from the Philipp Holzmann AG picture archive, Berlin-Brandenburgisches Wirtschaftsarchiv

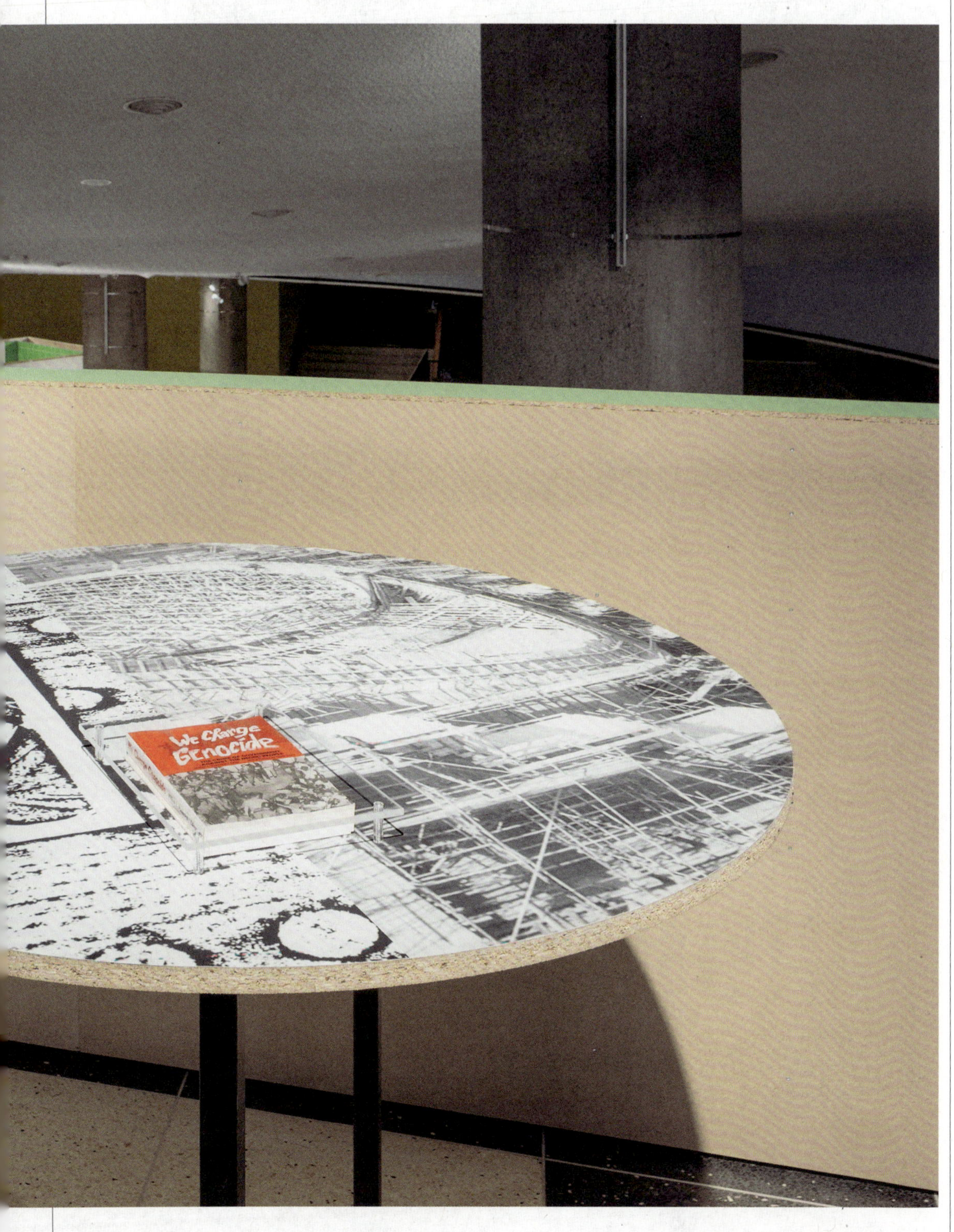

war das Gebäude ein Geschenk der USA unter derselben antikommunistischen Regierung der McCarthy-Ära, welche es den Robesons von 1950 bis 1957 untersagte, international zu reisen und zu arbeiten.

Transformative Fair Use der FBI-Akte „Enclosure – Bureau (1) NY 100-25857 Photograph of subject and his wife" (um 1945) und *stetig steigender Gerüstaufbau* des Bildarchivs der Philipp Holzmann AG, Berlin-Brandenburgisches Wirtschaftsarchiv.

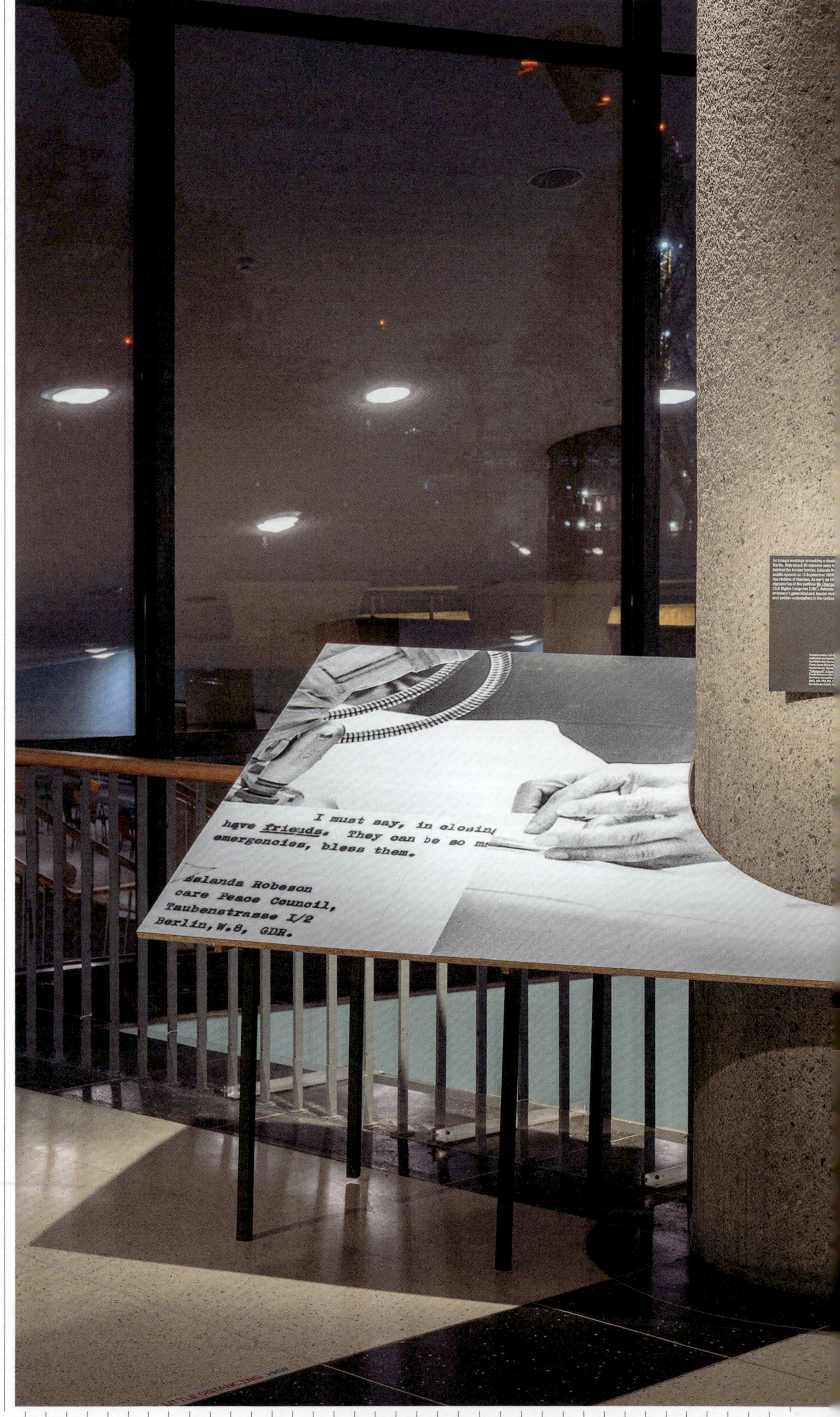
I must say, in closin
have friends. They can be so m
emergencies, bless them.

slanda Robeson
care Peace Council,
Taubenstrasse I/2
Berlin, W.8, GDR.

An image montage creating a viewing axis that looks toward East Berlin. Only about thirty minutes away from the HKW, which was then behind the Berlin Wall, Eslanda Robeson gave a public speech on September 13, 1959, to commemorate the victims of fascism. Back in 1951, as one of many signatories of the petition "We Charge Genocide" by the Civil Rights Congress (CRC), Eslanda related White supremacy's genocidal and fascist violence to slavery and settler colonialism in the United States, accusing the US government of genocide based on the UN Genocide Convention, which was presented to the United Nations in Paris in December 1951.

Transformative fair use: Horst Sturm, "Massenkundgebung anlässlich des Gedenktages für die Opfer des faschistischen Terrors," September 13, 1959, Paul Robeson Archive Akademie der Künste Berlin, PRA 612.11 and "'Kidnapped!' A True Story," written by Eslanda Goode Robeson after her arrival as guest of the Peace Council in East Berlin on August 27, 1963, PRA 345.

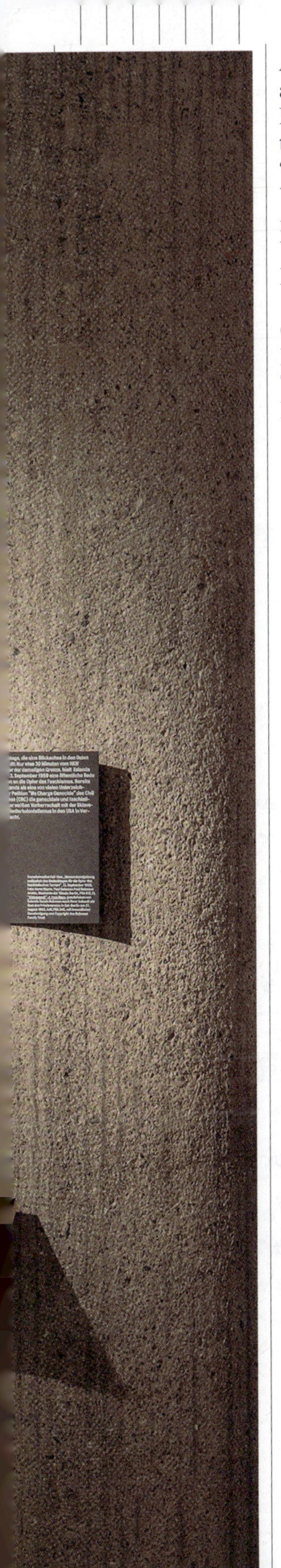

Bild-Montage, die eine Blickachse in den Osten Berlins herstellt: Nur etwa 30 Minuten vom HKW entfernt, hinter der damaligen Grenze, hielt Eslanda Robeson am 13. September 1959 eine öffentliche Rede zum Gedenken an die Opfer des Faschismus. Bereits 1951 hatte Eslanda als eine von vielen Unterzeichner·innen der Petition „We Charge Genocide" des Civil Rights Congress (CRC) die genozidale und faschistische Gewalt der weißen Vorherrschaft mit der Sklaverei und dem Siedlerkolonialismus in den USA in Verbindung gebracht. Die Regierung der Vereinigten Staaten wurde auf Grundlage der UN-Völkermordkonvention, welche im Dezember 1951 bei den Vereinten Nationen in Paris vorgestellt wurde, des Völkermordes beschuldigt.

Transformative Fair Use: Horst Sturm, „Massenkundgebung anlässlich des Gedenktages für die Opfer des faschistischen Terrors", 13. September 1959, Paul Robeson Archiv, Akademie der Künste Berlin, PRA 612.11, und *„Kidnapped!" A True Story*, geschrieben von Eslanda Goode Robeson nach ihrer Ankunft als Gast des Friedensrates in Ost-Berlin am 27. August 1963, PRA 345.

54

Eslanda Goode Robeson, an excerpt from "'Kidnapped!' A True Story," 9 Seiten. The essay was written in 1963, shortly after Paul and Eslanda's arrival at Berlin-Schönefeld airport as guests of the Peace Council. The diaristic report evokes their resistance to the experience of being hunted by the anti-communist media in London. Eslanda describes it as an "escape [that] reads like a movie thriller" in the November 1963 installment of her three-part text published in *The Afro-American*.

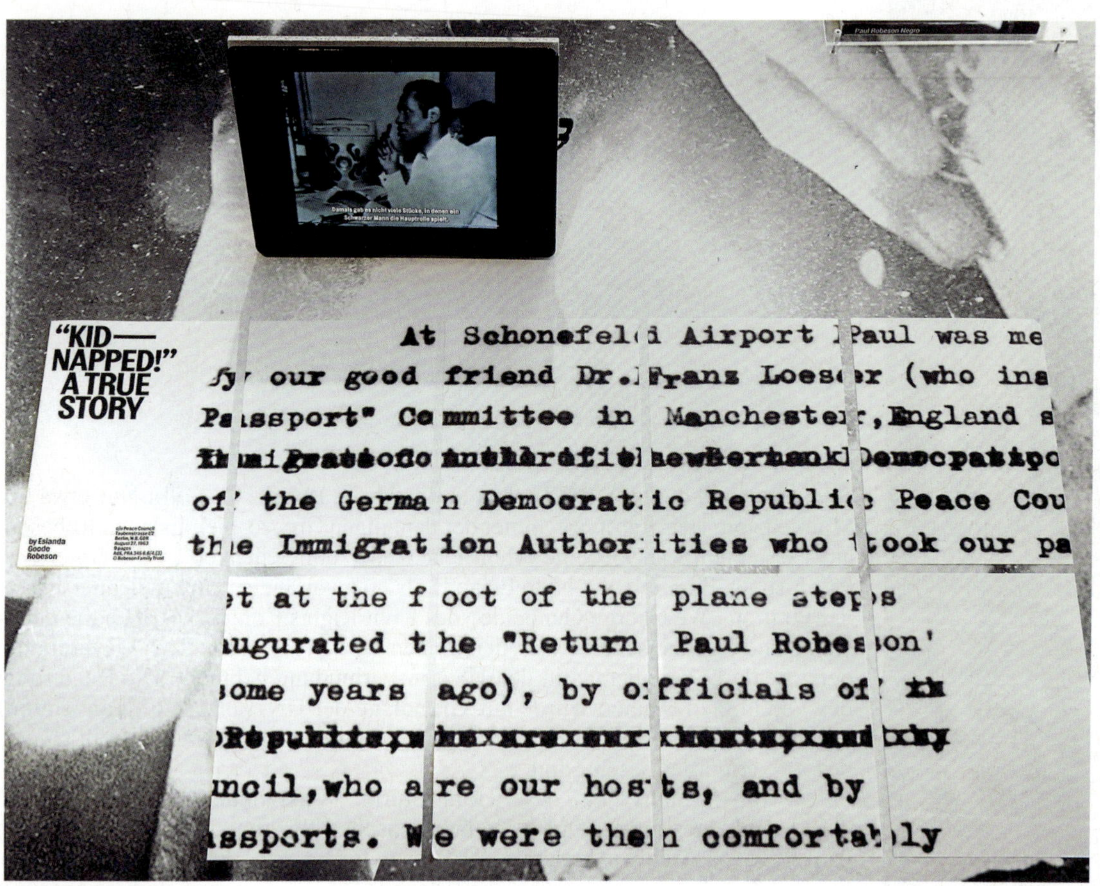

Eslanda Goode Robeson, Auszug aus „*Kidnapped!*" *A True Story*, 9 Seiten. Der Text entstand 1963, kurz nach Pauls und Eslandas Ankunft auf dem Flughafen Berlin-Schönefeld als Gäste des Friedensrates. Der tagebuchartig geschriebene Bericht reflektiert ihren Widerstand gegen die antikommunistische Hetzjagd von Journalisten in London, eine „Flucht [die] sich wie ein Film-Thriller liest", wie einer von drei Teilen ihres Textes in der Zeitung *The Afro-American* im November 1963 betitelt wurde.

Eslanda Goode Robeson, speech at the rally held on the day commemorating the victims of fascism, East Berlin, January 27, 1963, 2 pages, unpublished manuscript. Correspondence between Eslanda Robeson and Franz & Diana Loeser scheduling a visit to Berlin, October 1960, 2 pages. The visit took place between August and December 1963.

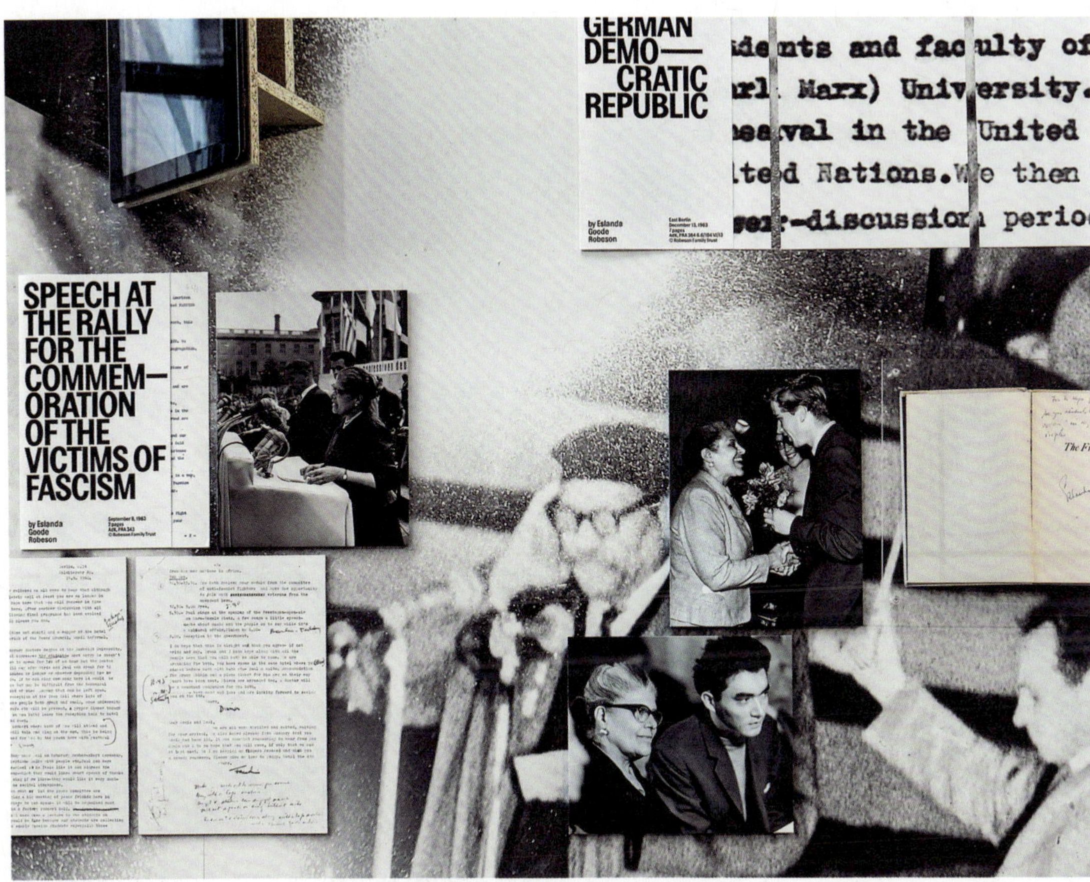

Eslanda Goode Robeson, Redebeitrag zur Kundgebung am Tag der Opfer des Faschismus, Ost-Berlin, 27. Januar 1963, 2 Seiten, unveröffentlichtes Manuskript; Briefwechsel von Eslanda Robeson mit Franz und Diana Loeser zum Ablauf eines geplanten Besuchs in Berlin, Oktober 1960, 2 Seiten, der Besuch fand zwischen August und Dezember 1963 statt.

Eslanda Goode Robeson, excerpt from "In the German Democratic Republic," 1963, 7 pages. Written at the end of her stay in the GDR, the unpublished script narrates her many public, political and intellectual activities, including the visit of the International Documentary Film Festival and the African students meeting at the Herder Institute, both in Leipzig; a forum on the "Negro in the United States" at Berlin's

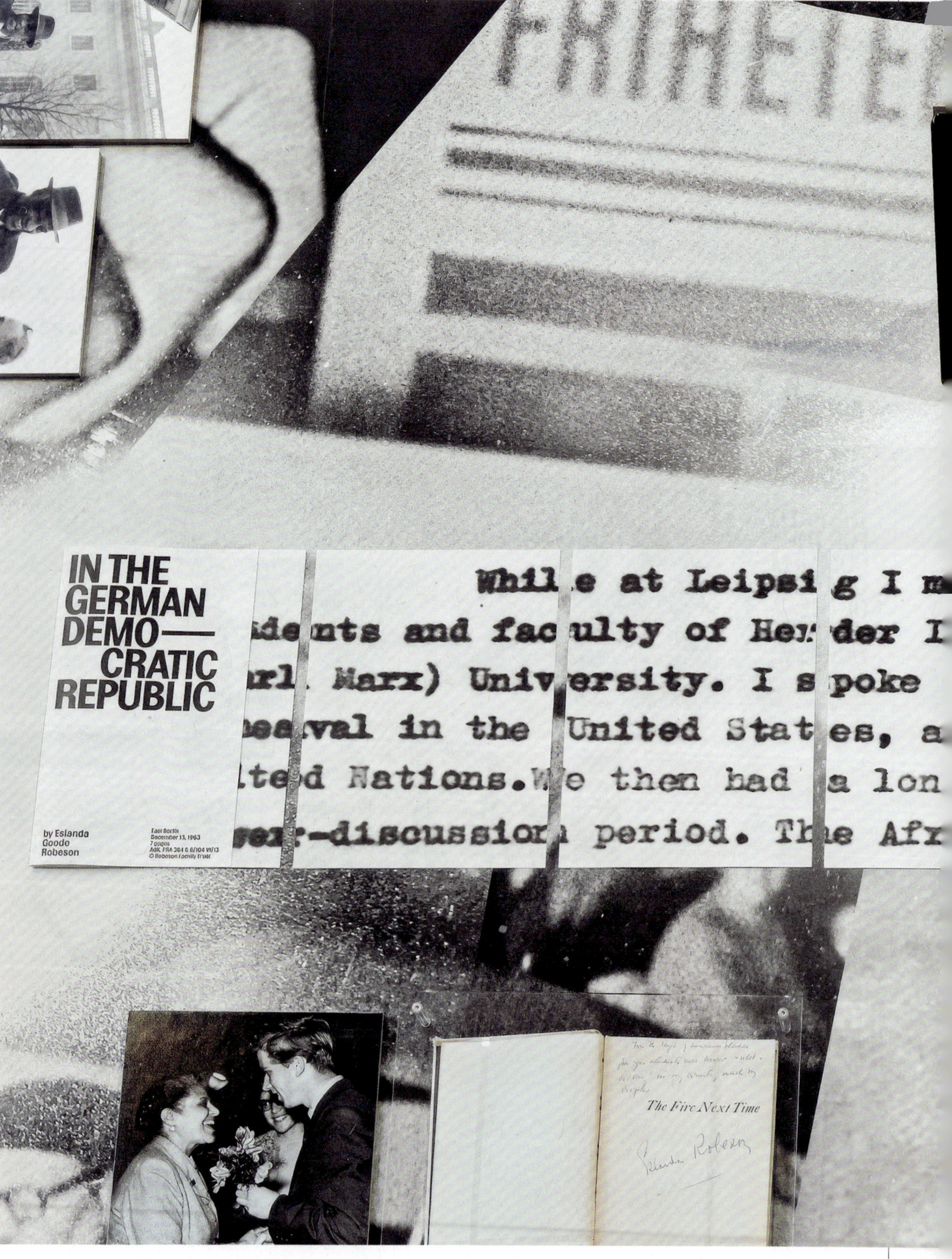

Eslanda Goode Robeson, Auszug aus *In der Deutschen Demokratischen Republik*, 1963, 7 Seiten. Das unveröffentlichte Skript, das am Ende ihres Aufenthalts in der DDR geschrieben wurde, schildert die verschiedenen öffentlichen, politischen und intellektuellen Aktivitäten, darunter den Besuch des Internationalen Dokumentarfilmfestivals und ein Treffen mit afrikanischen Studierenden am Herder-Institut, beides in Leipzig; ein Forum über den „Negro in the United States" an der Humboldt-Universität zu

Humboldt university with the lawyer Earl Dickerson, reverend Steven Fritchman, Mrs. Lay Cole, and Franz Loeser; a meeting with Jeanne Martin Cissé from the Republic of Guinea at the Women's International Democratic Federation in East Berlin on Unter den Linden; and her medical treatment at the clinic in Berlin Buch.

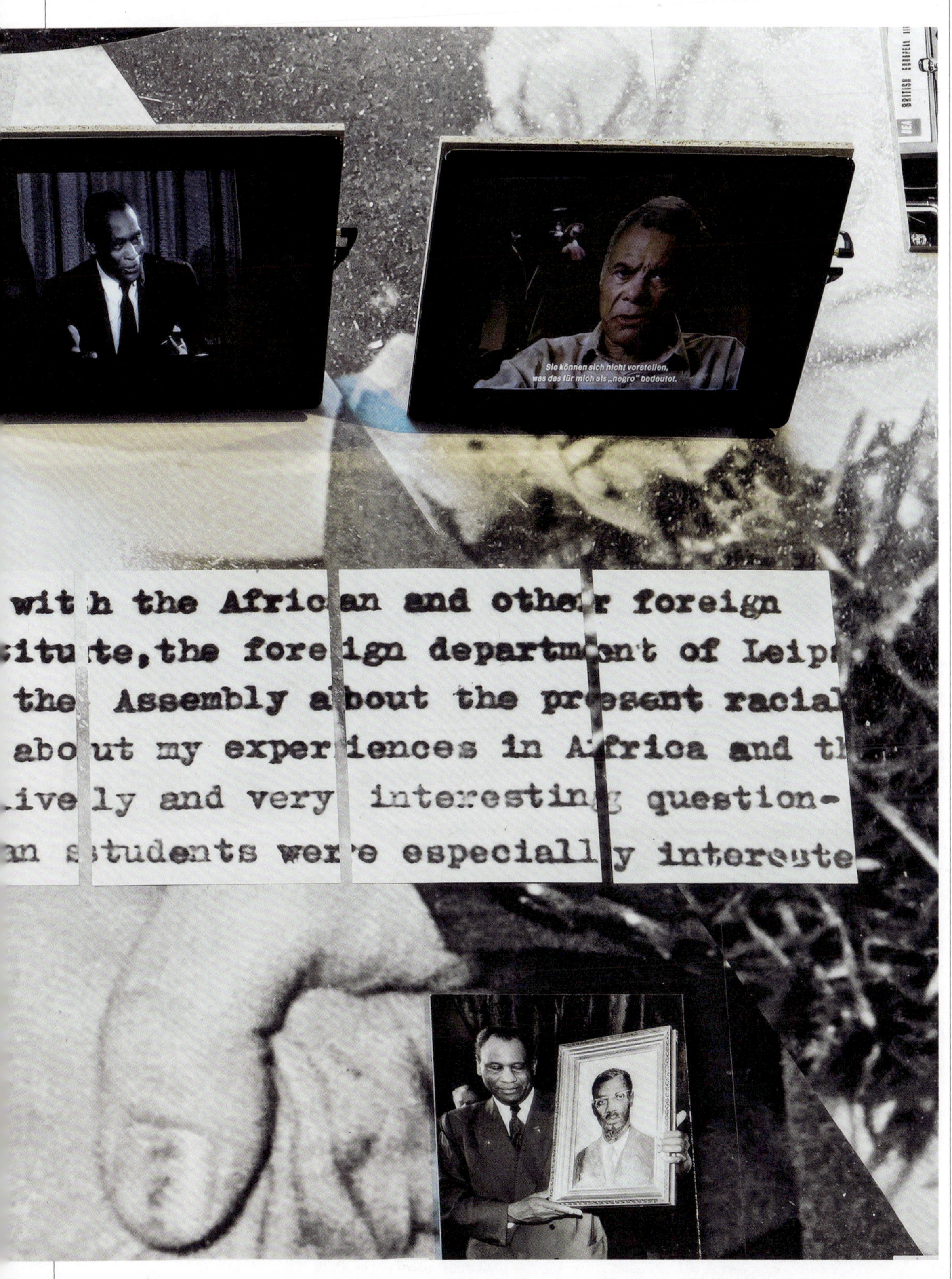

Berlin mit dem Rechtsanwalt Earl Dickerson, Reverend Steven Fritchman, Mrs. Lay Cole und Franz Loeser; ein Treffen mit Jeanne Martin Cissé aus der Republik Guinea bei der Internationalen Demokratischen Frauenföderation in Ost-Berlin in der Straße Unter den Linden sowie ihre medizinische Behandlung in der Klinik in Berlin-Buch.

Franz Loeser, *Die Abenteuer eines Emigranten: Erinnerungen* (Adventures of an Emigrant: Memories), Verlag Neues Leben, 1980, 349 pages, East German version of his autobiography

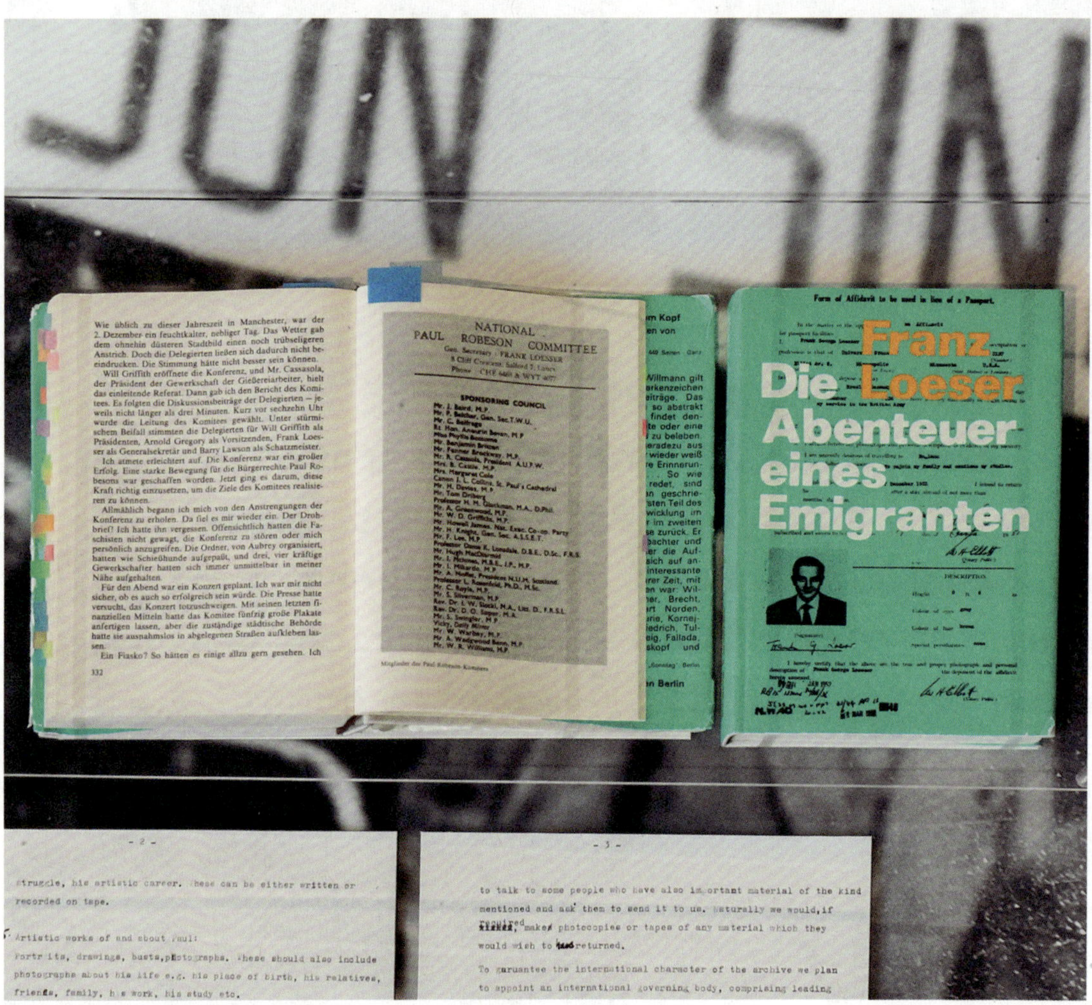

Franz Loeser, *Die Abenteuer eines Emigranten. Erinnerungen,* Berlin: Verlag Neues Leben 1980, 349 Seiten. DDR-Ausgabe seiner Autobiografie.

Eslanda Robeson, *African Journey*, Victor Gollancz, 1946, 187 pages. Eslanda Goode Robeson's second book, *African Journey*, is a diaristic account of her travels to Congo, Uganda, South Africa, and other countries on the African continent during the mid-1930s. There, she took notes from meetings with women groups and photographs of everyday life, including of herself and her son, Paul Jr. Robeson's images reveal a sensitivity toward the situations she both observed and participated in. Her photographic practice, which Leigh Raiford described as a "pan-African gaze," did away with the ethnological separation between continental Africans and people of African descent living in the US or Europe.

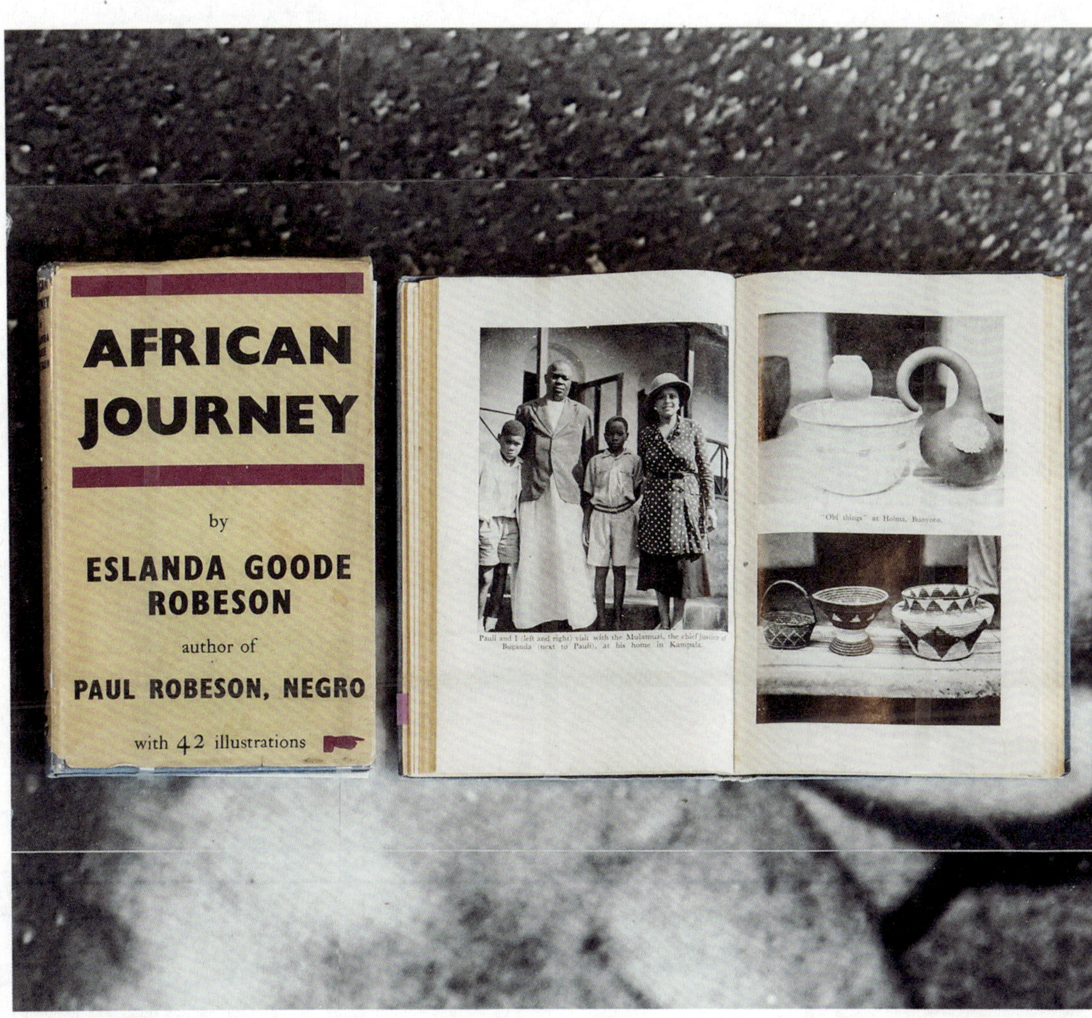

Eslanda Robeson, *African Journey*, London: Victor Gollancz Ltd. 1946, 187 Seiten. Das zweite Buch von Eslanda Goode Robeson, *African Journey*, ist ein tagebuchartiger Erfahrungsbericht über ihre Reisen in den Kongo, nach Uganda, Südafrika und zu anderen Orten auf dem Kontinent Mitte der 1930er Jahre. Sie beschrieb Begegnungen mit Frauengruppen und machte Fotos vom Alltagsleben, auch von sich selbst und ihrem Sohn Paul Jr. Robesons Bildpraxis zeigt eine Sensibilität für Situationen, welche sie beobachtet und deren Teil sie ist. Leigh Reiford spricht mit Bezug auf ihre Fotografien von einem „panafrikanischen Blick", der die ethnologische Trennung zwischen Menschen afrikanischer Abstammung auf dem afrikanischen Kontinent von denen in den USA oder Europa aufhebt.

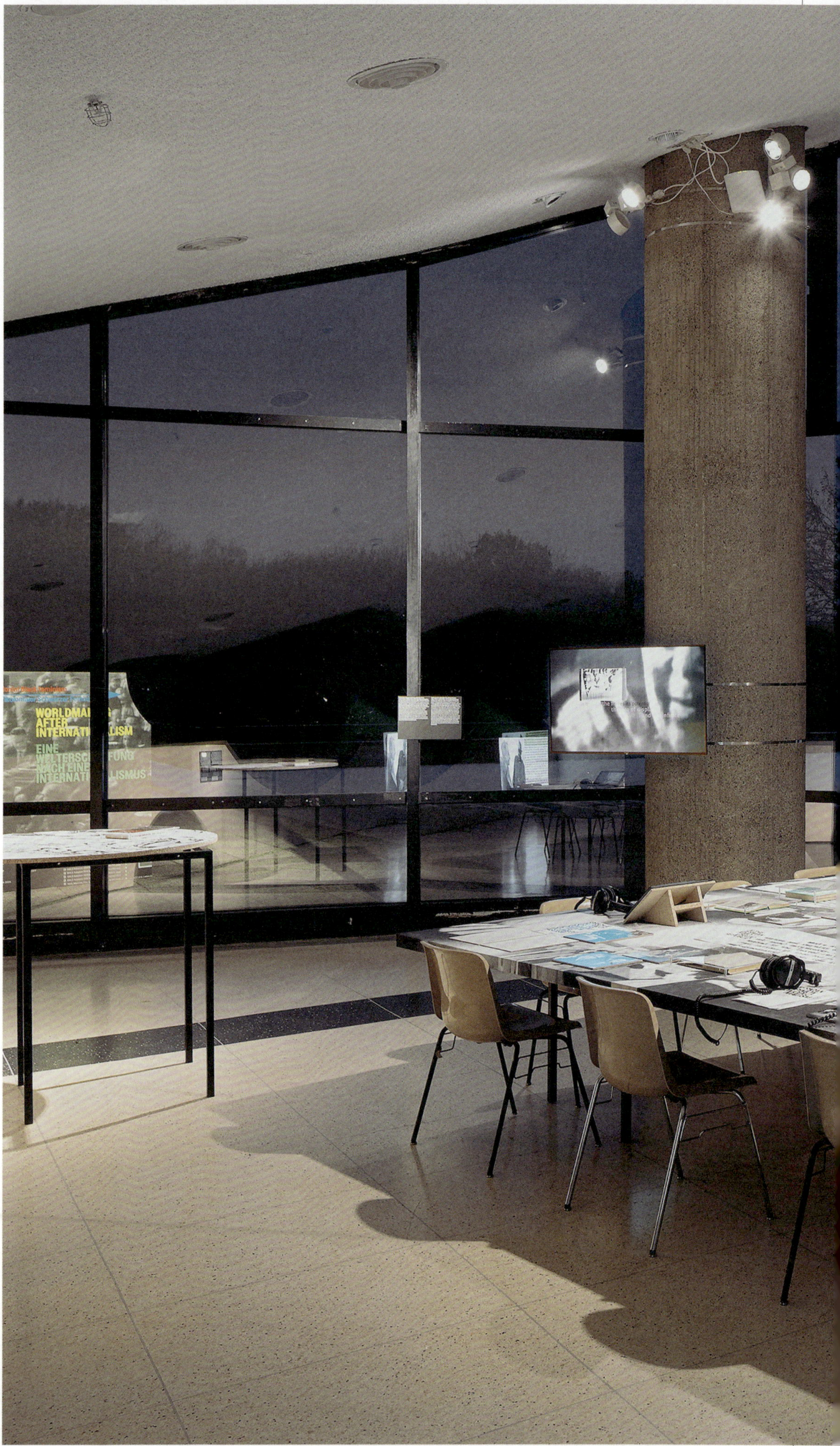

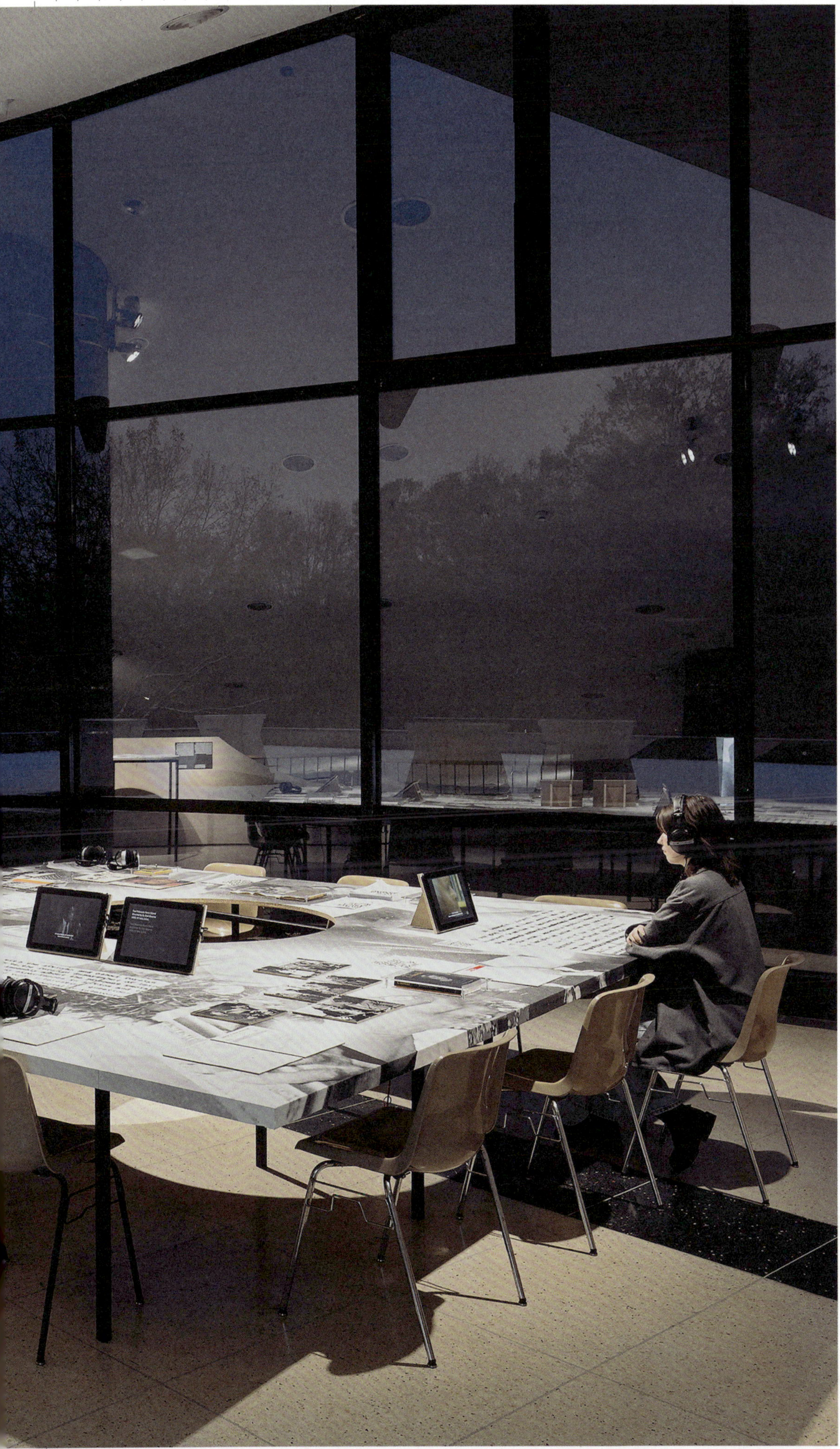

PIXEL CLARITY LIGHT

Aarti Sunder

PIXEL KLARHEIT LICHT

once a photograph
　　　then a newspaper cutout

　　now a digitized image

become
samples to
code and
re-code

infinite
samples
exist
　　it is
　　impossible
　　to grasp them all

looking at digital images is like looking at the
infinite

　　A compressed digital image exists like an
　　abbreviation

it reappears
when it is displayed as
light or sound

　　and then it disappears

referring to itself to construct itself, in a state of
constant reinvention

in this reinvention lies its potential

between the finite
　　the site of display
　　　　and the infinite

　　　　in the moment the
　　　　image is opened and
　　　　encountered again

never to be fully saturated,

always leaving something unsaid

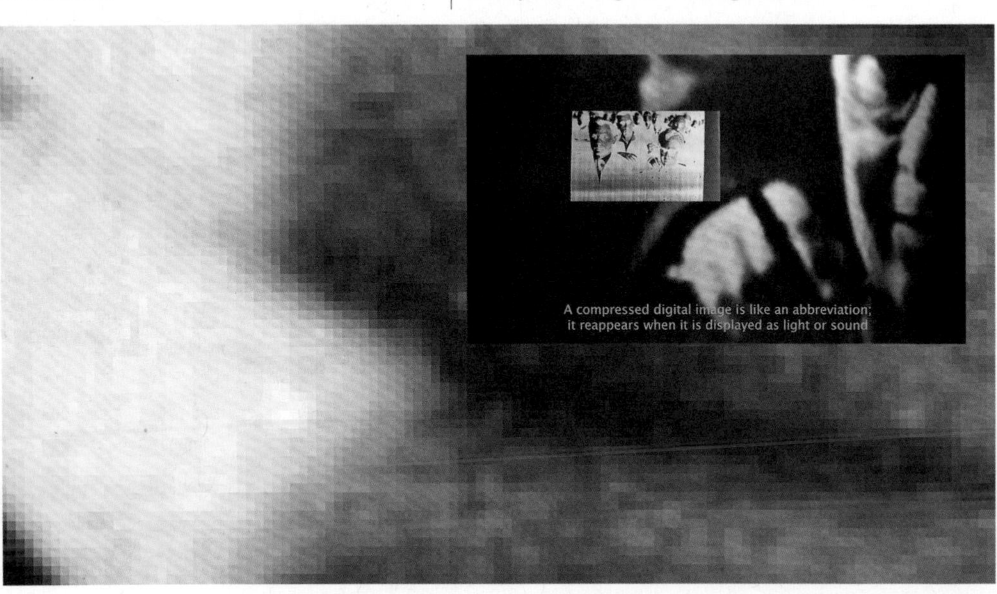

Detail of a photograph of Eslanda Robeson and Franz Loeser as observers in the criminal trial of Hans Globke (in absentia), Supreme Court of the GDR, Berlin, July 8, 1963, overlaid with video stills from Aarti Sunder's work *Pixel Clarity Light*

erst ein Foto
　　　　dann ein Zeitungsausschnitt

　　jetzt ein digitales Bild

werden zu
Schnipseln
kodiert und
umkodiert

unendlich viele
Schnipsel
existieren
　　es ist
　　unmöglich
　　sie alle zu begreifen

das Betrachten digitaler Bilder ist wie das
Betrachten des Unendlichen

　　Ein komprimiertes digitales Bild ist wie
　　eine Abkürzung

　　　　es erscheint wieder

wenn es gezeigt wird als
Licht oder Ton

　　und dann verschwindet es

es bezieht sich auf sich selbst, um sich selbst zu
erschaffen, in einem Zustand ständiger Neuerfindung

in dieser Neuerfindung liegt sein Potenzial

zwischen dem Endlichen
　　dem Ort der Darstellung
　　　　und dem Unendlichen

　　　　in dem Augenblick,
　　　　in dem das Bild
　　　　geöffnet und wieder
　　　　wahrgenommen wird

ohne jemals vollständig gesättigt zu sein,

immer etwas ungesagt lassend

die Voraussetzung der Kommunikation erfüllend.

fulfilling the premise of communication.

The moment of reconstitution where 1963
meets the present, is the site of friction

      friction

travels
between
people

organizations

machines   friction

meeting
resistance

expansion   friction

reproduction
is immaterial   friction

creative

contigent   friction

unstable

is translatable   friction

always existing

increasing   friction

always being
encountered

this image
also contains
metadata

information
about
information

aiding its

Der Augenblick der Wiederherstellung in dem
das Jahr 1963
auf die Gegenwart trifft ist ein Ort der Reibung
      Reibung

bewegt sich
zwischen
Menschen

Organisationen

Maschinen   Reibung

trifft auf Widerstand

Ausdehnung   Reibung

Reproduktion
ist nichtmateriell   Reibung

schöpferische

bedingte   Reibung

unbeständige

ist übersetzbar   Reibung

immer gegeben

zunehmend   Reibung

immer wieder
anzutreffen

dieses Bild
beinhaltet
Metadaten

Informationen
über
Informationen

unterstützen seine
Wiederverwendung

Austausch
über verschiedene

reuse

sharing
across
surfaces

people

contexts

time zones

generations

metadata
gets built
over time

it is always   fragmented
divergent
iterative
incomplete

ambiguous
corrupted
divergent
iterative
incomplete
ambiguous
corrupted

reparing it
involves
conversing
with
the original
inhabitants of
the image

its creators

its actors

its contenders

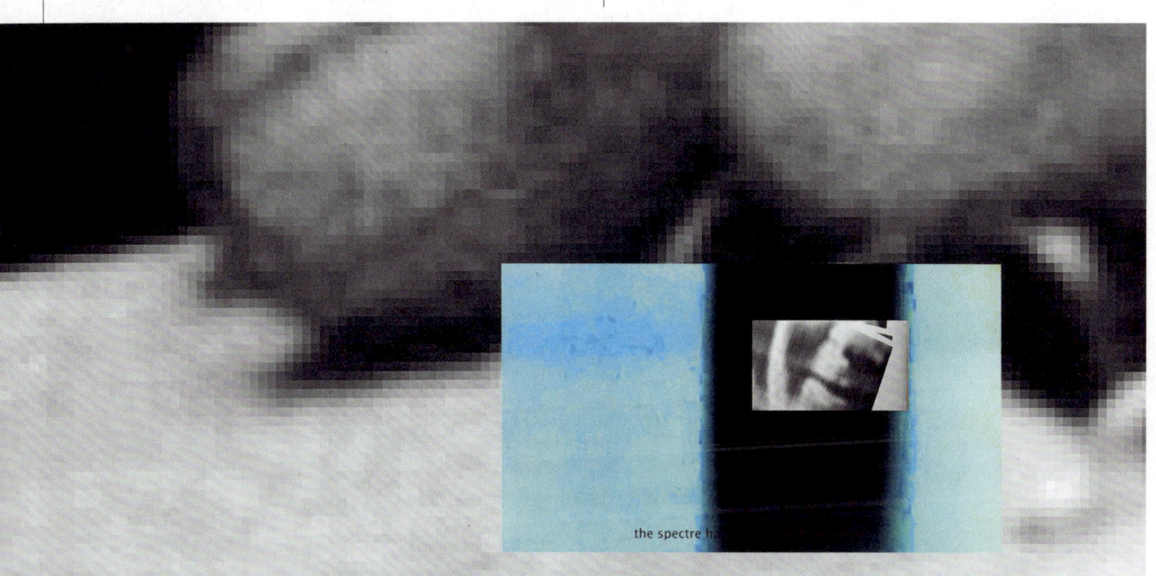

Oberflächen

Menschen

Zusammenhänge

Zeitzonen

Generationen

im Laufe der Zeit
werden Metadaten
zusammengetragen

sie sind immer   fragmentiert
abweichend
wiederholend
unvollständig
mehrdeutig
verfälscht
abweichend
wiederholend
unvollständig
mehrdeutig

verfälscht

sie zu reparieren
beinhaltet
einen Dialog
mit
denen
die ursprünglich
im Bild lebten

die es schufen

die darin handelten

die es herausforderten

diese von Reibung
durchdrungenen
Dialoge
laufen zwischen

Berufen
Maschinen
Generationen

these friction
soaked
conversations
happen across

professions
machines
generations

metadata generation then becomes a process
inscribed
with time

like evolving organizational diagrams deeply
entangled
with turbulence

that requires patience and energy to make
intelligible

frictions of reconstitution encounter

frictions of invisibility, scale and volume

the frictional encounter is
embedded in uncertainty.

focibly reducing
it ensures
its return with
haunting force

the spectre has
taken time to
reappear

recognising it is a
moment of intense
power,
and should not be
misdiagnosed as a
weakness.

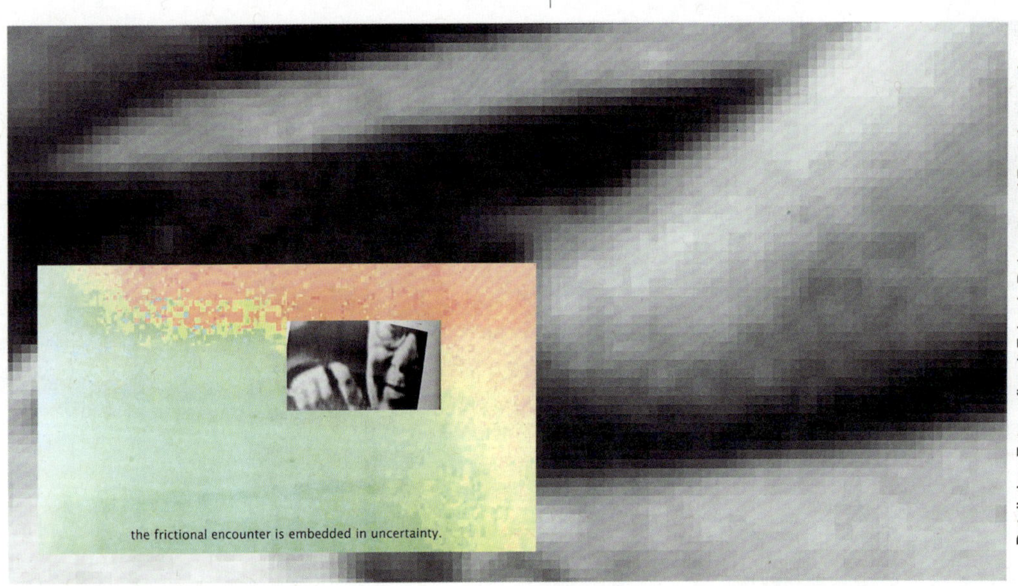

Detail einer Fotografie mit Eslanda Robeson und Franz Loeser als Beobachter im Strafprozess gegen Hans Globke (in absentia), Berlin, Oberstes Gericht der DDR, 8. Juli 1963, gerahmt durch Videostils aus Aarti Sunders *Pixel Clarity Light*

die Erzeugung von Metadaten wird dann zu
einem Prozess, dem die Zeit eingeschrieben ist

wie sich laufend verändernde Organigramme, tief
verquickt
in Turbulenzen

die nur mit Geduld und Energie verständlich
gemacht werden können

Reibungen der Wiederherstellung begegnen

Reibungen der Unsichtbarkeit, des Maßstabs und
der Lautstärke

die spannungsgeladene
Begegnung
ist eingebettet in
Unbestimmtheit.

Seine erzwungene
Verkleinerung gewährleistet
seine Rückkehr mit
gespenstischer Kraft

es brauchte Zeit
bis das Gespenst
wieder auftauchte

dies zu erkennen ist ein
Augenblick eindringlicher
Macht
und sollte nicht
fälschlich als Schwäche
diagnostiziert werden.

ESLANDA GOODE ROBESON: A RADICAL INTERNATIONALIST WRITER, OR "IF I AM A WRITER"

Katharina Warda

ESLANDA GOODE ROBESON. EINE RADIKALE INTERNATIONALISTISCHE SCHRIFTSTELLERIN – ODER: „FALLS ICH EINE SCHRIFTSTELLERIN BIN"

Script by Eslanda Robeson, 403 Archivnummer, Akademie der Künste, Berlin.

"How I became a writer (if I am a writer)" is the title of a 1949 essay by Eslanda Goode Robeson that is now all but forgotten. The words "if I am a writer" also reverberated in my repeated rereading of Robeson's texts. For me, it is not so much a matter of the modesty of these words and the humility they express in the presence of literature. On the contrary, the effect they have is rather to awaken in me the question of what constitutes real literature, of how this art form has traditionally been informed by a White, bourgeois, male perspective, and of the extent to which Robeson's writing practice defies this—or rather, how it counters it with a different way of writing.

As a Black woman born in East Germany, I was brought up with the idea of working-class art as a new artistic ideal. But by the same token, as a Black woman, I also grew up with artistic silence. White voices and texts were dominant, along with literary conceptions colored by a patriarchal viewpoint—no matter how hard they tried or professed to challenge the bourgeois nature of the genre. What I would have given to read voices like Robeson's instead. A Black, pan-African, feminist, and overtly internationalist voice whose writing posits connections rather than conjuring with the idea of original genius. A voice, moreover, that takes Black experiences out of their marginalized singularity and places them in a vital global network.

I would thus like to start this introduction to Eslanda Robeson with a photograph of her. Since I am looking at her particularly through her writing practice, the most obvious choice would have been a picture of her sitting down, reading, writing, or busying herself with ink and paper. However, as a writer myself,

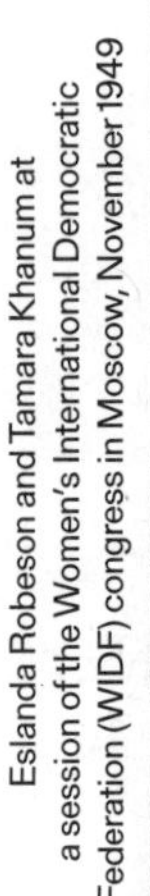

Eslanda Robeson and Tamara Khanum at a session of the Women's International Democratic Federation (WIDF) congress in Moscow, November 1949

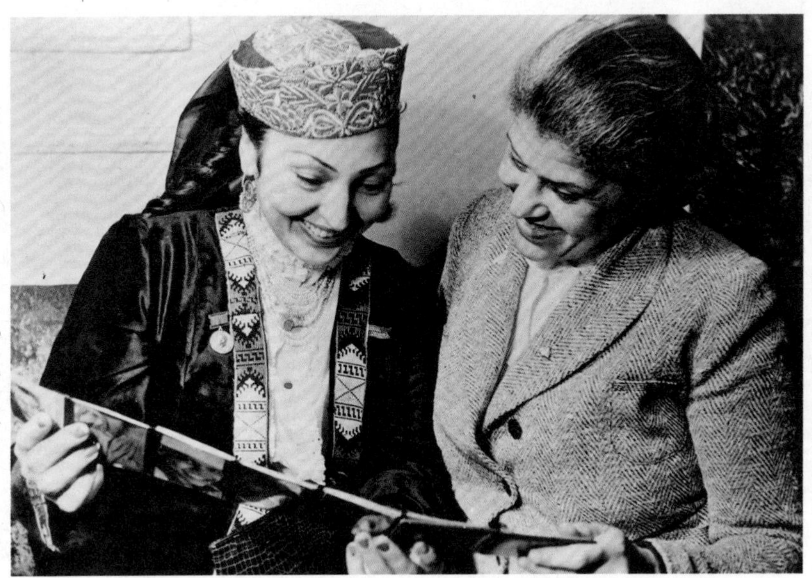

Eslanda Robeson und Tamara Khanum auf der Sitzung der Internationalen Demokratischen Frauenföderation (IDFF) in Moskau, November 1949

„Wie ich eine Schriftstellerin wurde (falls ich eine Schriftstellerin bin)" lautet der Titel eines nahezu in die Vergessenheit geratenen Essays von Eslanda Goode Robeson aus dem Jahr 1949. „Falls ich eine Schriftstellerin bin", diese Worte hallten auch bei meiner immer wieder neuen Lektüre von Robesons Texten nach. Es geht mir dabei weniger um die Bescheidenheit dieser Worte, um die Demut vor der Literatur. Ganz im Gegenteil wecken sie in mir eher die Frage nach dem, was richtige Literatur sei, wie weiß, bürgerlich und männlich diese Kunstform traditionell geprägt ist und inwiefern Robesons Schreibpraxis sich dem verwehrt – mehr noch: ihm ein anderes Schreiben entgegensetzt.

Als Schwarze Frau, die in der DDR geboren ist, bin ich mit der Idee einer Kunst der Arbeiterschaft als neuem künstlerischem Ideal aufgewachsen. Ebenfalls als Schwarze Frau bin ich aber auch mit einem künstlerischen Schweigen aufgewachsen. Einer Dominanz weißer Stimmen und Texte und patriarchal geprägten Auffassungen von Literatur – egal wie sehr sie versuchten oder vorgaben, die Bürgerlichkeit des Genres herauszufordern. Was hätte ich dafür gegeben, Stimmen wie die von Eslanda Robeson an ihrer Stelle zu lesen. Eine Schwarze, panafrikanische, feministische und offen internationalistische Stimme, deren Schreiben Verbindungen anstelle des beschworenen Originalgenies setzt. Und eine Stimme, die Schwarze Erfahrungen aus ihrer marginalisierten Singularität holt und sie in ein lebendiges Weltgeflecht setzt.

Ich möchte meine Einführung zu Eslanda Robeson daher mit einem Foto von ihr beginnen. Da mein Blick auf sie vor allem ihrer Schreibpraxis gilt, wäre es naheliegend gewesen, eine Abbildung zu wählen, auf der sie sitzt, schreibt, liest oder sich mit Tinte und Papier beschäftigt. Da auch ich Schriftstellerin bin, finde ich, dass ein

Script Eslanda Robeson AdK Archiv Nummer 403

I think such a picture would have missed the mark. Writing is an individual, more or less solitary practice. As a writer, one is constantly trapped in one's own ideas, feelings, and views—isolated from the world but at the same time addressing it. But Robeson's long-term writing practice proposes an alternative image to this classic rendering of "the writer." Robeson's writings practice unfold, over the trajectory of her life and practice, as a politics of sociality and network building.

It was thinking along these lines that led me to choose a different visual instead. Here, Robeson is at the congress of the Women's International Democratic Federation (WIDF), which convened in Moscow in November 1949. The WIDF was an international organization that had made it its mission to campaign for women's rights and against Fascism; established in Paris in 1945 and later operating from East Berlin, it was most active during the Cold War. Robeson was vice president of the American Women's Congress; in the picture next to her is Tamara Khanum, People's Artist of the Uzbek Republic. During a break at the congress, the two women share a look at a brochure, evidently in the form of a concertina-fold series of pictures. In their encounter and especially in the context of the congress, we can start to outline the intersectional and transcontinental feminism that Robeson championed. How did these political views manifest concretely in her writing practice?

WRITING AS A WEAPON OF DEFENSE

In her essay "How I became a writer (if I am a writer)," published in Moscow in 1949, Robeson invites us on a brief journey through her main works, debating whether or not she could call herself a writer. She explains that she was always writing things here and there, but that the work that made her writing public and brought her to a large readership was her biography of her husband Paul Robeson.

Toward the end of the 1920s, Paul Robeson, then already a law student, and chemistry student Eslanda Cardozo Goode met at Columbia University, fell in love, and married. Soon after, Paul's performing career took off as an actor and musician, and the couple settled in London. Despite being the first Black woman in the position, Eslanda left her job as a chemist at New York-Presbyterian Hospital to support Paul's growing success.

solches Bild unzutreffend gewesen wäre. Schreiben ist eine individuelle, fast einsame Praxis. Als Schriftsteller·in ist man immer in seinen eigenen Ideen, Gefühlen und Sichtweisen verfangen – man ist von der Welt isoliert und richtet sich doch gleichzeitig an sie. Im Vergleich mit dieser klassischen Auffassung der „Schriftstellerin" bietet uns Eslanda Robesons langjährige Schreibpraxis ein anderes Bild. Über die Zeitspanne ihres gesamten Lebens und Schaffens entfaltet sich Robesons Schreiben vielmehr als eine Politik der Geselligkeit und des Netzwerkens.

In diesem Sinne wähle ich also ein anderes Bild. Es zeigt Robeson auf dem Kongress der Internationalen Demokratischen Frauenföderation (IDFF), der im November 1949 in Moskau stattfand. Die IDFF war eine internationale Organisation, die sich den Einsatz für Frauenrechte und Antifaschismus zur Aufgabe gemacht hatte. Sie wurde 1945 in Paris gegründet und arbeitete später von Ost-Berlin aus, wobei sie während des Kalten Krieges am aktivsten war. Eslanda Robeson war die Vizepräsidentin der US-amerikanischen Sektion (American Women's Congress); neben ihr auf dem Foto sieht man die Volkskünstlerin Tamara Khanum aus der usbekischen Sowjetrepublik. Während einer Kongresspause sehen sich die beiden Frauen eine Broschüre an, offensichtlich ein Bilderleporello. Anhand dieser Begegnung und insbesondere im Rahmen des Kongresses können wir beginnen, den intersektionalen und transkontinentalen Feminismus zu skizzieren, den Robeson vertrat.

Wie haben sich diese politischen Ansichten konkret in ihrer Schreibpraxis niedergeschlagen?

SCHREIBEN ALS VERTEIDIGUNGSWAFFE

In dem Essay „How I became a writer. (If I am a writer)", der 1949 in Moskau veröffentlicht wurde, lädt uns Eslanda Robeson auf eine kurze Reise durch ihre Hauptwerke ein und erörtert, ob sie sich eine Schriftstellerin nennen kann oder nicht.

Weiterhin erklärt sie, dass sie schon immer hier und da etwas geschrieben habe, das Werk aber, das ihr Schreiben zu einem öffentlichen gemacht habe und mit dem sie ein großes Publikum erreichte, die Biografie ihres Mannes Paul Robeson gewesen sei.

Gegen Ende der 1920er Jahre lernten sich Paul Robeson, damals Jurastudent, und die Chemiestudentin Eslanda Cardozo Goode an der Columbia

1. Eslanda Goode Robeson, *African Journey* (John Day Company, 1945).

In London, she took up the role of Paul's manager—organizing and supporting the growth of his blossoming career as an internationally celebrated singer, actor, and activist. One of the best-known Black figures and public intellectuals of the day, he was seen and watched by a largely white audience, while being interviewed and written about by mainly white journalists. This was very unusual. At the time, the press was sharply divided between white and Black writers, a white and Black press, and white and Black interests. Paul and Eslanda often felt dissatisfied with their portrayal in the media and the inappropriate way in which Paul was depicted.

Eslanda initially put together some facts about Paul in a press sheet and eventually started to write his biography, which was published in 1930 under the title *Paul Robeson, Negro*. She later called the book—her first-ever publication—a "weapon of defense," having written it in order to give the two of them the power of authorship over their own lives and the way the public saw them. She used this to counter the perceptions of his White audience who formed their opinion of him based on the racist preconceptions that dominated public discourse about him and his work. Can this notion of writing as a "weapon of defense" be expanded as a frame for understanding and classifying Eslanda Robeson's practice more broadly beyond this specific book project? What forms can such a "weapon of defense" take when used as an expression of her writing's anti-racist, pan-African, feminist, and socialist potency?

WRITING AS A TOOL OF PROXIMITY AND AS A POLITICAL ACT

Robeson's writing practice continued to develop, moving into other methodological spaces. As an anthropology student of Bronisław Malinowski at the London School of Economics and as a world traveler, she published her second book, *African Journey*, in the US, the UK, and Czechoslovakia in 1945, and in the Soviet Union in 1958, using the notes from her trip to Uganda, Belgian Congo, and South Africa in 1936 as a foundation.[1] At the time, very few books depicted the lives, struggles, and visions of African people and communities, especially the women's voices in these communities. Various characters appear in Robeson's

University kennen, verliebten sich ineinander und heirateten. Bald darauf nahm Pauls Bühnenkarriere als Schauspieler und Musiker Fahrt auf und das Paar ließ sich in London nieder. Obwohl sie die erste Schwarze Frau in dieser Position war, gab Robeson ihren Job als Chemikerin am New York Presbyterian Hospital auf, um Pauls zunehmenden Erfolg zu unterstützen.

In London wurde sie seine Managerin: Sie organisierte und unterstützte seine zunehmend aufblühende Karriere als international gefeierter Sänger, Schauspieler und Aktivist. Als eine der bekanntesten Schwarzen Persönlichkeiten und öffentlichen Intellektuellen jener Zeit war er einem überwiegend weißen Publikum bekannt, auch die Journalisten, die über ihn schrieben und ihn interviewten, waren größtenteils weiß. Das war eine große Seltenheit. Zu jener Zeit war die Presse stark unterteilt in weiße und Schwarze Schreibende, weiße und Schwarze Presse, weiße und Schwarze Interessen. Paul und Eslanda waren mit ihren Porträts in den Medien und den unzutreffenden Darstellungen von Paul oft nicht einverstanden.

Zunächst fasste Eslanda Robeson einige Fakten über Paul in einem Presseheft zusammen, schießlich begann sie, seine Biografie zu verfassen, die 1930 unter dem Titel *Paul Robeson, Negro* veröffentlicht wurde.

Später bezeichnete sie dieses Buch – ihre allererste Veröffentlichung überhaupt – als „Verteidigungswaffe", denn sie hatte es geschrieben, damit die beiden selbst zu Autor*innen ihres eigenen Lebens und dessen öffentlicher Wahrnehmung wurden. Dies setzte sie gegen die Wahrnehmung seines weißen Publikums ein, das sich seine Meinung über Paul Robeson anhand der rassistischen Vorurteile bildete, die den öffentlichen Diskurs über ihn und seine Arbeit dominierten. Lässt sich diese Auffassung von Schreiben als „Verteidigungswaffe" ausweiten, um ihre Praxis über dieses spezifische Buchprojekt hinaus zu begreifen und einzuordnen? Welche Formen kann eine solche „Verteidigungswaffe" als Ausdruck der antirassistischen, panafrikanischen, feministischen und sozialistischen Potenz ihres Schreibens annehmen?

SCHREIBEN ALS INSTRUMENT DER NÄHE UND ALS POLITISCHER AKT

Robesons Schreibpraxis entwickelte sich weiter und bewegte sich in andere methodische Gebiete. Als Weltreisende und Anthropologiestudentin bei Bronisław

2. Leigh Raiford, "The Here and Now of Eslanda Robeson's African Journey," *Journal of Transnational American Studies* 8, no. 1 (2017): 134–52, esp. 149

3. Annette Joseph-Gabriel, "Eslanda Robeson's African Journeys," *Black Perspectives* (blog), March 17, 2016, https://www.aaihs.org/eslanda-robesons-african-journeys/.

4. Pearl S. Buck and Eslanda Goode Robeson, *American Argument* (John Day Company, 1949).

book: for example, Susie Yergans and Frieda Matthews, two Black scholars and community social workers from Alice in South Africa.

In *African Journey*, Robeson takes particular care over women and gender relations in addressing what she and others called at the time "the negro question." But instead of focusing on those usually placed at the forefront of this debate, she explored the ideas, perspectives, and experiences of struggle and resistance through her encounters with women in Uganda and South Africa, connecting them with the wider global debate and with her own perspective. *African Journey* is thus both an anthropological book and a political work that attempts to foster a sense of affinity and build connections between Black perspectives from different countries, cultures, and continents, and even between the political West and East in the Cold War period. In other words, it can be read as a proposal advocating a practice of Black Internationalism.

The ambiguous nature of such an internationalism is further strengthened by Robeson's "pan-African gaze," as Leigh Raiford argues, by narrating a relationship between the people she meets in Belgian Congo and the African Americans of her community in Harlem.[2]

At the same time, as Annette Joseph-Gabriel aptly expresses it, the journey to Africa "is also about asserting an *American* identity. She describes her pilgrimage as both a black diasporic story of displacement through the slave trade and a uniquely American story of migration that cuts across racial identification. Defining Africa as 'the old country' is also a project of defining the United States as a nation of immigrants and asserting Black Americans' belonging to this imagined nation because they too have their own 'old country.' In short, Robeson performs the composite identity of 'African American' *avant la lettre*."[3]

WRITING AS A GLOBAL NETWORK

Over time, she made personal connections more and more the focus of her writing. Robeson wrote her third book, *American Argument*, published in 1949, together with the Nobel laureate in literature and China scholar Pearl S. Buck.[4] In the form of dialogues and commentaries, the two women discuss a wide range of

---

Malinowski an der London School of Economics veröffentlichte sie ihr zweites Buch, *African Journey*, 1945 in den USA, England und der Tschechoslowakei sowie 1958 in der Sowjetunion.[1] Sie verarbeitete hierin die Aufzeichnungen ihrer Reise 1936 nach Uganda, Kongo und Südafrika. Zu dieser Zeit gab es nur sehr wenige Bücher, die das Leben, die Kämpfe und die Visionen afrikanischer Menschen und Gemeinschaften darstellten, insbesondere die Stimmen der Frauen in diesen Gemeinschaften. Verschiedene eindrucksvolle Persönlichkeiten tauchen im Buch auf, so zum Beispiel Susie Yergans und Frieda Matthews, zwei Schwarze Intellektuelle und Sozialarbeiterinnen aus Alice, Südafrika.

Robeson befasst sich in *African Journey* mit dem, was sie und andere die „Negro-Frage" nannten, und schenkt dabei der Betrachtung von Frauen und Geschlechterverhältnissen besondere Aufmerksamkeit. Anstatt sich allerdings auf diejenigen zu konzentrieren, die in dieser Debatte üblicherweise zuerst genannt werden, geht sie den Ideen, Perspektiven und Erfahrungen aus Kampf und Widerstand anhand ihrer Begegnungen mit Frauen in Uganda und Südafrika nach und verbindet diese mit der umfassenderen globalen Debatte sowie der eigenen Sichtweise. Daher ist *African Journey* sowohl ein anthropologisches als auch ein politisches Werk, das versucht, eine Nähe zu schaffen und Verbindungen herzustellen zwischen Schwarzen Perspektiven aus verschiedenen Ländern, Kulturen und Kontinenten, sogar zwischen dem politischen Westen und Osten in der Ära des Kalten Kriegs. Es kann als Vorschlag für eine Praxis des Schwarzen Internationalismus gelesen werden.

Die Ambivalenz eines solchen Internationalismus wird, wie Leigh Raiford schreibt, durch Robesons panafrikanische Perspektive verstärkt, da es auch von der Beziehung zwischen den Menschen, denen sie im Kongo begegnet, und den Afroamerikaner·innen aus ihrer Community in Harlem erzählt.[2]

Gleichzeitig geht es, wie Annette Joseph-Gabriel es treffend ausdrückt, bei ihrer Reise nach Afrika „auch um die Behauptung einer amerikanischen Identität. Sie beschreibt ihre Reise sowohl als eine Geschichte der Schwarzen Diaspora, der durch den Sklavenhandel Vertriebenen, als auch als eine einzigartige amerikanische Geschichte der Migration, die die Rassengrenzen überschreitet. Afrika als ‚the old country' zu benennen, ist auch ein Projekt, das die Vereinigten Staaten als Nation von Einwanderern definiert und die Zugehörigkeit Schwarzer Amerikaner zu dieser imaginierten Nation bekräftigt, denn auch sie haben ihr eigenes ‚old

1. Eslanda Goode Robeson, *African Journey*, New York: John Day Company 1945.

2. Leigh Raiford, „The Here and Now of Eslanda Robeson's African Journey", in: *Journal of Transnational American Studies*, 8/1, 2017, S. 134–152.

pertinent topics: US American society, Soviet Union, racial segregation, gender relations and the role of women, education, and childrearing. The book explores political differences and similarities between the women, while insisting upon a dialogical approach, focusing on exchange rather than disagreement. Buck shares Robeson's criticism of US Cold War politics yet broadly rejects her position on Communism, and more specifically the role of the Soviet Union.

Besides her published books, Robeson left behind a range of lively correspondence with a variety of people. She exchanged letters over a period of years with left-wing intellectuals such as the German Jewish philosopher Franz Loeser and his wife Diana Loeser, through whom Eslanda and Paul Robeson found their way to East Germany, where they stayed for several weeks for medical treatment in 1963. There was also a vivid exchange of letters with Shirley Graham Du Bois and W. E. B. Du Bois. In Robeson's idiosyncratic private letter writing, in particular, we find a strategy that runs through her entire oeuvre and legacy: the creation of networks and an appreciation of exchange—or, in other words, her ability to explore the political potential of friendship.

In this way, Robeson maps out a writing practice that builds on connection without erasing difference—a Black internationalist socialist feminism that pushed, in its language and form, against the model of the individualistic writer as a singular genius. Of the many techniques she used as an author, chemist, anthropologist, photographer, actress, and activist, writing was one of the chief elements in her armory.

country'. Kurz gesagt, Robeson führt die zusammengesetzte Identität des ‚Afroamerikaners' avant la lettre vor."[3]

SCHREIBEN ALS WELTNETZWERK

Mit der Zeit rückte sie in ihrem Schreiben immer mehr die persönlichen Verbindungen in den Mittelpunkt. Robeson schrieb 1949 ihr drittes Buch, *American Argument*,[4] gemeinsam mit der Literaturnobelpreisträgerin und China-Kennerin Pearl S. Buck. In Form von Dialogen und Kommentaren diskutieren die beiden Frauen eine breite Spanne relevanter Themen wie die US-amerikanische Gesellschaft, die Sowjetunion, Rassentrennung, Geschlechterverhältnisse, die Rolle der Frau, Bildung und das Aufziehen von Kindern. Das Buch lotet die politischen Differenzen und Ähnlichkeiten zwischen den beiden Frauen aus, wobei es auf einer dialogischen Form beharrt, die sich mehr auf Austausch statt auf Uneinigkeit konzentriert.

Buck teilt Robesons Kritik an der US-Politik im Kalten Krieg, lehnt deren Haltung zum Kommunismus und insbesondere zur Rolle der Sowjetunion jedoch weitgehend ab.

Neben ihren Büchern hinterließ Eslanda Robeson lebhafte Korrespondenzen mit verschiedenen Personen. Über Jahre stand sie im Briefwechsel mit linken Intellektuellen wie dem deutsch-jüdischen Philosophen Franz Loeser und seiner Frau Diana Loeser, über die Eslanda und Paul Robeson ihren Weg in die DDR gefunden haben, wo sie sich im Jahr 1963 einige Wochen für eine medizinische Behandlung aufhielten. Es gab ebenfalls einen lebhaften Briefkontakt mit Shirley Graham Du Bois und W. E. B. Du Bois. Vor allem in Eslanda Robesons eigener Art des privaten Briefeschreibens spiegelt sich eine Strategie wider, die sich durch ihr gesamtes Werk und Vermächtnis zieht: die Schaffung von Netzwerken und das Wertschätzen von Austausch – oder anders ausgedrückt: ihre Fähigkeit, das politische Potenzial von Freundschaften auszuloten.

Insofern entwirft Eslanda ein Schreiben, das auf Verbindungen aufbaut, ohne Unterschiede auszulöschen – ein internationalistischer Schwarzer, sozialistischer Feminismus, der sich in Sprache und Form gegen das Modell der individualistischen Schriftsteller·in als singuläres Genie wandte. Vor allem war Schreiben eine der vielen Techniken, die Eslanda Robeson als Schriftstellerin, Chemikerin, Anthropologin, Fotografin, Schauspielerin und Aktivistin einsetzte.

3. Annette Joseph-Gabriel, „Eslanda Robeson's African Journeys" (2016), in: *Black Perspectives*, AAIHS, https://www.aaihs.org/eslanda-robesons-african-journeys/; letzter Zugriff: 10.10.2022

4. Pearl S. Buck und Eslanda Goode Robeson, *American Argument*, New York: John Day Company 1949.

BLACK RADICAL HISTORIES IN GERMANY

Tiffany N. Florvil

GESCHICHTEN DES SCHWARZEN RADIKALISMUS IN DEUTSCHLAND

1. Cedric J. Robinson, *Black Marxism: The Making of the Black Radical Tradition* (University of North Carolina, 1980), 171.

2. May Ayim, *Blues in Black and White: A Collection of Essays, Poetry, and Conversations*, trans. Anne V. Adams (Africa World Press, 2003), 57–58.

The Black radical tradition [called for] the continuing development of a collective consciousness informed by the historical struggle for liberation and motivated by the shared sense of obligation to preserve the collective being, the ontological totality.

Cedric Robinson[1]

Racism and anti-Semitism were some of the undesirable ingredients of the upbringing that I experienced. I am conscious of it and I won't let it go until I have rooted it out and dismantled it from myself.
… I am convinced that we—and I am referring to all people in this country who do not tolerate racism and anti-Semitism—are desirous of and capable of coalitions.…
… We can bring about change!

May Ayim[2]

I began with two quotations from Black diasporic scholars. The first is African American political theorist Cedric Robinson, who advanced the field of Black Studies, especially with his important 1983 book *Black Marxism: The Making of a Black Radical Tradition*. He also spent time in Europe, refining his theories on racial capitalism and Black radicalism. The second is Black German writer May Ayim who expanded the field of Black German Studies in critical ways through her 1986 co-edited feminist volume *Farbe bekennen: Afro-deutsche Frauen auf den Spuren ihrer Geschichte* in late Cold War West Germany. She, too, traveled the globe, refining her ideas about Black history. Through their words, Robinson and Ayim described what the Black radical tradition is. In many ways, the quotations illustrate how Black radicalism is both a praxis and a consciousness that entails fighting for Black liberation and combating racist, oppressive forces across the globe. This radicalism also recognizes the humanity of Black people despite the persistence of anti-Black racism and white supremacy. Robinson and Ayim also forged transnational connections and produced Black knowledge that challenged hegemonic frameworks and structures.

Die Schwarze radikale Tradition [verlangte nach] der kontinuierlichen Entwicklung eines kollektiven Bewusstseins, das Wissen um den historischen Befreiungskampf in sich trägt und angetrieben wird durch ein gemeinsames Gefühl der Verpflichtung, das Kollektivwesen zu bewahren, die ontologische Totalität.

Cedric Robinson[1]

Rassismus und Antisemitismus waren einige der unliebsamen Ingredienzien der Erziehung, die ich erfahren habe. Das ist mir bewußt, und ich werde nicht lockerlassen, bevor ich sie innerhalb und außerhalb von mir aufgespürt und abgebaut habe.
… Aber ich bin überzeugt, daß wir – und damit meine ich alle Menschen in diesem Land, die Rassismus und Antisemitismus nicht dulden – zu Bündnissen willig und fähig sind.
…Wir können verändern!

May Ayim[2]

Ich habe zwei Zitate Schwarzer diasporischer Wissenschaftler·innen an den Anfang dieses Textes gesetzt. Der Erste ist der afroamerikanische politische Theoretiker Cedric Robinson, der das Feld der Black Studies entschieden vorangetrieben hat, insbesondere mit seinem 1983 erschienenen einflussreichen Buch *Black Marxism: The Making of a Black Radical Tradition*. Er hat sich auch einige Zeit in Europa aufgehalten und dort seine Theorien zu „racial capitalism" und Schwarzem Radikalismus weiterentwickelt. Die zweite ist die Schwarze deutsche Schriftstellerin May Ayim, die das Feld der Black German Studies im Westdeutschland der späten Jahre des Kalten Krieges mit dem 1986 von ihr mitherausgegebenen feministischen Band *Farbe bekennen: Afro-deutsche Frauen auf den Spuren ihrer Geschichte* kritisch erweitert hat. Auch sie bereiste die Welt, um ihre Vorstellungen über Schwarze Geschichte zu schärfen. Mit ihren Worten beschreiben Robinson und Ayim die Schwarze radikale Tradition. Die Zitate illustrieren, dass der Schwarze Radikalismus eine Praxis wie auch ein Bewusstsein ist und einen Kampf für Schwarze Befreiung und die Bekämpfung rassistischer, unterdrückerischer Kräfte auf der ganzen Welt beinhaltet. Dieser Radikalismus

1. Cedric J. Robinson, *Black Marxism: The Making of the Black Radical Tradition*, Chapel Hill: The University of North Carolina Press 1980, S. 171.

2. May Ayim, „Das Jahr 1990. Heimat und Einheit aus afro-deutscher Perspektive", in: dies., *Grenzenlos und unverschämt*, Berlin: Orlanda Frauenverlag 1997, S. 88–103, hier S. 99, 100, 102.

3. Joshua Myers, *Cedric Robinson: The Time of the Black Radical Tradition* (Polity, 2021).

4. Tracy Denean Sharpley-Whiting, *Negritude Women* (University of Minnesota, 2002), Brent Hayes Edwards, *The Practice of Diaspora: Literature, Translation, and the Rise of Black Internationalism* (Harvard University, 2003), Minkah Makalani, *In the Cause of Freedom: Radical Black Internationalism from Harlem to London, 1917–1939* (University of North Carolina, 2011), Marc Matera, *Black London: The Imperial Metropolis and Decolonization in the Twentieth Century* (University of California, 2015), Barbara Ransby, *Eslanda: The Large and Unconventional Life of Mrs. Paul Robeson* (Yale University, 2013), and Dayo Gore, *Radicalism at the Crossroads: African American Women Activists in the Cold War* (NYU, 2011).

Joshua Myers's recent biography on Robinson has detailed his dynamic life and oeuvre.[3] By contrast, Ayim is still not as well known by those outside of the Black German community or German Studies circles, even though she made key contributions with her poetry and prose in and beyond Germany. Both were Black radicals, and their words allow me to reflect on this tradition in the Germanies.

This chapter explores the tradition of Black radicalism in Germany with figures such as Trinidadian George Padmore (1903–1959), African American Ollie Harrington (1912–1995), African American Shirley Graham Du Bois (1896–1977), and Black German May Ayim (1960–1996). The study of Black radicalism in Europe is often associated with cities such as Paris or London, and scholars including Dayo Gore, Minkah Makalani, and Barbara Ransby have written about the "routes and roots" of radicalisms and internationalisms.[4] But Black radicalism also traveled to Central Europe (Germany), where Padmore, Harrington, Graham Du Bois, and Ayim worked, strategized, networked, and positioned the region as a critical site for Black diasporic activism in the twentieth century. I argue that these individuals drew upon their expertise and experiences to underscore the pervasiveness of intersecting oppressions of racism, Fascism, classism, and sexism. Traveling abroad informed their cosmopolitanism, and these Black radicals advocated for basic human rights and demanded political changes locally and internationally.

This chapter also situates Ayim, a Black woman born and raised in Germany, in this rich lineage of Black radicalism in Europe. With her activism, she boldly created new vocabularies and shifted discourses, bringing the margins to the center on her terms. Ayim focused on the needs and conditions of the Black German community and other minoritized communities in Germany, while also imparting knowledge about the country's colonial history, which had been simultaneously silenced and ignored. In so doing, she urged Germany to reckon with its racist past and present.

In the first section, I explore the presence of Black radicalism in Germany with Padmore, Harrington, and Graham Du Bois. Their perspectives and politics were internationalist in content and form. Their work in Germany opened it up

---

ist auch eine Würdigung der Menschlichkeit von Schwarzen Menschen angesichts des Fortbestehens von anti-Schwarzem Rassismus und weißem Vorherrschaftsgebaren. Robinson und Ayim schmiedeten auch transnationale Bündnisse und produzierten Schwarzes Wissen, das hegemoniale Bezugssysteme und Strukturen infrage stellte. Joshua Myers' kürzlich erschienene Robinson-Biografie hat dessen dynamisches Leben und Werk detailreich nachgezeichnet.[3] Im Gegensatz zu Robinson ist Ayim außerhalb der Community der Afrodeutschen oder Kreisen der Black German Studies immer noch nicht sonderlich bekannt. Beide waren Schwarze Radikale, und ihre Worte erlauben es mir, über diese Tradition in den verschiedenen deutschen Staaten nachzudenken.

Dieser Text erkundet die Tradition des Schwarzen Radikalismus in Deutschland anhand von Figuren wie dem Trinidader George Padmore (1903–1959), dem Afroamerikaner Ollie Harrington (1912–1995), der Afroamerikanerin Shirley Graham Du Bois (1896–1977) und der Schwarzen Deutschen[4] May Ayim (1960–1996). Die Erforschung des Schwarzen Radikalismus in Europa wird oft mit Städten wie Paris oder London assoziiert, und Forscher·innen wie Dayo Gore, Minkah Makalani und Barbara Ransby haben über die „Wege und Wurzeln" von Radikalismen und Internationalismen geschrieben.[5] Aber der Schwarze Radikalismus kam auch nach Mitteleuropa (Deutschland), wo Padmore, Harrington, Graham Du Bois und Ayim arbeiteten, Strategien entwarfen, Netzwerke knüpften und so die Region als einen Schauplatz von herausragender Bedeutung für den Schwarzen diasporischen Aktivismus im 20. Jahrhundert etablierten. Meine These ist, dass sie sich auf ihre Expertise und ihre Erfahrungen stützten, um die Allgegenwart der sich überschneidenden Unterdrückungsformen von Rassismus, Faschismus, Klassismus und Sexismus hervorzuheben. Auslandsreisen beförderten ihren Kosmopolitismus, und die Schwarzen Radikalen setzten sich für grundlegende Menschenrechte ein und forderten auf lokaler wie internationaler Ebene politische Veränderungen.

Dieser Text verortet zudem Ayim, eine Schwarze Frau, die in Deutschland geboren wurde und aufgewachsen ist, innerhalb dieser beeindruckenden Traditionslinie des Schwarzen Radikalismus in Europa. Als Aktivistin schuf sie entschlossen ein neues Vokabular und veränderte Diskurse, indem sie das Marginalisierte zu ihren Bedingungen ins Zentrum rückte. Ayim konzentrierte sich

3. Joshua Myers, *Cedric Robinson: The Time of the Black Radical Tradition*, Cambridge, UK: Polity 2021.

4. Anm. d. Ü.: Während Florvil hier und im Folgenden fast ausschließlich von „Black Germans" spricht, was in der Übersetzung mit „Schwarze Deutsche" wiedergegeben wird, hat sich Ayim selbst zumeist als „Afro-Deutsche" bezeichnet, ein von ihr mitgeprägter Begriff. Im Vorwort zu *Farbe bekennen* schreiben May Ayim, Katharina Oguntoye und Dagmar Schultz 1986: „Mit Audre Lorde entwickelten wir den Begriff ‚afro-deutsch' in Anlehnung an afro-amerikanisch, als Ausdruck unserer kulturellen Herkunft. ‚Afro-deutsch' schien uns einleuchtend, da wir fünf eine deutsche Mutter und einen afrikanischen oder afro-amerikanischen Vater haben. Inzwischen lernten wir Afro-Deutsche kennen, deren Eltern beide aus Afrika stammen oder deren einer Elternteil afro-deutsch ist und der andere aus Afrika kommt. Dadurch wurde uns klar, daß unsere wesentliche Gemeinsamkeit kein biologisches, sondern ein soziales Kriterium ist: das Leben in einer

5. Tiffany N. Florvil, *Mobilizing Black Germany: Afro-German Women and the Making of a Transnational Movement* (University of Illinois, 2020).

6. Noaquia N. Callahan, "A Rare Colored Bird: Mary Church Terrell, Die Fortschritte der farbigen Frauen, and the International Council of Women's Congress in Berlin, Germany, 1904," Bulletin of the German Historical Institute 113 (2017): 93.

as a site for political possibility and Black political culture. Padmore, Harrington, and Graham Du Bois all used their voices and talents in the service of Black people and to speak out about social injustice. The second section examines Ayim's cultural and political work through the Black German movement of the 1980s and 1990s. During these years, she was active in the Initiative Schwarze Deutsche (Initiative of Black Germans, ISD—now Initiative Schwarze Menschen in Deutschland, or the Initiative of Black People in Germany), a cultural-political organization she cofounded in 1985 in Berlin.[5] Exemplifying the radicalism of Padmore, Harrington, and Graham Du Bois, Ayim pursued intersectional change with her literature and politics and cultivated solidarities with White allies and many people across the Black diaspora. I conclude by sharing why studying Ayim alongside Padmore, Harrington, and Graham Du Bois helps scholars understand the contours of Black German forms of radicalism, and why Black German radicalism matters.

CENTURIES OF BLACK AND GERMAN ENTANGLEMENTS

Much like France and Great Britain, Germany, before and after unification in 1871, was also an important site for Black radicalism. There, individuals such as James W. C. Pennington, Mary Church Terrell, Martin Luther King Jr., Paul and Eslanda Robeson, and Helga Emde championed the political and civil rights of minoritized communities. Pennington, for example, delivered speeches for the abolition of slavery across Germany and received an honorary doctoral degree in divinity from Heidelberg University in 1849. Later in 1850, he also presided over an antislavery meeting and served on committees at the Frankfurt Peace Congress. He remained in Europe until 1852, attending other congresses and participating in speaking tours. In 1904, Terrell spoke at the International Congress of Women (ICW), which comprised multiple feminist groups advocating for women's suffrage and pacificism. At this ICW meeting in Berlin, Terrell was the only Black woman in attendance and presented her speech, "The Progress of Colored Women," in German before a large international crowd of activists.[6] As Noaquia Callahan Banks has written, "Terrell successfully wove the mission of the black

---

auf die Bedürfnisse und Lebensbedingungen der afrodeutschen Community und anderer minorisierter Gruppen in Deutschland und vermittelte Wissen über die koloniale Geschichte des Landes, die zugleich beschwiegen und ignoriert wurde. Dadurch forderte sie die deutsche Öffentlichkeit dazu auf, sich mit der rassistischen Vergangenheit und Gegenwart des Landes auseinanderzusetzen.

Im ersten Teil betrachte ich die Präsenz des Schwarzen Radikalismus in Deutschland anhand von Padmore, Harrington und Graham Du Bois. Ihre Perspektiven und politischen Ansichten und Betätigungen waren dem Inhalt und der Form nach internationalistisch. Ihr Wirken in Deutschland ermöglichte politische Interventionen und schuf Orte für Schwarze politische Kultur. Alle drei, Padmore, Harrington und Graham Du Bois, stellten ihre Stimmen und ihre Talente in den Dienst Schwarzer Menschen und machten soziale Ungerechtigkeit zum Thema. Der zweite Teil untersucht Ayims kulturelle und politische Arbeit im Lichte der afrodeutschen Bewegung der 1980er und 1990er Jahre. Während dieser Jahre war sie aktiv in der Initiative Schwarze Deutsche (ISD), heute: Initiative Schwarze Menschen in Deutschland, einer kulturell-politischen Organisation, die sie mit anderen Aktivist·innen 1985 in Berlin begründete.[6] Den Radikalismus von Padmore, Harrington und Graham Du Bois in beispielhafter Weise verkörpernd, verfolgte Ayim mit ihrer Literatur und Politik das Ziel, intersektionelle Veränderungen herbeizuführen und praktizierte Solidarität mit weißen Verbündeten und vielen Menschen aus der Schwarzen Diaspora. Abschließend möchte ich darlegen, warum die Beschäftigung mit Ayim neben Padmore, Harrington und Graham Du Bois der Forschung helfen kann, die Konturen Schwarzer deutscher Formen des Radikalismus zu verstehen, und warum Schwarzer deutscher Radikalismus so wichtig ist.

JAHRHUNDERTE SCHWARZER UND DEUTSCHER VERFLECHTUNGEN

Ähnlich wie Frankreich und Großbritannien war auch Deutschland vor und nach der Reichsgründung von 1871 ein wichtiger Schauplatz des Schwarzen Radikalismus. Hier kämpften etwa James W. C. Pennington, Mary Church Terrell, Martin Luther King Jr., Paul und Eslanda Robeson und Helga Emde für die politischen und die Bürgerrechte minorisierter Communitys. Pennington beispielsweise hielt in ganz Deutschland Reden zur Abschaffung der Sklaverei und wurde 1849 von

weißen deutschen Gesellschaft." (May Ayim, Katharina Oguntoye, Dagmar Schultz (Hg.), *Farbe bekennen: Afro-deutsche Frauen auf den Spuren ihrer Geschichte*, Berlin: Orlanda Frauenverlag 1986, S. 10).

5. Tracy Denean Sharpley-Whiting, *Negritude Women*, Minneapolis: University of Minnesota Press 2002; Brent Hayes Edwards, *The Practice of Diaspora: Literature, Translation, and the Rise of Black Internationalism*, Cambridge, MA: Harvard University Press 2003; Minkah Makalani, *In the Cause of Freedom: Radical Black Internationalism from Harlem to London, 1917–1939*, Chapel Hill: The University of North Carolina Press 2011; Marc Matera, *Black London: The Imperial Metropolis and Decolonization in the Twentieth Century*, Oakland: University of California Press 2015; Barbara Ransby, *Eslanda: The Large and Unconventional Life of Mrs. Paul Robeson*, New Haven, CT: Yale University Press 2013; Dayo Gore, *Radicalism at the Crossroads: African American Women Activists in the Cold War*, New York: NYU Press 2011.

7.   Callahan, "A Rare Colored Bird," 94.

8.   Maria Höhn and Martin Klimke, *A Breath of Freedom: The Civil Rights Struggle, African American GIs, and Germany* (Palgrave, 2010), and Florvil, *Mobilizing Black Germany*.

9.   Höhn and Klimke, *A Breath of Freedom*; Kira Thurman, Singing Like Germans: *Black Musicians in the Land of Bach, Beethoven, and Brahms* (Cornell University Press, 2021), 242–70; Eslanda Goode Robeson, "Why He 'Sneaked' to East Germany," *The Afro-American*, November 2, 1963, 20.

10.   Quinn Slobodian, "Socialist Chromatism: Race, Racism, and the Racial Rainbow in East Germany," in *Comrades of Color: East Germany in the Cold War World*, ed. Quinn Slobodian (Berghahn, 2015), 27–31; Höhn and Klimke, *A Breath of Freedom*, 123–41.

women's club movement into the agenda of a predominantly white and predominantly transatlantic women's organization and the broader European public."[7] She left her mark in and beyond Europe.

Sixty years later, in 1964, King visited West and East Berlin and pursued cultural diplomacy. King gave sermons and attended multiple official events in both West Germany (Federal Republic of Germany, FRG) and East Germany (German Democratic Republic, GDR). In the GDR, he also connected with African and Asian students at Humboldt University.[8] Eslanda and Paul Robeson, who used their power to promote the liberation of colonized and oppressed people, were also no strangers to the GDR. Paul was revered, and he performed at Humboldt University, where he also received an honorary doctorate in 1960. In 1963, the Robesons returned to the GDR, where Paul received medical care, and Eslanda was honored with the Clara Zetkin medal for her antiracist and human rights activism.[9] She also witnessed in court the prosecution, in absentia, of former Nazi Hans Globke.

In the GDR, officials and journalists also practiced a "racial rainbow," and this egalitarian and anti-racist ethos informed their anti-colonialist solidarity. The government's politics of solidarity (*Solidaritätspolitik*) supported other socialist liberation movements.[10] The GDR provided financial assistance for African independence fighters from the South West Africa People's Organization (SWAPO

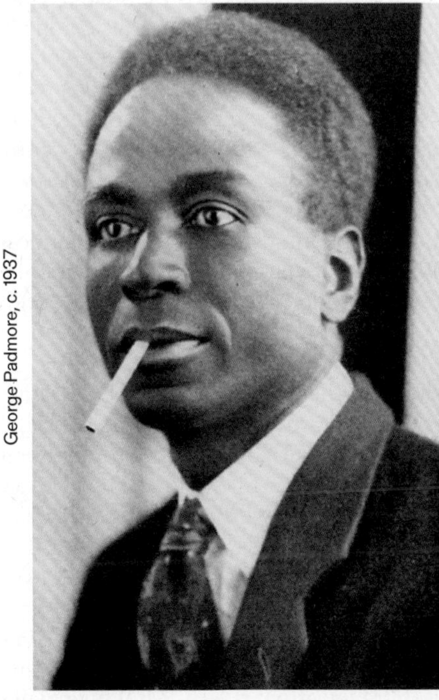

der Universität Heidelberg mit der Ehrendoktorwürde in Theologie ausgezeichnet. Später, im Jahr 1850, führte er den Vorsitz bei einem Antisklaverei-Treffen und beteiligte sich an Ausschusssitzungen auf dem Weltfriedenskongress in Frankfurt am Main. Er blieb bis 1852 in Europa, besuchte weitere Kongresse und nahm an Vortragsreisen teil. Terrell sprach 1904 auf dem Internationalen Frauen-Kongress des International Council of Women (ICW), an dem zahlreiche feministische Gruppen teilnahmen, die sich für das Frauenwahlrecht und den Pazifismus einsetzten. Bei dem Treffen des ICW in Berlin war Terrell die einzige Schwarze Teilnehmerin und hielt ihre ins Deutsche übersetzte Rede mit dem Titel „Die Fortschritte der farbigen Frauen" vor einem großen internationalen Publikum von Aktivistinnen.[7] Noaquia Callahan Banks schreibt dazu: „Terrell brachte erfolgreich die Mission der Bewegung Schwarzer Frauenklubs in die Agenda einer überwiegend weißen und überwiegend transatlantischen Frauenorganisation ein und präsentierte sie einem breiten europäischen Publikum."[8] Sie hinterließ ihre Spuren in Europa und außerhalb.

60 Jahre später, im Jahr 1964, besuchte Martin Luther King West- und Ost-Berlin und betätigte sich in Kulturdiplomatie. Er hielt Predigten und nahm an zahlreichen offiziellen Anlässen sowohl in der BRD als auch in der DDR teil. In der DDR knüpfte er auch Verbindungen zu afrikanischen und asiatischen Studierenden an der Humboldt-Universität.[9] Auch Eslanda und Paul Robeson, die ihren Einfluss dazu verwendeten, für die Befreiung kolonisierter und unterdrückter Völker einzutreten, waren keine Unbekannten in der DDR. Paul Robeson wurde verehrt und trat an der Humboldt-Universität auf, wo er 1960 auch die

6.   Tiffany N. Florvil, *Mobilizing Black Germany: Afro-German Women and the Making of a Transnational Movement*, Chicago: University of Illinois Press 2020.

7.   Noaquia N. Callahan, „A Rare Colored Bird: Mary Church Terrell, *Die Fortschritte der farbigen Frauen*, and the International Council of Women's Congress in Berlin, Germany, 1904", in: *Bulletin of the German Historical Institute* 113, 2017, S. 93–107.

8.   Ebd., S. 94.

9.   Maria Höhn und Martin Klimke, *A Breath of Freedom: The Civil Rights Struggle, African American GIs, and Germany*, New York: Palgrave 2010, und Florvil, *Mobilizing Black Germany*.

11. Jan Behrends, Thomas Lindenberger, and Patrice Poutrus, eds., *Fremde und Fremd-Sein in der DDR: Zu historischen Ursachen der Fremdenfeindlichkeit in Ostdeutschland* (Metropol, 2003).

12. Florvil, *Mobilizing Black Germany*; Pamela Ohene-Nyako, "Black European Women's Intersectional Thought and Internationalism, 1965–2001," (PhD diss., University of Geneva, 2024).

13. Larry Greene and Anke Ortlepp, eds., *Germans and African Americans: Two Centuries of Exchange* (University of Mississippi, 2011); Tiffany N. Florvil, "Zur Beständigkeit der Graswurzel: Transnationale Perspektiven auf Schwarzen Antirassismus im Deutschland des 20. Jahrhunderts," in "(Anti-)Rassismus," special issue, *Aus Politik und Zeitgeschichte* 70, nos. 42–44 (2020): 33–38.

Party of Namibia) and the Mozambique Liberation Front (FRELIMO). It also advocated for African American activists, including Angela Davis and the Robesons, who regarded the country as a beacon of antiracist and anti-colonialist solidarity. Thus, with its international antiracist image, the country performed its anti-Fascism and distinguished itself from its capitalist counterpart. But sadly, the rhetoric of diversity differed on the ground.[11]

On the other side of the Berlin Wall, Emde, along with other Black Germans, hosted the first national gathering in the Frankfurt area, catalyzing a modern Black German civil rights movement. She also cofounded a local Frankfurt chapter of the ISD. In addition to her activism within the movement, Emde was a Black internationalist who used ecumenical and feminist organizations based in Europe to push for anti-racist and feminist change and draw attention to the particularities of the Black European experience.[12] Emde's contributions were no small feat. Taken together, these are just a few examples of the narratives that demonstrate centuries of radical exchanges and soft power in Germany.[13]

THE GERMANIES AND BLACK DIASPORIC ACTIVISTS

The aftermath of the Great War led to Germany's first political experiment with democracy—the Weimar Republic. The war also resulted in political instability due to Communist uprisings and uncertainty on the part of conservatives and others within President Friedrich Ebert's own Social Democratic Party regarding his leadership. Germany dealt with the "loss" of its colonial territorial possessions and economic instability caused by the Treaty of the Versailles and later the Great Depression. During this period, a great deal of activism on the part of Black people from Germany's former colonies, the United States, and the Caribbean occurred. One of those diasporic figures was Trinidadian-born Communist journalist and writer George Padmore—a figure whom Robinson also wrote about in *Black Marxism*.

Padmore's radicalism was deeply connected to anti-colonialism, Pan-Africanism, and Communism, owing to his upbringing in the British colony of Trinidad and his experiences in the United States and the Soviet Union. Scholars such as Robinson, Hakim Adi, Theo Williams, and others have described him as

---

Ehrendoktorwürde erhielt. 1963 kehrten die Robesons in die DDR zurück, wo Paul medizinisch versorgt wurde, Eslanda wurde für ihren unermüdlichen Einsatz für Antirassismus und Menschenrechte mit der Clara-Zetkin-Medaille geehrt.[10] Sie verfolgte auch den Gerichtsprozess gegen den ehemaligen Nazi Hans Globke, der in Abwesenheit des Angeklagten abgehalten wurde.

Das egalitäre und antirassistische Ethos, das in der DDR von Offiziellen und Journalist·innen hochgehalten wurde, prägte auch deren antikolonialistische Solidarität. Die Solidaritätspolitik der Regierung unterstützte andere sozialistische Befreiungsbewegungen.[11] Die DDR stellte afrikanischen Unabhängigkeitskämpfer·innen der South-West Africa People's Organisation (SWAPO Party of Namibia) und der Mosambikanischen Befreiungsfront (FRELIMO) finanzielle Hilfen zur Verfügung. Sie setzte sich auch für afroamerikanische Aktivist·innen wie Angela Davis und die Robesons ein, die das Land als einen Leitstern antirassistischer und antikolonialistischer Solidarität betrachteten. Auf diese Weise vertrat das Land mit seinem internationalen antirassistischen Image seinen Antifaschismus und setzte sich von seinem kapitalistischen Gegenpart ab. Leider sah die Alltagsrealität ganz anders aus, als diese Rhetorik der Diversität vermuten ließe.[12]

Auf der anderen Seite der Berliner Mauer richtete Emde gemeinsam mit anderen Schwarzen Deutschen ein erstes bundesweites Treffen bei Frankfurt am Main aus und rief damit eine moderne Schwarze Deutsche Bürgerrechtsbewegung ins Leben. Sie war auch Mitbegründerin des ISD-Ortsverbandes Frankfurt am Main. Über ihren Aktivismus innerhalb der Bewegung hinaus war Emde eine Schwarze Internationalistin, die mit der Hilfe in Europa ansässiger ökumenischer und feministischer Organisationen für antirassistisch und feministisch motivierte Veränderungen kämpfte und die Aufmerksamkeit auf die Besonderheiten der Erfahrungen Schwarzer Europäer·innen lenkte.[13] Emde hat dabei Bemerkenswertes geleistet. Dies sind nur einige Beispiele für die Geschichten, die Jahrhunderte des radikalen Austauschs und des kulturellen Einflusses in Deutschland belegen.[14]

DIE DEUTSCHEN STAATEN UND DIE AKTIVIST·INNEN DER SCHWARZEN DIASPORA

Die Nachwehen des Ersten Weltkriegs führten zu Deutschlands erstem Experiment mit der Demokratie – zur Weimarer Republik. Dem Krieg folgte auch eine

10. Höhn und Klimke, *A Breath of Freedom*; Kira Thurman, *Singing Like Germans: Black Musicians in the Land of Bach, Beethoven, and Brahms*, Ithaca, NY: Cornell University Press 2021, S. 242–270; Eslanda Goode Robeson, „Why He ‚Sneaked' to East Germany", in: *The Afro-American*, 2. November 1963, S. 20.

11. Quinn Slobodian, „Socialist Chromatism: Race, Racism, and the Racial Rainbow in East Germany", in: ders. (Hg.), *Comrades of Color: East Germany in the Cold War World*, New York: Berghahn 2015, S. 27–41; Höhn und Klimke, *A Breath of Freedom*, S. 123–141.

12. Jan Behrends, Thomas Lindenberger und Patrice Poutrus (Hg.), *Fremde und Fremd-Sein in der DDR: Zu historischen Ursachen der Fremdenfeindlichkeit in Ostdeutschland*, Berlin: Metropol 2003.

13. Florvil, *Mobilizing Black Germany*; Pamela Ohene-Nyako, *Black European Women's Intersectional Thought and Internationalism, 1965–2001*, Diss. Universität Genf 2024.

14. Larry Greene und Anke Ortlepp (Hg.), *Germans and

a Black internationalist figure who had connections with many across the Black intelligentsia and who wanted to lead the "Negro proletariat." In 1930, Padmore organized the "International Conference of Negro Workers" in Hamburg. Padmore strove to create an anti-colonial and anti-racist alliance of people across the Black diaspora. Delegates from the Caribbean, Europe, Africa, and the United States formulated demands that included universal workers' rights, the complete independence of all colonies, and the right of self-determination for all nations. In their conference report, delegates also wrote about the conditions of Black people under British, French, Belgian, Portuguese, and American rule, signaling the widespread nature of imperialist exploitation. Padmore's involvement in the conference was heralded as a success.

In Hamburg, he also edited *The Negro Worker*, the mouthpiece of the International Trade Union Committee of Negro Workers (ITUCNW). The ITUCNW was part of the Red International of Labor Unions and the Communist Third International or Comintern. Officially established in July 1930, *The Negro Worker* was headquartered in Hamburg in November 1930, and Padmore was appointed editor in 1931. Padmore's Black thought was prominently articulated across the pages of this journal and in his essays and books. His writings publicized the multifaceted nature of racism and provided solutions that targeted the eradication of class exploitation and racial and colonial oppression on a global scale. He also drew connections between the dynamics in the United States and in Africa, linking oppressed peoples worldwide. Moreover, his radicalism was decidedly Marxist. As a Communist, his anti-racism was inherently international, as evinced in *The Negro Worker*. In 1933, the Comintern suspended *The Negro Worker* and disbanded the ITUCNW, causing Padmore to criticize and split with the Communist Party. Shortly after this, the Nazis came to power, and Padmore was arrested and deported to England.

In London, he joined a dynamic community of activists committed to African independence and anti-Fascism. With his work, Padmore advocated for the oppressed and exploited classes and supported pan-Africanist initiatives, including the Pan-African Congresses of subsequent years. In his 1937 book *Africa and*

Phase politischer Instabilität als Folge der kommunistischen Aufstände und der Unsicherheiten hinsichtlich der Führungsrolle von Reichspräsident Friedrich Ebert nicht nur bei konservativen Kräften innerhalb der Sozialdemokratischen Partei. Deutschland musste mit dem „Verlust" seiner kolonialen Gebietsansprüche und mit der durch den Vertrag von Versailles und die nachfolgende Wirtschaftskrise ausgelösten ökonomischen Instabilität umgehen. In dieser Zeit gab es einen regen Aktivismus Schwarzer Menschen aus den ehemaligen deutschen Kolonien, den Vereinigten Staaten und der Karibik. Eine dieser Figuren der Diaspora war der in Trinidad zur Welt gekommene kommunistische Journalist und Schriftsteller George Padmore, den auch Robinson in *Black Marxism* erwähnt.

Padmores Radikalismus war tief verknüpft mit seinem Antikolonialismus, Panafrikanismus und Kommunismus und er war den Umständen seines Aufwachsens in der britischen Kolonie Trinidad wie auch seinen Erfahrungen in den Vereinigten Staaten und der Sowjetunion geschuldet. Forscher·innen wie Robinson, Hakim Adi, Theo Williams und andere haben ihn als Vertreter des Schwarzen Internationalismus beschrieben, der Verbindungen zu zahlreichen Akteur·innen der Schwarzen Intelligenzija unterhielt und der das „Schwarze Proletariat" anführen wollte. 1930 organisierte Padmore die „Internationale Konferenz Schwarzer Arbeiter der Liga gegen den Imperialismus". Er war bestrebt, Menschen aus der gesamten Schwarzen Diaspora zu einer antikolonialen und antirassistischen Allianz zusammenzuschweißen. Delegierte aus der Karibik, Europa, Afrika und den Vereinigten Staaten formulierten Forderungen, darunter universelle Arbeiterrechte, die vollständige Unabhängigkeit aller Kolonien und das Recht auf Selbstbestimmung für alle Völker. In ihrem Konferenzbericht schreiben die Delegierten auch über die Lebensbedingungen Schwarzer Menschen unter britischer, französischer, belgischer, portugiesischer und amerikanischer Herrschaft und verdeutlichten so die Verbreitung der imperialistischen Ausbeutung. Padmores Mitwirkung an der Konferenz wurde als Erfolg gepriesen.

In Hamburg gab er auch die Monatszeitschrift *The Negro Worker*[15] heraus, das Sprachrohr des International Trade Union Committee of Negro Workers (ITUCNW). Das ITUCNW war Teil der Roten Internationale der Gewerkschaften und der III. Kommunistischen Internationale (Komintern). Offiziell im Juli 1930 gegründet, bezog *The Negro Worker* im November 1930 sein Redaktionsbüro in

African Americans: Two Centuries of Exchange, Jackson: University of Mississippi Press 2011; Tiffany N. Florvil, „Zur Beständigkeit der Graswurzel: Transnationale Perspektiven auf Schwarzen Antirassismus im Deutschland des 20. Jahrhunderts", in: „(Anti-) Rassismus", Sonderheft der Zeitschrift *Aus Politik und Zeitgeschichte* 70, Nr. 42–44, 2020: S. 33–38.

15. Anm. d. Ü.: Der Begriff „Negro", der von Padmore u. a. auch für die im vorigen Absatz erwähnte Konferenz benutzt wurde, fand von der Jahrhundertwende (Booker T. Washington und W. E. B. DuBois) über die Harlem Renaissance der 1920er und 1930er Jahre bis in die Zeit der Bürgerrechtsbewegung der 1960er Jahre (Martin Luther King) hinein Verwendung als diskursiver Begriff und als Eigenbezeichnung von Afroamerikaner·innen.

14. Theo Williams, "Theorizing the 1930s: Black Radicalism, Antifascism and Anticolonialism in Interwar Britain," JHI Blog, January 12, 2022, https://www.jhiblog.org/2022/01/12/theorizing-the-1930s-black-radicalism-antifascism-and-anticolonialism-in-interwar-britain.

15. Stephanie Brown, "'Bootsie' in Berlin: An Interview with Helma Harrington on Oliver Harrington's Life and Work in East Germany, 1961–1995," *African American Review* 44, no. 3 (2011): 358.

16. See also Oliver W. Harrington, *Why I Left America and Other Essays* (1993; University of

World Peace, for instance, Padmore wrote, "'Democratic' Imperialism and 'Fascist' Imperialism are merely interchanging ideologies corresponding to the economic and political conditions of capitalism within a given country on the one hand, and the degree to which the class struggle has developed on the other."[14] Yet his years in Hamburg enabled him to advance his Black radicalism and political thought.

From Hamburg to East Berlin, African American writer, journalist, and cartoonist Oliver "Ollie" Wendell Harrington's Black radicalism continued to manifest itself in his numerous illustrations. In 1961, he traveled to East Berlin, where he requested political asylum after the suspicious death of his friend Richard Wright in Paris.[15] While in East Berlin, he sent his cartoons and articles to the United States, where they regularly appeared in books, leftist periodicals, satirical magazines, and major Black newspapers like the *Pittsburgh Courier*. In his cartoons, Harrington attacked institutionalized racism, imperialism, poverty, political corruption, homelessness, and other pressing issues.[16]

The GDR heightened Harrington's artistry and global anti-Fascist politics in significant ways. Richard Powell has noted, "Harrington's cartoons of the 1960s—meticulous, virtuosic, and acerbic—might suggest that his East Berlin base and proximity to the graphic arts traditions of the German Renaissance and later may have played a key role in his artistic turn toward a more refined drawing technique."[17] Additionally, Brian Dolinar considered Harrington to be part of the

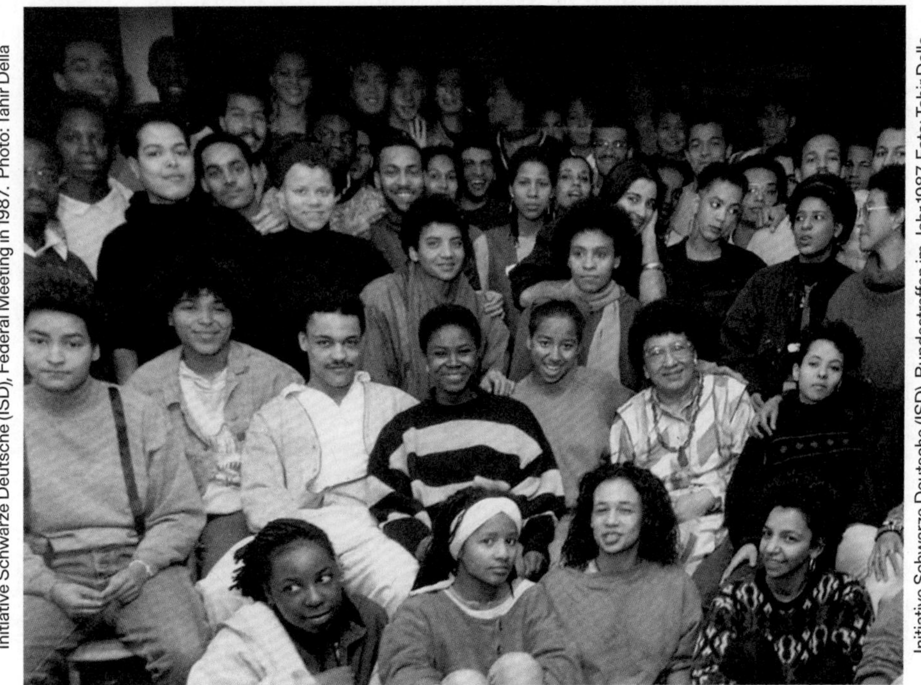

Initiative Schwarze Deutsche (ISD), Federal Meeting in 1987. Photo: Tahir Della

Initiative Schwarze Deutsche (ISD), Bundestreffen im Jahr 1987. Foto: Tahir Della

Hamburg und 1931 wurde Padmore zum Herausgeber ernannt. Padmores Schwarzes Denken fand prominenten Ausdruck auf den Seiten dieser Zeitschrift wie auch in seinen Essays und Büchern. Seine Schriften zeigten das vielfältige Gesicht des Rassismus und formulierten Lösungsvorschläge, die auf eine weltweite Ausradierung von Klassenausbeutung sowie rassistischer und kolonialer Unterdrückung abzielten. Er zog auch Verbindungslinien zwischen den Dynamiken in den Vereinigten Staaten und in Afrika und schuf so Verflechtungen zwischen unterdrückten Menschen in aller Welt. Mehr noch, sein Radikalismus war entschieden marxistisch. Als Kommunist war sein Antirassismus von Haus aus international, wie sich in *The Negro Worker* zeigte. 1933 suspendierte die Komintern *The Negro Worker* und löste das ITUCNW auf, was Padmore dazu veranlasste, die Kommunistische Partei zu kritisieren und sich von ihr zu trennen. Kurze Zeit später kamen die Nazis an die Macht und Padmore wurde inhaftiert und nach England ausgewiesen.

In London schloss er sich einer tatkräftigen Gemeinschaft von Aktivist·innen an, die sich der afrikanischen Unabhängigkeit und dem Antifaschismus verschrieben hatten. Mit seiner Arbeit setzte sich Padmore für die unterdrückten und ausgebeuteten Klassen ein und unterstützte panafrikanistische Initiativen, etwa die Panafrikanischen Kongresse der folgenden Jahre. In seinem 1937 erschienen Buch *Africa and World Peace* schreibt Padmore: „Der ‚demokratische' Imperialismus und der ‚faschistische' Imperialismus sind austauschbare Ideologien, die einerseits den jeweiligen ökonomischen und politischen Bedingungen innerhalb eines Landes entsprechen und andererseits dem Grad, bis zu dem sich

16. Mississippi, 2010); Anna Duensing, "Fascists Without Labels: Jim Crow, Civil Rights, and the Making of a Black Antifascist Tradition, 1933–1977" (PhD diss., Yale University, 2022), 364–429.

17. Richard J. Powell, *Going There: Black Visual Satire* (Yale University Press, 2020), 88.

18. Quoted in Powell, *Going There*, 88.

19. Powell, *Going There*, 90.

"Black Cultural Front," which was a group of politically left-leaning Black artists and intellectuals that included Paul Robeson, Frank Marshall Davis, Charles White, Shirley Graham Du Bois, and more. This group increasingly saw their "artistic mission in geopolitical terms" and linked African Americans with the struggles of oppressed people across the globe.[18]

In East Berlin, he also wrote for satirical magazines, including *Eulenspiegel* and *Das Magazin*. While Padmore organized and wrote, Harrington's preferred medium was art. It allowed him to criticize the problems of America (national) while also attending to issues of marginalization and exploitation across the Global South (international). His socialist ideals did not wane. He never refrained from criticizing American imperialism in Vietnam or British colonialism in Rhodesia (modern-day Zimbabwe), showing the interplay between the international and the national in his artistic and political work.

In an untitled 1969 cartoon with the text "I believe it is not only acceptable to Rhodesians, but with a clear conscience we can argue this constitution outside the borders of our country," Harrington responded to prime minister Ian Smith's comments about producing a new written constitution that would strengthen the autonomy of the White minority and limit the number of elected Black members to the Rhodesian parliament in Rhodesia.[19] I am unable to analyze the cartoon in its entirety, but I want to flag two points about its radicalism. First, this image was included in *The Daily World*, a New York–based Communist newspaper. Through this potent cartoon, Harrington linked Black Rhodesians to African Americans, suggesting their struggles and conditions were analogous. Both populations endured White supremacist violence. In this way, British imperialism and US Jim Crow were not entirely different. Harrington was like Padmore, who made similar connections in his own work. Second, this was a radical image to produce and submit to *The Daily World* because it centered on Black people. It advanced racial equality and called out White supremacy. Harrington acknowledged the plight of Black Rhodesians and the manifold costs of European colonialism.

Even while being watched by the FBI and the Stasi, his cartoons in the GDR tackled American themes on social integration and bussing in 1970s Boston.

der Klassenkampf entwickelt hat."[16] Seine Jahre in Hamburg halfen ihm, seinen Schwarzen Radikalismus und sein politisches Denken weiterzuentwickeln.

Szenenwechsel von Hamburg nach Ost-Berlin: Der Schwarze Radikalismus des afroamerikanischen Schriftstellers, Journalisten und Karikaturisten Oliver „Ollie" Wendell Harrington schlug sich immer wieder in seinen Illustrationen nieder. 1961 reiste er nach Ost-Berlin, wo er nach dem Tod seines Freundes Richard Wright, dessen Umstände ihm suspekt erschienen, politisches Asyl beantragte.[17] Während seiner Zeit in Ost-Berlin schickte er seine Karikaturen und Artikel in die Vereinigten Staaten, wo sie regelmäßig in Büchern, linken Zeitschriften, Satiremagazinen und wichtigen Schwarzen Zeitungen wie dem *Pittsburgh Courier* veröffentlicht wurden. In seinen Karikaturen attackierte Harrington institutionalisierten Rassismus, Imperialismus, politische Korruption, Obdachlosigkeit und andere drängende Themen.[18]

Die Zeit in der DDR hatte spürbar Einfluss auf Harringtons künstlerisches Schaffen und seine globale antifaschistische Politik. Richard Powell schreibt: „Harringtons Karikaturen der 1960er Jahre – poetisch, virtuos und bissig – legen die Vermutung nahe, dass sein Leben in Ost-Berlin und die Nähe zu den grafischen Traditionen der deutschen Renaissance und späterer Perioden eine Schlüsselrolle bei seiner künstlerischen Hinwendung zu einer verfeinerten Zeichentechnik gespielt haben könnten."[19] Brian Dolinar rechnet Harrington zudem der „Schwarzen Kulturfront" zu, einer Gruppe linker Schwarzer Künstler·innen und Intellektueller, der unter anderem Paul Robeson, Frank Marshall Davis, Charles White und Shirley Graham Du Bois angehörten. Diese Gruppe begriff ihre „künstlerische Aufgabe" zunehmend „in geopolitischen Begriffen" und verknüpfte das Schicksal der Afroamerikaner·innen mit den Kämpfen unterdrückter Menschen auf dem gesamten Erdball.[20]

In Ost-Berlin schrieb er auch für satirische Publikationen wie den *Eulenspiegel* und *Das Magazin*. Während Padmore sich aufs Organisieren und Schreiben konzentrierte, war Harringtons bevorzugtes Medium die Kunst. Sie ermöglichte es ihm, die nationalen Probleme in Amerika zu kritisieren und sich zugleich den internationalen Themen von Marginalisierung und Ausbeutung im Globalen Süden zu widmen. Seine sozialistischen Ideale erlahmten nicht. Er hielt sich nie zurück mit Kritik am amerikanischen Imperialismus in Vietnam oder am britischen Kolonialismus in Rhodesien (dem heutigen Simbabwe), wobei

16. Theo Williams, „Theorizing the 1930s: Black Radicalism, Antifascism and Anticolonialism in Interwar Britain", in: *Journal of the History of Ideas Blog*, 12. Januar 2022, https://www.jhiblog.org/2022/01/12/theorizing-the-1930s-black-radicalism-antifascism-and-anticolonialism-in-interwar-britain

17. Stephanie Brown, „Bootsie' in Berlin: An Interview with Helma Harrington on Oliver Harrington's Life and Work in East Germany, 1961–1995", in: *African American Review*, 44, Nr. 3, 2011, S. 353–372, hier S. 358.

18. Siehe auch Oliver W. Harrington, *Why I Left America and Other Essays* (1993), Jackson: University of Mississippi Press 2010; Anna Duensing, *Fascists Without Labels: Jim Crow, Civil Rights, and the Making of a Black Antifascist Tradition, 1933–1977*, Diss. Yale University 2022, S. 364–429.

19. Richard J. Powell, *Going There: Black Visual Satire*, New Haven, CT: Yale University Press 2020, S. 88.

20. Zit. nach ebd.

20. Gerald Horne, *Race Woman: The Lives of Shirley Graham Du Bois* (NYU, 2002), 175.

21. Jennifer Blaylock, "The Mother, the Mistress, and the Cover Girls: Ghana Broadcasting Corporation and the Coloniality of Gender," *Feminist Media Histories* 8, no. 1 (2022): 107.

22. Shirley Graham Du Bois FBI file 018, p. 18, accessed September 26, 2024, https://archive.org/details/ShirleyGraham-DuBoisFBIFile/Shirley%20Graham%20Du%20Bois%20018/page/n17/mode/2up.

23. Blaylock, "The Mother, the Mistress, and the Cover Girls," 108.

He also appeared on radio and a television discussion panel. Yet he never stopped focusing on the suffering of communities in the Global South, the West's indifference, and the presence of Fascism. Again, Harrington's radicalism was channeled through his art, and his art and politics remained inextricably linked.

Radicalism was not only the purview of Black men, as Shirley Graham Du Bois was another Black Communist radical who used her time in the GDR to learn and share knowledge with Ghanaian people after its independence in 1957. She was also good friends with Eslanda Robeson. After her husband's death in 1963, she did not resign herself to a life of inaction. Instead, she "beg[a]n preparation for a very important post … an educational and creative post."[20] After his death, she began a career in television, which first included being a guest speaker at a twelve-day seminar on educational television held at the Ghana Broadcasting Corporation's Television Training School.[21] The first president of Ghana, Kwame Nkrumah, appointed her director of Ghana Television in 1964. Graham Du Bois worked to devise and build successful television in Ghana, engendering a version of Black feminist and pan-Africanist broadcasting that was inclusive and paid attention to women. Her work in broadcasting in Ghana was an act of meaning making and a labor of love.

Before and during her directorship, she traveled to the GDR (and other countries) to study their television systems. While there, she met with East German elites such as the editor of *Neues Deutschland* and gained access to factories and equipment associated with the state television broadcaster, Deutscher Fernsehfunk, which furthered the cause of socialism. Graham Du Bois also spoke with managers and developed additional techniques and strategies. Her FBI files referenced her efforts to stock Ghana's libraries and universities with books from the East Berlin publishing imprint Seven Seas, which was a forum for East German writings in English translation. She purchased and compiled publications for the television system as well.[22] Yet her time in East Germany was fruitful, and it allowed her to continue her radical vision of making Ghana Television "a symbol for African liberation and unity and transnational Black solidarity."[23] Moreover, it was a radical move for her to turn to East Germany before Chancellor Willy

internationale und nationale Geschehnisse in seiner künstlerischen und politischen Arbeit zusammenspielen.

In einer unbetitelten Karikatur aus dem Jahr 1969 mit dem Text „Ich glaube, dass sie nicht nur für Rhodesier akzeptabel ist, sondern dass wir diese Verfassung mit gutem Gewissen auch außerhalb der Grenzen unseres Landes vertreten können" reagierte Harrington auf die Äußerungen von Premierminister Ian Smith, der eine neue schriftliche Verfassung ausarbeiten wollte, die die Autonomie der weißen Minderheit stärken und die Zahl der gewählten Schwarzen Mitglieder des rhodesischen Parlaments begrenzen würde.[21] Ich kann an dieser Stelle die Karikatur nicht in Gänze analysieren, aber ich möchte zwei Punkte im Hinblick auf ihren Radikalismus hervorheben. Erstens wurde die Abbildung in *The Daily World* abgedruckt, einer kommunistischen Zeitschrift aus New York. Mit dieser eindrücklichen Karikatur stellte Harrington eine Verbindung zwischen den Schwarzen Rhodesier·innen und den Afroamerikaner·innen her und deutete an, dass ihre Kämpfe und Lebensbedingungen vergleichbar seien. Beide erlitten die Gewalt des weißen Herrschaftsdenkens. In dieser Hinsicht waren der britische Imperialismus und die als „Jim Crow" bekannte Rassendiskriminierung in den USA nicht völlig verschieden. Auch Padmore zog in seinem Werk ähnliche Verbindungslinien. Zweitens war es radikal, dieses scharfe Bild zu produzieren und bei *The Daily World* einzureichen, weil es die Schwarzen in den Mittelpunkt stellte. Es setzte sich für Gleichberechtigung ein und prangerte die weiße Vorherrschaft an. Harrington würdigte die Notlage der Schwarzen Rhodesier und lenkte den Blick auf die vielfältigen Kosten des europäischen Kolonialismus.

Selbst während er unter Beobachtung sowohl des FBI als auch der Stasi stand, adressierten seine in der DDR entstandenen Karikaturen amerikanische Themen wie die soziale Integration und das Bussing – also den Einsatz von Schulbussen zur Abschaffung der Rassentrennung in Schulen – im Boston der 1970er Jahre. Er hatte auch Auftritte in Radiosendungen und nahm an einer Fernsehdiskussion teil. Doch zugleich hörte er nie auf, seinen Blick auf notleidende Communitys im Globalen Süden zu richten, auf die Gleichgültigkeit des Westens und auf die Gegenwart des Faschismus. Auch hier brachte Harrington seinen Radikalismus in seiner künstlerischen Arbeit zum Ausdruck, Kunst und Politik blieben bei ihm immer unauflöslich miteinander verknüpft.

21. Ebd., S. 90.

24. Horne, *Race Woman*, 210.

25. Quoted in Leah Bassel and Akwugo Emejulu, *Minority Women and Austerity: Survival and Resistance in France and Britain* (Policy, 2017).

Brandt's Ostpolitik and "opening to the East" had begun. She was already practicing openness to the East, making East Germans real and comprehensible to Ghanaians, and vice versa.

Her radicalism established Ghana Television as a critical anti-colonial, pan-African, and socialist network that reflected bold innovation and African traditions. It also served as a model for other decolonized African countries. Her willingness to draw on East Germany reflected an understanding that the country offered a viable model for Ghana's new media, both present and future. The 1966 military coup that overthrew President Kwame Nkrumah ended that dream and forced her to look for a new residence. Shortly after the coup, Graham Du Bois traveled back to East Germany and contemplated moving there, remarking, "Every day I have been in the GDR has strengthened my desire to make Berlin my home—if I cannot go back to Ghana."[24] While she didn't move to East Berlin, the city certainly made an impression.

AYIM'S RADICALISM

Undeniably, Berlin also made an impression on Black German activist and author May Ayim, who moved to the city in 1984. There, her radicalism operated in several directions until her tragic death in 1996. Indeed, Black Germans' creation of a diasporic community was spurred on by the collective diasporic radicalism of people like Ayim, John Kantara, Katharina Oguntoye, Eleonore Wiedenroth-Coulibaly, Helga Emde, David Nii Addy, and Abenaa Adomako. No longer remaining silent, Black Germans, especially Ayim, united to challenge the presence of political racelessness, in which "race is to have no social place, no explicit markings. It is to be excised from any characterizing of human conditions, relations[, or] formations."[25] In the postwar Germanies, there was a disavowal and obscuring of race along with its colonial legacy, and concepts such as race and racism remained simultaneously invisible and taboo, on the one hand, while having actual material implications for minoritized communities on the other. Black Germans challenged these entrenched discriminatory practices and beliefs.

Der Radikalismus war nicht allein eine Domäne Schwarzer Männer, wie man an Shirley Graham Du Bois sehen kann, einer weiteren Schwarzen kommunistischen Radikalen, die ihre Zeit in der DDR dazu nutzte, sich weiterzubilden und ihr Wissen mit der Bevölkerung Ghanas nach der Erlangung der Unabhängigkeit des Landes 1957 zu teilen. Sie war eng befreundet mit Eslanda Robeson. Nach dem Tod ihres Ehemanns im Jahr 1963 fand sie sich nicht mit einem untätigen Leben ab. Stattdessen „begann sie sich auf eine sehr wichtige Aufgabe vorzubereiten … eine aufklärerische und kreative Aufgabe".[22] Nach seinem Tod startete sie eine Karriere im Fernsehen, die damit begann, dass sie als Gastrednerin an einem zwölftägigen Seminar im Bildungsfernsehen teilnahm, das in der Television Training School des nationalen Fernsehsenders von Ghana stattfand.[23] Der erste Präsident Ghanas, Kwame Nkrumah, ernannte sie 1964 zur Direktorin des Fernsehsenders von Ghana. Graham Du Bois arbeitete an der Entwicklung und dem Aufbau eines erfolgreichen Fernsehsenders in Ghana und schuf einen Schwarzen feministischen und panafrikanistischen Rundfunk, der inklusiv war und sich den Belangen von Frauen zuwandte. Ihre Arbeit im Rundfunk in Ghana war ein Akt der Sinnstiftung und der Leidenschaft.

Vor und während ihrer Amtszeit als Direktorin reiste sie in die DDR (und weitere Länder), um deren Fernsehsysteme zu studieren. Während ihres Aufenthaltes traf sie mit Vertreter·innen der ostdeutschen Eliten wie dem Herausgeber der Zeitung *Neues Deutschland* zusammen und erhielt Zugang zu Fabriken und Anlagen, die mit dem staatlichen Sender Deutscher Fernsehfunk verbunden waren, der die Sache des Sozialismus vorantrieb. Graham Du Bois sprach auch mit Betriebsleitern und entwickelte zusätzliche Strategien und Techniken. Ihr FBI-Dossier verzeichnet ihre Versuche, die Bibliotheken und Universitäten Ghanas mit Büchern des Ost-Berliner Verlags Seven Seas auszustatten, bei dem Texte von DDR-Autor·innen in englischer Übersetzung erschienen. Sie erwarb und sammelte auch Publikationen für das Fernsehsystem.[24] Ihre Zeit in Ostdeutschland erwies sich als fruchtbar und ermöglichte ihr die Fortführung ihrer radikalen Vision, den Sender Ghana Television zu „einem Symbol der afrikanischen Befreiung und Einheit und der transnationalen Schwarzen Solidarität" zu erheben.[25] Zudem war es ein Zeichen ihrer Radikalität, sich der DDR zuzuwenden, noch bevor Bundeskanzler Willy Brandt seine Ostpolitik initiierte und die „Öffnung nach

22. Gerald Horne, *Race Woman: The Lives of Shirley Graham Du Bois*, New York: NYU Press 2002, S. 175.

23. Jennifer Blaylock, „The Mother, the Mistress, and the Cover Girls: Ghana Broadcasting Corporation and the Coloniality of Gender", in: *Feminist Media Histories*, 8, Nr. 1, 2022, S. 102–133, hier S. 107.

24. FBI-Akte zu Shirley Graham Du Bois, S. 18, https://archive.org/details/ ShirleyGrahamDuBois- FBIFile/Shirley%20Graham%20Du%20Bois%20 018/page/n17/mode/2up

25. Blaylock, „The Mother, the Mistress, and the Cover Girls", S. 108.

26. Florvil, *Mobilizing Black Germany*, 131–32.

Ayim sparked this new stage of Black German activism, which entailed the organization of conferences, exhibitions, and demonstrations. These events were not only radical but also radicalizing. The annual Black History Month (BHM) celebrations in Berlin, inaugurated by the ISD in 1990, were one such event. The BHM made Black German radicalism legible in the public sphere in several ways. First, the BHMs reflected the revolutionary objectives of Black German spatial politics, and the ISD's use of different spaces throughout Berlin and its creation of a "Black sense of place" rooted Blackness across the city.[26] Second, ISD organizers and members publicly (re)introduced Black history, enabling the BHMs to function as a disruption to the White German status quo and traditional racist hierarchies. The Black German organizers of these annual celebrations, including Ayim, publicly discussed race and called out German discourses of racelessness. In so doing, they reimagined possibilities, allowing the past, in all its horror and violent totality, to speak to and with the present. From events on Black Europe,

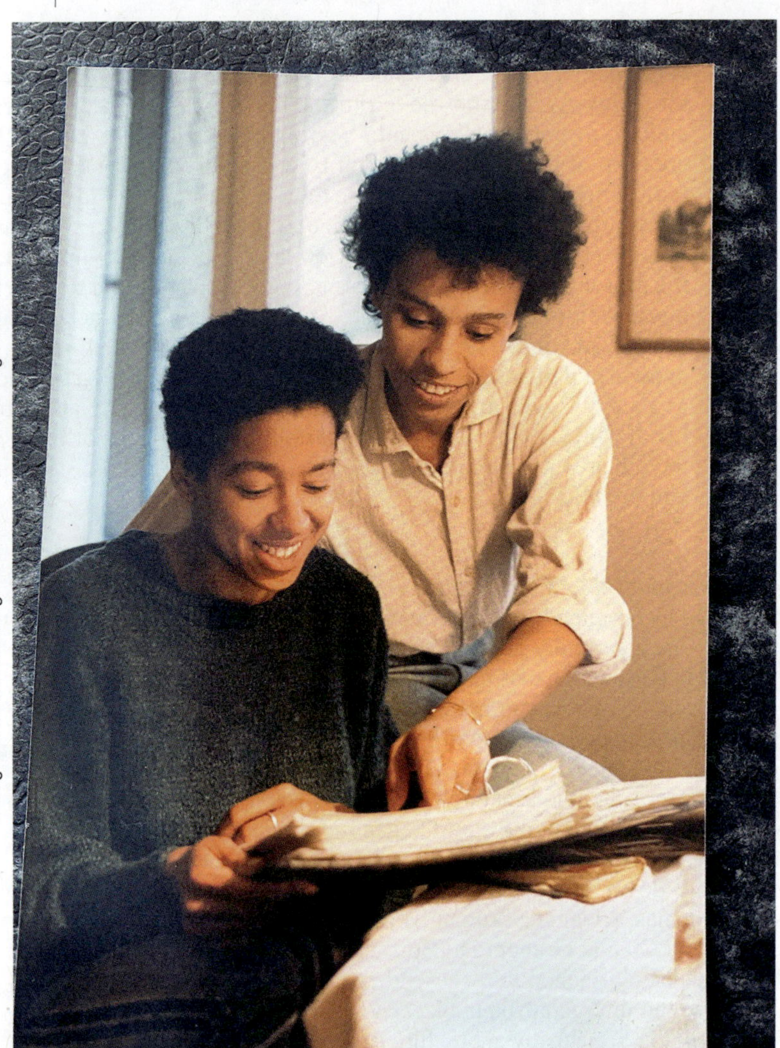

May Ayim and Katharina Oguntoye during their work on *Showing our Colors* in 1985. Photo: Dagmar Schultz

May Ayim und Katharina Oguntoye im Jahr 1985 bei der Arbeit an *Farbe bekennen*. Foto: Dagmar Schultz

Osten" begonnen hatte. Sie praktizierte bereits eine Offenheit gegenüber dem Osten und vermittelte den Ghanaer·innen so ein realistisches und verständliches Bild der Ostdeutschen und umgekehrt.

Dank ihres Radikalismus etablierte sich Ghana Television als kritischer antikolonialer, panafrikanischer und sozialistischer Sender, der mutige Innovationen ebenso wie afrikanische Traditionen widerspiegelte. Er diente auch als Vorbild für andere dekolonialisierte afrikanische Länder. Ihre Bereitschaft, sich an der DDR zu orientieren, zeugt von der Einsicht, dass dieses Land ein tragfähiges Modell für die Gegenwart und Zukunft der neuen Medien in Ghana darstellen könnte. Der Militärputsch von 1966, bei dem Präsident Kwame Nkrumah gestürzt wurde, beendete diesen Traum und zwang sie, eine neue Heimstatt zu suchen. Kurz nach dem Putsch reiste Graham Du Bois zurück nach Ostdeutschland und erwog, dorthin umzusiedeln. Sie äußerte, dass „jeder Tag meines Aufenthalts in der DDR meinen Wunsch bestärkt hat, Berlin zu meiner Heimat zu machen – falls ich nicht nach Ghana zurückkehren können sollte".[26] Auch wenn sie am Ende doch nicht nach Ost-Berlin umsiedelte, hinterließ die Stadt einen bleibenden Eindruck bei ihr.

26. Horne, *Race Woman*, S. 210.

27. See Tiffany N. Florvil, "May Ayim's Cosmopolitanism from Below in Europe," History Workshop, October 2, 2023, https://www.historyworkshop.org.uk/feminism/may-ayims-cosmopolitanism-from-below-in-europe/.

28. May Ayim, "Racism and Resistance in United Germany," speech, May 9–11, 1994, 2; Florvil, Mobilizing Black Germany.

slavery, and colonialism, as well as presentations by Theodor Michael, Tina Campt, Tsitsi Dangarembga, Ika Hügel-Marshall, and others, Black Germans recognized that this history had been out of reach for so many for too long. The BHMs were restorative.

Ayim committed herself to a variety of pan-African initiatives as well as causes that focused on migrant and Black women as thinkers, writers, and artists. She centered their humanity, limiting the reach of White supremacy in the process. In the 1990s, she worked with the Pan-European Women's Network for Intercultural Action and Exchange (AKWAABA), a group that sought to secure funding from the Council of Europe, the European Commission, and other institutions in the European Union. Members of AKWAABA attempted to increase Black women's representation in the continent, especially in the field of art. Ayim "knew that multicultural collaborations fostered meaningful change in Europe" and beyond.[27]

In 1994, Ayim's radicalism took her to the United States. While there, she presented at Carleton College as the Christopher U. Light Lecturer for Literature in the German and Russian Department and an international conference at the University of Minnesota. Ayim's "Racism and Resistance in United Germany" speech offers a compelling example of her radicalism in praxis. Her work always disseminated the historical truths about racism, colonialism, and Fascism and brought Black people out of obscurity in Europe, while also helping them survive in the present.

Ayim drew on her research and honored Black ancestors in her speech. In this respect, she not only recognized Anton Wilhelm Amo, an eighteenth-century Enlightenment thinker, but also other lesser-known people, including an African family who died in the Berlin Tierpark in 1920. She acknowledged their humanity during an anti-Black moment. The family was included in a *Völkerschau* or human zoo exhibition. Ayim remarked, "They were kept there barely dressed and couldn't survive the cold winter. The German audience was delighted about [these] 'exotic shows' and scientists were excited to use [non-White] people of different cultures for their explorations and experiments."[28] Anti-Blackness was

AYIMS RADIKALISMUS

Zweifellos machte Berlin auch einen starken Eindruck auf die Schwarze Deutsche Aktivistin und Autorin May Ayim, die 1984 in die Stadt zog. Einmal dort angekommen, entfaltete sich ihr radikaler Aktivismus in unterschiedliche Richtungen, bis er mit ihrem tragischen Tod 1996 ein jähes Ende fand. Die von Schwarzen Deutschen vorangetriebe Schaffung einer Diaspora-Gemeinschaft wurde beflügelt durch den kollektiven diasporischen Radikalismus von Ayim, John Kantara, Katharina Oguntoye, Eleonore Wiedenroth-Coulibaly, Helga Emde, David Nii Addy, Abenaa Adomako und anderen. Schwarze Deutsche, vor allem Ayim, wollten nicht länger schweigen und taten sich zusammen, um die vorherrschende politische Blindheit gegenüber *race* herauszufordern, der gemäß „Rasse keinen Platz in der Gesellschaft haben und nicht explizit gekennzeichnet werden soll. Sie soll aus jeglicher Charakterisierung menschlicher Lebensbedingungen, Beziehungen [oder] Gruppen getilgt werden."[27] In den beiden deutschen Staaten der Nachkriegszeit wurde das Konzept der Rasse mitsamt seinem kolonialen Erbe entwertet und verschleiert, Rasse und Rassismus blieben einerseits gleichermaßen unsichtbar und tabuisiert, andererseits hatten sie konkrete materielle Auswirkungen auf minorisierte Gemeinschaften. Schwarze Deutsche stellten diese tief verwurzelten diskriminierenden Praktiken und Überzeugungen infrage.

Ayim gab den Anstoß zu dieser neuen Phase ikes Schwarzen deutschen Aktivismus, die mit der Organisation von Konferenzen, Ausstellungen und Demonstrationen einherging. Diese Veranstaltungen waren nicht nur radikal, sondern wirkten auch radikalisierend. Die jährlichen Feierlichkeiten zum Black History Month (BHM) in Berlin, die 1990 von der ISD ins Leben gerufen wurden, waren eine solche Veranstaltung. Der BHM machte den Schwarzen deutschen Radikalismus in der Öffentlichkeit in mehrfacher Hinsicht lesbar. Erstens spiegelten die BHMs die revolutionären raumpolitischen Ziele der Schwarzen Deutschen wider und zeigten, wie die ISD unterschiedliche Räume in ganz Berlin nutzte und ein „Schwarzes Ortsbewusstsein" schuf, das Schwarzsein in der ganzen Stadt verankerte.[28] Zweitens machten die Organisator·innen und Mitglieder der ISD die Schwarze Geschichte öffentlichkeitswirksam (wieder) zum Thema und ermöglichten es den BHMs, einen Bruch mit dem weißen deutschen Status quo und den traditionellen rassistischen Hierarchien zu vollziehen. Die Schwarzen

27. Zitiert in Leah Bassel und Akwugo Emejulu, *Minority Women and Austerity: Survival and Resistance in France and Britain*, Bristol, UK: Policy 2017.

28. Florvil, *Mobilizing Black Germany*, S. 131–132.

29. Ayim, "Racism and Resistance," 3-4.

30. Ayim, "Racism and Resistance," 8.

felt and experienced and resulted in the family's and other Black peoples social and physical deaths. Angela Zimmerman and others have written that nineteenth-century Germany's racist tradition of the *Völkerschau* claimed that African-descended people were allegedly "primitive" and devoid of culture. Ayim explained that the "past and present of Afro-Germans are connected with the facts and the repression of Germany's colonial and fascist history, but besides the effects of racism and exclusion, the Black German experience also reflects an ongoing movement of resistance and courage of a not yet very strong and visible, but constantly growing Black Community."[29] She was a key figure in this "growing Black Community."

Interweaving her historical research, personal experiences, and compelling poetry, Ayim disrupted positive depictions of unified or post-*Wende* Germany as an inclusive and tolerant space. She disclosed that "a ten-year-old African boy was kicked out of a train, in order to give a place to a white person. . . . These were incidents in November 1989 in West Berlin, and since 1990 reports of racist attacks mainly against Black people, mostly in the east part of Germany, have increased."[30] Ayim reclaimed the power that silenced certain voices over others and remedied the layers of violence in her speech. She grappled with the totality of anti-Blackness and offered a politics of care for all Black ancestors.

Interestingly, her 1994 speech was an indictment of both West and East Germany for their overt racism; neither side was deemed innocent. Ayim argued that while the GDR's international solidarity politics allied it with liberatory struggles in communities of the Global South, their diplomatic and political act of solidarity rang hollow, owing to "racist and antisemitic thoughts" and the erasure of the presence and history of Black people in the Communist country. Regardless of differing ideologies, both Germanies were complicit in their practices of everyday and structural racism. She stated, "It is remarkable that most of the German politicians are very concerned about the reputation of their country, but [care] little about the victims or those who could be victims of racist attacks. The specific situation of Black people in Germany is usually not mentioned, and only expressed in terms of numbers or warnings about refugees and asylum seekers

---

deutschen Organisator·innen dieser jährlichen Feierlichkeiten, darunter Ayim, diskutierten öffentlich das Konzept Rasse und prangerten deutsche Diskurse der Rassenblindheit an. Auf diese Weise schufen sie neue Möglichkeiten, indem sie der Vergangenheit in all ihrem Schrecken und ihrer gewalttätigen Totalität erlaubten, zu und mit der Gegenwart zu sprechen. In Veranstaltungen zu Schwarzem Europa, Sklaverei und Kolonialismus sowie in Vorträgen von Theodor Michael, Tina Campt, Tsitsi Dangarembga, Ika Hügel-Marshall und anderen erkannten Schwarze Deutsche, dass diese Geschichte für viele zu lange unzugänglich gewesen war. Die BHMs waren ein Mittel der Regeneration.

Ayim engagierte sich in zahlreichen panafrikanischen Initiativen wie auch für Anliegen, die sich auf migrantische und Schwarze Frauen als Denkerinnen, Schriftstellerinnen und Künstlerinnen konzentrierten. Sie stellte ihre Menschlichkeit in den Mittelpunkt und begrenzte dadurch den Wirkungsbereich weißer Vorherrschaft. In den 1990er Jahren arbeitete sie mit dem Pan European Women's Network for Intercultural Action and Exchange (AKWAABA) zusammen, einer Gruppe, die sich um finanzielle Unterstützung durch den Europarat, die Europäische Kommission und andere Institutionen der Europäischen Union bemühte. Mitglieder von AWAABA versuchten, die Repräsentation Schwarzer Frauen auf dem Kontinent zu erhöhen, insbesondere auf dem Feld der Kunst. Ayim „wusste, dass multikulturelle Kollaborationen echte Veränderungen in Europa beförderten" – und auch über Europa hinauswirkten.[29]

Im Jahr 1994 brachte Ayims Radikalismus sie in die Vereinigten Staaten. Während ihres dortigen Aufenthaltes hielt sie Vorträge am Carleton College als Christopher U. Light Lecturer for Literature am German and Russian Department und auf einer internationalen Konferenz an der University of Minnesota. Ihre Rede „Racism and Resistance in United Germany" (Rassismus und Widerstand im vereinten Deutschland) liefert ein überzeugendes Beispiel ihres Radikalismus in der Praxis. Ihre Arbeit diente der Verbreitung historischer Tatsachen über Rassismus, Kolonialismus und Faschismus und bewahrte Schwarze Menschen in Europa vor dem Vergessen, während sie ihnen zugleich half, in der Gegenwart zu überleben.

In ihrer Rede stützte Ayim sich auf ihre Forschungen und würdigte die Schwarzen Vorfahren. In dieser Hinsicht zollte sie nicht nur Anton Wilhelm Amo Respekt, einem Denker der Aufklärung aus dem 18. Jahrhundert, sondern auch

29. Vgl. Tiffany N. Florvil, „May Ayim's Cosmopolitanism from Below in Europe", in: *History Workshop*, 2. Oktober 2023, https://www.historyworkshop.org.uk/feminism/may-ayims-cosmopolitanism-from-below-in-europe/.

31. Ayim, "Racism and Resistance," 13.

who 'overflood' and 'overrun' Germany. With these talks, politicians do encourage and increase the rejection of Black people. The open violence is putting into practice what leading politicians delegate."[31] She called out the entrenched discursive and structural bigotry.

* * *

So why does discussing Ayim along with Padmore, Harrington, and Graham Du Bois matter? What does Ayim's radicalism actually mean for us today? What shape did Black German radicalism take? These examples of Black radicalism demonstrate that Germany was a site of transnational radical political culture, and it did not take one shape or linear path. Padmore and Harrington used their radicalism to demand racial, social, and political changes that certainly had implications for African Americans and others in the Global South. Padmore organized, edited, and wrote, while Harrington drew, wrote, and satirized. One approach was not superior to the other as both men pursued similar ends in their bid to combat all forms of discrimination and end Western imperialism. Graham Du Bois's radicalism was tied to making Ghana stand out as a modern decolonial country. Ghana's potential lay in its ability to build and sustain a broadcasting network geared to all. Graham Du Bois opened East Germany to Ghana and vice versa. Coming to Germany required them all to learn new strategies and advance their political objectives. Ayim differed slightly because she was born in Germany. Her radicalism was homegrown and in the service of Black Germans and other minoritized communities, and she used her creative talents as a vehicle for transformation, much like her diasporic predecessors.

Undergirding Ayim's radicalism was an urgency to transform German society and affirm the importance of its history. Recovering the past with ISD events, Ayim and her compatriots pursued epistemic change that challenged hierarchies and paradigms. These forms of Black German radicalism were intellectual, affective, cultural, and political. Their efforts are often not seen in such a light, which is why it is important to show how Ayim and her Black German compatriots were radicals.

anderen, weniger bekannten Menschen, darunter eine afrikanische Familie, die 1920 im Berliner Tierpark starb. Sie würdigte ihre Menschlichkeit in einer Zeit, die voller Rassismus gegen Schwarze war. Die Familie wurde bei einer Völkerschau wie in einem menschlichen Zoo ausgestellt. Ayim bemerkte: „Sie wurden dort kaum bekleidet gehalten und konnten den kalten Winter nicht überleben. Das deutsche Publikum war begeistert von [diesen] ‚exotischen Darbietungen', und Wissenschaftler waren darauf erpicht, [nicht-weiße] Menschen aus unterschiedlichen Kulturen für ihre Forschungen und Experimente zu benutzen."[30] Anti-Schwarzsein wurde gefühlt und erlebt und führte zum sozialen und physischen Tod der Familie und anderer Schwarzer Menschen. Angela Zimmerman und andere haben daran erinnert, dass die rassistische Tradition der Völkerschau im Deutschland des 19. Jahrhunderts der Annahme folgte, Menschen afrikanischer Abstammung wären „primitiv" und ohne Kultur. Ayim erklärte, dass die „Vergangenheit und Gegenwart der Afro-Deutschen eng verbunden ist mit den Fakten und der Verdrängung von Deutschlands kolonialer und faschistischer Geschichte, doch jenseits der Effekte von Rassismus und Ausgrenzung spiegelt sich in der Erfahrung Schwarzer Deutscher auch eine anhaltende Bewegung des Widerstands und der Mut einer noch nicht sonderlich starken und sichtbaren, aber stetig wachsenden Schwarzen Community".[31] Sie selbst war eine Schlüsselfigur in dieser „wachsenden Schwarzen Community".

Indem sie ihre historischen Forschungen mit persönlichen Erfahrungen und einer bezwingenden Lyrik verwebte, störte Ayim positive Deutungen, die das vereinigte Deutschland der Nachwendezeit als einen inklusiven und von Toleranz geprägten Ort darstellten. Sie wies darauf hin, dass „ein zehnjähriger afrikanischer Junge aus dem Zug geschmissen wurde, um Platz für eine weiße Person zu machen … Das waren Vorfälle, die sich im November 1989 in West-Berlin ereigneten, und seit 1990 haben Berichte über rassistische Angriffe, vorwiegend auf Schwarze Menschen, zumeist im Ostteil Deutschlands, zugenommen."[32] Ayim forderte die Macht zurück, die bestimmte Stimmen hörbar machte und andere zum Schweigen brachte, und versuchte, der vielschichtigen Gewalt in ihrer Rede eine heilende Perspektive entgegenzusetzen. Sie setzte sich mit dem Hass auf Schwarze in seiner Totalität auseinander und entwarf eine Politik der Fürsorge für alle Schwarzen Vorfahren.

Interessanterweise attackierte ihre 1994 gehaltene Rede West- wie Ostdeutschland gleichermaßen für ihren offenen Rassismus; keine Seite konnte

30. May Ayim, „Racism and Resistance in United Germany", Vortrag bei der Konferenz „Xenophobia in Germany", University of Minnesota, 11.–14. Mai 1994, S. 2; Florvil, *Mobilizing Black Germany*.

31. Ebd., S. 3–4.

32. Ebd., S. 8.

Ayim's radical activism highlighted the specific lived experiences of Black people that racelessness hoped to elide in Germany. Her work remains prescient and urges us to center radical Black narratives that have been both ignored and erased in Germany. Just as she did on countless occasions, we must speak out about the contours of race, racecraft, and ethnonationalism in Germany, the United States, and elsewhere. In our increasingly Fascist moment, we must use our words, voices, and actions as weapons in a crucial fight for equality and liberation.

Unschuld für sich reklamieren. Ayim argumentierte, dass die internationale Solidaritätspolitik der DDR sich zwar mit den Befreiungskämpfen in Communitys des Globalen Südens verbündete, ihre diplomatischen und politischen Solidaritätsbekundungen jedoch hohl klangen angesichts des „rassistischen und antisemitischen Denkens" und der Ausradierung der Gegenwart und Geschichte Schwarzer Menschen in dem kommunistischen Land. Ungeachtet ihrer unterschiedlichen Ideologien erschienen die beiden deutschen Staaten in ihrem alltäglichen und strukturellen Rassismus als Komplizen. Sie stellte fest: „Es ist auffällig, dass die meisten deutschen Politiker sich äußerst besorgt zeigen über den Ruf ihres Landes, sich aber kaum um die Opfer und potenziellen Opfer rassistischer Angriffe scheren. Die besondere Situation Schwarzer Menschen in Deutschland wird für gewöhnlich nicht erwähnt und findet höchstens Ausdruck in Zahlen oder in Warnungen vor Flüchtlingen und Asylsuchenden, die Deutschland ‚überfluten' und ‚überrennen'. Mit solchen Reden ermutigen und verstärken die Politiker die Ablehnung Schwarzer Menschen. Die offene Gewalt setzt in die Praxis um, was führende Politiker zur Aufgabe erklären."[33] Sie prangerte die tief verankerte diskursive und strukturelle Bigotterie an.

***

Warum ist es also wichtig, Ayim gemeinsam mit Padmore, Harrington und Graham Du Bois zu diskutieren? Was bedeutet Ayims Radikalismus für uns? Wie gestaltete sich der Schwarze deutsche Radikalismus? Diese Beispiele des Schwarzen Radikalismus zeigen, dass Deutschland Schauplatz einer transnationalen radikalen politischen Kultur war, die nicht nur eine einzige Gestalt annahm oder einen linearen Pfad beschritt. Padmore und Harrington nutzten ihren Radikalismus, um rassische, soziale und politische Veränderungen zu fordern, die sicherlich auch Auswirkungen auf Afroamerikaner·innen und Menschen im Globalen Süden hatten. Padmore organisierte, redigierte und schrieb, während Harrington zeichnete, schrieb und persiflierte. Der eine Ansatz war dem anderen nicht überlegen, da beide Männer in ihrem Werben für den Kampf gegen alle Formen der Diskriminierung und für ein Ende des westlichen Imperialismus ganz ähnliche Ziele verfolgten. Graham Du Bois' Radikalismus stand im Zeichen ihres Wunsches, Ghana zu einem modernen dekolonialisierten Land zu machen. Ghanas

33. Ebd., S. 13.

Potenzial sollte sich in seiner Fähigkeit offenbaren, einen Fernsehsender aufzubauen und zu betreiben, der sich an alle richtete. Graham Du Bois öffnete die DDR für Ghana und umgekehrt. Nach Deutschland zu kommen, bedeutete für sie alle, neue Strategien zu erlernen und ihre politischen Ziele voranzutreiben. Ayims Position war eine etwas andere, da sie in Deutschland geboren wurde. Ihr Radikalismus war hausgemacht und stand im Dienste Schwarzer Deutscher und anderer minorisierter Gruppen, und sie nutzte ihre kreativen Talente als Vehikel für den Wandel, ähnlich wie ihre Vorgänger·innen in der Diaspora.

Hinter Ayims Radikalität stand der Drang, die deutsche Gesellschaft zu verändern und die Bedeutung ihrer Geschichte zu bekräftigen. Durch die Aufarbeitung der Vergangenheit mit Veranstaltungen der ISD strebten Ayim und ihre Mitstreiter·innen einen epistemischen Wandel an, der Hierarchien und Paradigmen infrage stellte. Diese Formen des Schwarzen deutschen Radikalismus waren intellektuell, affektiv, kulturell und politisch. Ihre Bemühungen werden oft nicht in einem solchen Licht gesehen, weshalb es wichtig ist, zu zeigen, wie radikal Ayim und ihre Schwarzen deutschen Mitstreiter·innen waren.

Ayims radikaler Aktivismus betonte die spezifischen Lebenserfahrungen Schwarzer Menschen, die mit der Vorstellung der Rassenblindheit in Deutschland annulliert werden sollten. Ihr Werk ist nach wie vor aktuell und fordert uns dazu auf, radikale Schwarze Erzählungen in den Blick zu rücken, die in Deutschland ignoriert und ausgelöscht wurden. So wie sie es bei unzähligen Gelegenheiten getan hat, sollten wir die Konturen von Rasse, Rassismus und Ethnonationalismus in Deutschland, den Vereinigten Staaten und anderswo ohne Scheu offenlegen. In dieser zunehmend faschistischen Zeit müssen wir unsere Worte, Stimmen und Taten zu Waffen machen und sie in einem entscheidenden Kampf für Gleichheit und Befreiung einsetzen.

A Conversation with George E. Lewis,
Doreen Mende, Matana Roberts, and Kira Thurman

RESONATING STRUGGLES: PAUL AND ESLANDA ROBESON IN EAST BERLIN

RESONATING STRUGGLES: PAUL UND ESLANDA ROBESON IN OST-BERLIN

George E. Lewis im Gespräch mit Doreen Mende,
Matana Roberts und Kira Thurman

The panel discussion "Resonating Struggles: Paul and Eslanda Robeson in East Berlin" took place as a live-stream broadcast from the Plenarsaal at the Akademie der Künste in Berlin on June 1, 2021. The panel consisted of composer, musician, and mixed media artist Matana Roberts, professor of German language, musician, and musicologist Kira Thurman, and curator, theorist, and professor of curatorial/ politics Doreen Mende. The moderator was professor of American music, composer, and musician George E. Lewis.

The panel discussion was a part of the overarching program "Arbeit am Gedächtnis: Transforming Archives." In engaging with this important topic, the Akademie der Künste was reflecting anew on its own institution as a repository of memory and on the political and critical dimension of memory. The examination of the Akademie's own archives also led us to the Paul Robeson Archive, whose existence there is the product of a revealing history of entanglements with close connections to the history of Germany, both East and West, and the Cold War. The Robeson archive, which also includes the Eslanda Robeson Archive, was founded in 1965 at the Akademie der Künste in East Berlin based on the work of the Paul Robeson Committee, which was established at the Akademie in 1958.

Central to the founding of the archive was the German Jewish philosopher Franz Loeser. While he was a student at the University of Minnesota, he protected Paul Robeson during the Peekskill Race Riots of 1949. After being exiled from the anticommunist McCarthyite US to the UK, Loeser founded the Robeson Passport Committee in Manchester, England, and then migrated in 1957 to the GDR. In East Germany, he continued his work for and with Robeson, which resulted in the foundation of the Archive of the Paul Robeson Committee, housed at the Akademie der Künste in East Berlin on Robert-Koch-Platz, where it is still located today. Invoking these geopolitical entanglements as a way of remembering the friendships, encounters, and journeys of Paul and Eslanda Robeson—who faced the same questions of racism, colonialism, and Fascism that continue to be structures of violence in the twenty-first century—is the starting point for the panel conversation.

Das Panelgespräch „Resonating Struggles: Paul und Eslanda Robeson in Ost-Berlin" wurde am 1. Juni 2021 als Livestream aus dem Plenarsaal der Akademie der Künste (AdK) in Berlin übertragen. An der Diskussion nahmen Matana Roberts, Komponist·in, Musiker·in und Mixed-Media-Künstler·in, Kira Thurman, Professorin für Germanistik, Musikerin und Musikwissenschaftlerin, und Doreen Mende, Kuratorin, Theoretikerin und Professorin für Kuratorik / Politik, teil. Die Moderation übernahm George E. Lewis, Professor für amerikanische Musik, Komponist und Musiker. Die Podiumsdiskussion war Teil des übergreifenden Programms „Arbeit am Gedächtnis. Archive verwandeln". Mit diesem wichtigen Thema reflektierte sich die Akademie der Künste erneut als Institution und Erinnerungsspeicher und betonte dabei die politische Dimension der Erinnerung. Die Untersuchung der akademieeigenen Archive führte auch zum Paul-Robeson-Archiv, dessen Existenz in der Akademie der Künste das Ergebnis einer aufschlussreichen Geschichte von Verstrickungen ist, die eng mit der deutsch-deutschen Geschichte und dem Kalten Krieg verflochten ist. Das Paul-Robeson-Archiv, zu dem auch das Eslanda-Robeson-Archiv gehört, wurde 1965 an der Akademie der Künste in Ost-Berlin auf der Grundlage des Archivs des Paul-Robeson-Komitees gegründet, das seit 1958 an der Akademie bestand.

Zentral für die Gründung des Archivs war der deutsch-jüdische Philosoph Franz Loeser. Als Student an der University of Minnesota verteidigte er Paul Robeson während der Peekskill Riots 1949. Als Loeser aus den antikommunistischen USA der McCarthy-Ära nach Großbritannien verbannt wurde, gründete er das Robeson Passport Committee in Manchester und wanderte dann 1957 in die DDR aus. Dort setzte er seine Arbeit für und mit Paul Robeson fort, die zur Gründung des Archivs des Paul-Robeson-Komitees in der Akademie der Künste in Ost-Berlin am Robert-Koch-Platz führte, wo es sich auch heute noch befindet. Diese geopolitischen Verflechtungen in der Erinnerung an die Freundschaft, die Begegnungen und die Reisen von Paul und Eslanda Robeson zu jener Zeit, als sie in ähnlicher Weise mit Rassismus, Kolonialismus und Faschismus als den politisch dringlichen Fragen des 21. Jahrhunderts konfrontiert waren, bilden die Ausgangspunkte für das Panelgespräch.

MR: I am interested in the power of memory and the power of history, which—despite not being acquainted with them personally, of course— I know Paul Robeson and Eslanda Robeson drew on in order to stay committed to the futurist vision they had for themselves, while at the same time living very visionary lives.

In my opinion, Eslanda Robeson's biography is one for the ages. Reading about her and understanding the things that she goes through and the ways in which she created opportunities for Paul Robeson, and herself, was just amazing to see. It gave me a deeper understanding too of the ways in which the Robesons suffered in terms of trying to move forward with their vision, I was stunned time and again by how they could continue to get back up, day after day, having being knocked down, over and over again, by their own country of birth as well as being kind of paraded around as propaganda in some other aspects of their lives.

I took great inspiration from the ways in which they inserted themselves into different cultures, into different communities, the ways in which they broadened their reach and pure understanding of what it means to be a global citizen at a time when I'm not sure Americans, let alone African Americans, were being given a chance to think about that.

DM: I started working with Eslanda Cardozo Goode Robeson after reading about her in Franz Loeser's East German biography *Die Abenteuer eines Emigranten: Erinnerungen* (1980), and then in Barbara Ransby's biography *Eslanda: The Large and Unconventional Life of Mrs. Paul Robeson* (2013).

I chose to work with Eslanda not only as an interlocutor but also as a kind of trans-generational voice for the study of a Black intersectional feminism in tandem with an anti-colonial internationalism that cuts across the geographies of Eastern Europe, in the process tracing the repressed memory of Eslanda's presence in East Berlin, Leipzig, and Prague in the early 1960s. Without wanting to isolate the political geography of Communist realities in the GDR, I would, however, like to understand that aspect more as an entangled geography of different struggles, in much the same way as Eslanda Robeson was a writer, world traveler, photographer, and interlocutor.

MR: Mich interessiert die Kraft der Erinnerung und der Geschichte. Ich weiß – auch wenn ich sie natürlich nicht persönlich kannte –, dass Paul Robeson und Eslanda Robeson, die ein wirklich visionäres Leben führten, auf diese Kraft vertrauten, um ihrer sehr zukunftszugewandten Vision treu zu bleiben.

Ich denke, die Biografie von Eslanda Robeson wird lange Zeit beispielhaft bleiben. Es war sehr eindrucksvoll, über sie zu lesen und zu erfahren, was sie durchgemacht hat und wie sie es geschafft hat, Möglichkeiten für Paul Robeson und für sich selbst zu finden.

Auch, um ein besseres Verständnis dafür zu bekommen, wie viel Leid Paul und Eslanda Robeson ertragen haben, während sie an der Umsetzung ihrer Vision arbeiteten. Ich war nachhaltig beeindruckt, wie sie es Tag für Tag geschafft haben, wieder aufzustehen, obwohl ihr Geburtsland sie wieder und wieder versuchte kleinzuhalten und sie gleichzeitig, in anderen Bereichen ihres Lebens, gewissermaßen auch zu Propagandazwecken vorführte.

Für mich war es sehr inspirierend, zu sehen, wie sie in verschiedenen Kulturen und Gemeinschaften ihren Platz fanden, wie sie ihre Reichweite und ihre Auffassung dessen erweiterten, was es bedeutete, Weltbürger·in zu sein – und das zu einer Zeit, in der wohl die wenigsten US-Amerikaner·innen, geschweige denn Afro-Amerikaner·innen, die Möglichkeit hatten, darüber auch nur nachzudenken.

DM: Meine aktive Auseinandersetzung mit Eslanda Cardozo Goode Robeson begann, nachdem ich ihr in Franz Loesers ostdeutscher Autobiografie *Die Abenteuer eines Emigranten* (1980) begegnet war und dann die Biografie *Eslanda: The Large and Unconventional Life of Mrs. Paul Robeson* (2013) von Barbara Ransby gelesen hatte.

Ich habe Eslanda für meine Arbeit als Gesprächspartnerin gefunden, aber auch als eine Art generationsübergreifende Stimme eines Schwarzen intersektionalen Feminismus im Verbund mit einem antikolonialen Internationalismus, der durch die Geografien von Ost-Europa verlief. Es ging mir auch darum, der verdrängten Erinnerung an Eslandas Präsenz in Ost-Berlin, Leipzig und auch Prag in den frühen 1960er Jahren nachzugehen. Ohne die politische Geografie kommunistischer Realitäten in der DDR isolieren zu wollen, möchte ich diese als geografische Verflechtung von verschiedenen Kämpfen sehen;

My approach to the Paul Robeson Committee archive at the Akademie der Künste in Berlin is very much informed by acknowledging the struggles that both Eslanda and Paul Robeson experienced, and not just in 1963, a time that not only currently plays a special role in my reading about Eslanda in Europe but is also constitutive of their lives and thus inscribed in both the Robeson archive and throughout the archiving process. I am interested in the extent to which the Robesons' struggles would be inseparable from a transhistorical practice of researching. How do we engage with such an archive? Perhaps, borrowing Shana L. Redmond's term of an "antiphonal life" in relation to Paul Robeson, one could address the archive as an antiphonal substance. A substance that echoes, vibrates, and is still honored in the present. However, is it possible to do this without disregarding the violence of exclusions?

For me, above all, the rupture around 1990, when the world order was reforming, remains a condition for working out methods of archival metabolism, as I would call the need to recognize these exclusions and ruptures. With this in mind, I would think in relation to Eslanda Robeson about the creation of worlds after the internationalism that thwarted the GDR (and beyond).

KT: I would like to clarify that while I think in much the same way as Matana and Doreen about how extraordinary Paul Robeson and Eslanda Robeson were, at the same time, I would also like to point out that I think they were part of a larger context of African Americans coming to Germany, specifically East Germany, in the 1950s and 1960s.

It was a sort of symbiotic relationship—East Germany held up African Americans like Paul Robeson as political symbols, using them as a legitimizing tool for their own geopolitical existence. Also, and rightly so in a lot of ways, these people made clear that they stood in solidarity with African American civil rights, that they understood and were supportive of anti-colonialist and anti-capitalist struggles, and that they recognized the problems of racism.

In a lot of ways, therefore, East Germany positioned itself as a land and as a space that was welcoming to African American political activists: Angela Davis came to visit, Martin Luther King Jr. came to visit, Paul Robeson as well. I think

genauso wie Eslanda Robeson Autorin, Welt-Reisende, Fotografin und Gesprächspartnerin war.

In meiner Herangehensweise an das Archiv des Paul-Robeson-Komitees in der Akademie der Künste in Berlin geht es vor allem um eine Anerkennung der Kämpfe, die sowohl Eslanda als auch Paul Robeson zu meistern hatten, nicht nur im Jahr 1963, das aktuell in meinem Lesen über Eslanda in Europa eine besondere Rolle einnimmt, denn diese Kämpfe waren grundlegend für ihr Leben und sind damit sowohl in das Archiv als auch in den Archivierungsprozess eingeschrieben. Mich interessiert, inwiefern die Kämpfe der Robesons von einer transhistorischen Praxis des Forschens nicht zu trennen wären. Wie begegnet man so einem Archiv – vielleicht könnte man, Shana L. Redmonds Begriff des „antiphonalen Lebens" von Paul Robeson aufnehmend, das Archiv als antiphonale Substanz adressieren. Eine Substanz, die in der Gegenwart widerhallt, vibriert und geehrt wird. Jedoch ohne dabei die Gewalt der Ausschlüsse außer Acht zu lassen?

Für mich ist vor allem der Bruch um 1990, als sich die Weltordnung neu formierte, nach wie vor eine Bedingung, um Methoden eines archivarischen Metabolismus – wie ich die Notwendigkeit benennen würde, diesen Ausschlüssen und Brüchen Rechnung zu tragen – zu erarbeiten. In diesem Sinne würde ich mit Eslanda Robeson über Welterschaffungen nach dem Internationalismus, der die DDR durchkreuzte (und über diese hinausging), nachdenken.

KT: Ich möchte einerseits ähnlich wie Matana und Doreen hervorheben, wie außergewöhnlich Paul Robeson und Eslanda Robeson gewesen sind. Andererseits möchte ich aber auch darauf hinweisen, dass sie Teil eines größeren Zusammenhangs waren, in dem während der 1950er und 1960er Jahre Afro-Amerikaner·innen nach Deutschland, speziell nach Ostdeutschland kamen.

Es war eine Art symbiotische Beziehung: Die DDR zelebrierte Afro-Amerikaner·innen wie Paul Robeson als politische Symbole und nutzte sie zur Legitimierung ihrer eigenen geopolitischen Existenz. Und oft zu Recht, wurden damit doch Solidarität und Verständnis für afro-amerikanische Bürger·innenrechte sowie Unterstützung für antikoloniale und antikapitalistische Kämpfe bekundet und das Problem des Rassismus anerkannt.

what is perhaps surprising for people is that African American soldiers stationed in West Germany occasionally defected too; they left the military and crossed the wall, so to speak, and then lived in East Germany up until the fall of the wall.

There is this really fascinating, long history of African American entanglements with East Germany specifically. I think one other example I can give, if that's helpful, is that many of the translations of African American poetry were produced and created in East Germany. Langston Hughes's poetry, for example, and that of other African American poets, was translated in East Germany pretty prolifically and seriously.

So, when I think about Paul Robeson's tour in 1960 and him getting the Medal of Peace from Humboldt University and all of that, it very much fits that model.

GL: I'm thinking most about Shana L. Redmond's extraordinary hermeneutic treatment of Paul Robeson at the moment. In her recent book *Everything Man: The Form and Function of Paul Robeson*, which takes its title from an Eslanda Goode Robeson quote, she writes, "Everything, everybody, everybody asked him to be everywhere!" And it's kind of funny, you know, since I'm an African American academic in a sort of a big-time institution, and that really is still the case. I mean, the few Afro-diasporic academics are constantly called upon to be part of diversity committees or whatever in order, basically, to hide the lack of diversity in these institutions more generally. And I think that might resonate with some of the experiences people on this panel have had.

Now, a recurring theme in Redmond's book is the primary role of "voice," as productive of social status, cultural image. Doreen, I came across an article published in *e-flux*, titled "The Undutiful Daughters Concept of Archival Metabolism," where you write: "The problem with formative twentieth-century theories of the archive is their monocultural commitment to 'the law,' as if it was naturally given." I take archival metabolism as the sense in which an archive actually enacts a repertoire, so you get an apparently disembodied memory that nonetheless produces gestures, orality, dance, and movement. And that is, as it is in the case of Paul Robeson, voice.

In vielerlei Hinsicht positionierte sich Ostdeutschland als Land und Raum, wo afroamerikanische politische Aktivist·innen willkommen waren. Angela Davis kam zu Besuch. Martin Luther King Jr. kam zu Besuch. Und eben Paul Robeson. Den einen oder anderen mag vielleicht überraschen, dass es auch gelegentlich afro-amerikanische Soldat·innen gab, die in Westdeutschland stationiert waren, das Militär verließen und sozusagen die Seiten wechselten und bis zum Mauerfall in der DDR lebten.

Es gibt also diese faszinierende und lange Geschichte afro-amerikanischer Verflechtungen mit Ostdeutschland. Ein weiteres Beispiel sind die Übersetzungen afro-amerikanischer Lyrik, die in der DDR entstanden. Langston Hughes' Gedichte, aber auch andere afro-amerikanische Lyriker·innen wurden in Ostdeutschland ziemlich erfolgreich und seriös übersetzt.

Wenn ich an Paul Robesons Reise im Jahr 1960 denke und an die Verleihung der Deutschen Friedensmedaille durch die Humboldt-Universität und all das, dann passt das ziemlich gut in dieses Schema.

GL: Zunächst möchte ich vor allem die außergewöhnliche hermeneutische Betrachtung von Paul Robeson in Shana L. Redmonds jüngstem Buch erwähnen, *Everything Man: The Form and Function of Paul Robeson*. Der Titel ist nach einem Zitat von Eslanda Goode Robeson gewählt: „Everything, everybody, everybody asked him to be everywhere!" (Alles, jede, jeder bat ihn darum, überall zu sein.) Und es ist irgendwie lustig, ich bin afro-amerikanischer Akademiker in einer großen Institution, und es ist wirklich nach wie vor so: Die wenigen afro-diasporischen Akademiker·innen werden ständig aufgefordert, an Diversity-Ausschüssen oder was auch immer teilzunehmen, letztlich um den Mangel an Vielfalt in diesen Institutionen zu kaschieren. Ich denke, die Teilnehmer·innen dieses Panels kennen diese Erfahrung alle auf irgendeine Weise.

Nun, ein wiederkehrendes Thema in Redmonds Buch ist die vordringliche Rolle der „Stimme" als Produkt des sozialen Status, des kulturellen Images.

Doreen, ich bin auf einen Artikel gestoßen, veröffentlicht in e-flux, mit dem Titel „The Undutiful Daughters Concept of Archival Metabolism", in dem du schreibst: „Das Problem mit den einflussreichen Archivtheorien des 20. Jahrhunderts ist ihre monokulturelle Verpflichtung gegenüber ›dem Gesetz‹, als wäre es naturgegeben." Ich verstehe den archivarischen Metabolismus im Sinne eines

DM: This concept becomes necessary, specifically when working on archival substances that depart from political geographies or from forms of internationalism. Since 1990, infrastructurally as well as institutionally, these archives have all but disappeared; they have not just disappeared, they have been violently erased or repressed.

So, on the one hand, archival metabolism is an attempt to consider the historical inscription as a transhistorical moment, as a trans-generational process. On the other, it should also recognize the systemic rupture around 1990 that is part of our argument, as well, most importantly, as taking into account the extreme and conflictual tension between state-socialist—or macropolitical infrastructures—and micro-social encounters. Let's not forget, and I think Kira writes about this very aptly and persuasively, that state socialism in East Germany was White, patriarchal, geriatric, anti-intellectual socialism.

It is complex. I would like to link this and see it as a methodology for decolonizing socialism, decolonizing internationalism, which was not always only anti-colonial and anti-Fascist. Therefore, when it comes to decolonizing socialism, I am interested in the ambiguities and conflicts of these concrete moments. What portals are there into them? Which micro-social forms of practice do they operate in that could be used to open up the binarity of the Cold War? It is a difficult but necessary question. Because this binarity is still active, as part of contemporary memory politics, it must finally be complexified.

GL: Does your concept of archival metabolism transform a twentieth-century, nominally non-digital archive, like the Robeson archive?

DM: Let me answer you in this way: How might we not only critically mobilize the historical moment of Eslanda and Paul Robeson's encounter with Franz and Diana Loeser in the GDR in around 1963 as a trans-generational narrative but also metabolize it for thinking through contemporary problems? How might we think about a connection between a photographic record depicting speaker or headphone technologies, such as that used by Eslanda and Franz in the Supreme

---

Archivs, das tatsächlich einem Repertoire Wirkmacht verleiht. Es entsteht ein scheinbar körperloses Gedächtnis, das trotzdem aus Gesten, Mündlichkeit, Tanz und Bewegung besteht. Und im Fall von Paul Robeson auch aus Stimme.

DM: Dieses Konzept wurde vor allem für die Arbeit mit archivarischen Substanzen notwendig, deren Ausgangspunkt die politischen Geografien oder Formen des Internationalismus sind. Seit 1990 sind sie infrastrukturell und institutionell so gut wie verschwunden; nicht einfach verschwunden, sondern gewaltsam ausgelöscht oder verdrängt worden.

Der archivarische Metabolismus ist der Versuch, einerseits die historische Einschreibung als transhistorischen Moment, als transgenerationalen Prozess zu betrachten. Andererseits soll er dem systemischen Bruch Rechnung tragen, der um 1990 geschieht und Teil unserer Auseinandersetzung ist, sowie vor allem auch die extreme und konfliktreiche Spannung zwischen staatssozialistischen oder makropolitischen Infrastrukturen und mikrosozialen Begegnungen berücksichtigen. Denn vergessen wir nicht – und ich finde, Kira hat dazu sehr treffende und wichtige Dinge geschrieben –, dass der Staatssozialismus in Ostdeutschland ein weißer, patriarchaler, geriatrischer, antiintellektueller Sozialismus war.

Es ist komplex. Daran möchte ich anknüpfen als Methode zur Dekolonisierung des Sozialismus und des Internationalismus. Denn der Internationalismus war nicht nur antiimperialistisch und antifaschistisch. Bei der Dekolonisierung des Sozialismus interessieren mich Ambivalenzen und Konflikte solcher konkreten Momente. Welche Zugänge gibt es? Welche mikrosozialen Praxisformen nutzen sie, mit denen sich die Binarität des Kalten Kriegs überwinden ließen? Es ist eine schwierige, aber notwendige Frage. Denn diese Binarität wirkt immer noch nach, sie ist Teil gegenwärtiger Erinnerungspolitik. Das muss endlich komplexer betrachtet werden.

GL: Hat dein Konzept des archivarischen Metabolismus auch Konsequenzen für ein nicht digitales Archiv des 20. Jahrhunderts, zum Beispiel das Robeson-Archiv?

DM: Lass mich so antworten: Wie könnten wir den historischen Moment – die Begegnung von Eslanda und Paul Robeson mit Franz und Diana Loeser in der DDR um 1963 – als transgenerationale Erzählung nicht nur kritisch produktiv

Court of the GDR in 1963, and the speakers integral to a laptop as a research tool in 2021? Right now, I am asking students, former students, and colleagues to help advance this archival metabolism of the image—technologically and trans-generationally—which automatically implies the political or techno-political and discursive conceptual level.

GL: Matana, you talked about the futurist vision of Paul and Eslanda just now. Could you say more about that?

MR: I recognized in the Robesons a certain kind of dedication not only to the history of the past but also to the history of the future, because they come from a history that they were able to benefit from in some sense, from the sacrifices of people in their ancestral line that fought for some of the freedoms, those very limited freedoms but, still, freedoms that they were able to enjoy during their lifetime. But this also made them fully aware that the freedoms they were being given were not enough. That there was more to fight for. There was more to excavate, document, and bear witness to.

GL: Yeah, I mean, you wrote in your essay, "There have been times in my own life, when I've looked to history, to cope with my experiences with just being a Black body in a vast world." And to me, that points to a kind of empathy in your encounter with the Robeson Archive. Then later you write, "The term resonance can be defined as 'the quality and a sound of being deep, full, and reverberating' or when thinking about 'resonance' as applied to an image, it brings to mind ideas of clarity, of depending on your own associated memories and experience." For me, empathy is also a form of resonance.

MR: I have always looked to history as a means of coping with layers and layers of negative filters that I have to deal with as a Black body in the world. But as a Black artist who must answer to . . . I mean, I've recently come to the conclusion that everybody has to answer to somebody—but my work has to constantly be

machen, sondern auch für das Verständnis gegenwärtiger Probleme verstoff-wechseln? Welche Verbindung lässt sich zwischen einer Fotografie mit Laut-sprecher- bzw. Kopfhörertechnologie, die Eslanda und Franz im Obersten Gericht der DDR im Jahr 1963 nutzen, und den Lautsprechern unserer Laptops, unserer Forschungsinstrumente im Jahr 2021 herstellen? Im Moment bitte ich Studie-rende, frühere Studierende und Kolleg·innen, dazu beizutragen, diesen archi-varischen Metabolismus des Bildes technologisch-transgenerational voranzu-bringen, was automatisch auch die politische beziehungsweise techno-politische und diskursive Begriffsebene mit ins Spiel bringt.

GL: Matana, du hast gerade von der Zukunftsvision von Paul und Eslanda ge-sprochen. Könntest du das etwas ausführen?

MR: Ich sehe bei ihnen eine Hingabe an die vergangene, aber auch an die künf-tige Geschichte. Sie kamen aus einer Historie, in der sie gewissermaßen von den Opfern der Menschen ihrer anzestralen Linie profitierten. Sie hatten einige der Freiheiten erkämpft, begrenzte, aber immerhin Freiheiten, die sie zu Lebzeiten genießen konnten. Und sie waren sich auch bewusst, dass die Freiheiten, die ihnen gewährt waren, nicht ausreichten. Es gab mehr zu erkämpfen. Es gab mehr herauszufinden, zu dokumentieren und zu bezeugen.

GL: Ja, du schreibst in deinem Essay: „Es gab Zeiten in meinem Leben, da ver-suchte ich durch den Blick in die Geschichte mit meinen Erfahrungen als Schwar-zer Körper in einer riesigen Welt fertig zu werden."
    Für mich drückt das Empathie in deiner Begegnung mit dem Robeson-Archiv aus. Etwas später schreibst du: „Der Begriff ›Resonanz‹ lässt sich als eine Qualität und ein Klang definieren, der tief, voll und nachhallend ist, oder, wenn man über ›Resonanzen‹ als etwas Bildliches denkt, wird einem klar, wie viel von den eigenen, assoziativen Erinnerungen und Erfahrungen abhängt."
    Für mich ist Empathie auch eine Art Resonanz.

MR: Für mich war Geschichte immer ein Weg, um die vielen Schichten und negativen Filter zu bewältigen, mit denen ich als Schwarzer Körper in der Welt

filtered through a White gaze in order to garner support or, you know, criticality, but it's always filtered through the White gaze. Rarely do I get to intersect with the Black gaze first, other than my own, before having to let it filter through and then loop back around and hope that it reaches other people.

When looking at the archive, I just, you know, thought a lot about how the lives of Black artists through the generations are essentially variations on a theme. Like these same themes in relation to Paul and Eslanda, you know, there are things they have been through that I'm not certain I would have been able to handle. But still, because of the perniciousness of systematic racism, and the way it is still rooted in most institutions, I really just seem to recognize a certain sort of reminder to stay in the fight. Looking at the Robesons' work, they were able to stay in the fight and still thrived in some sense.

Also, what I very much took with me from the archive was seeing how hard they worked. Until the very end, really—you know, reading the letters Eslanda was writing from her hospital bed or getting an idea of the level of exhaustion that Paul was dealing with. I don't know if it's safe, even now, to talk about the CIA, about the ways in which the Robesons were being tortured—at least, so it seemed to me—by their own government, even while living abroad.

So thinking about resonance, it's a reminder of many things, but I also have to make sure that it's measured because there are times I wake up and go, well, you know, this is not going to be the greatest day, but at least I'm not on a plantation somewhere picking cotton, or in a big house having to, you know, do God only knows what in order to survive. Yet, the archive gave me just massive inspiration to remain a Black artist in the world, to continue to push through and hold my head as high as I can, within reason, to create the world that I wish to see.

GL: Kira, you just published this amazing book, *Singing like Germans: Black Musicians in the Land of Bach, Beethoven, and Brahms* (2021). In it, you recount the experiences of Afro-diasporic performers in Germany, stretching back more than a century. And you also bring out these kinds of hidden histories, as George Lipsitz would say, these hidden histories, often fraught with the German-speaking

konfrontiert bin. Aber als Schwarze Künstler·in, die sich vor irgendjemandem verantworten muss – und jeder muss sich vor irgendjemandem verantworten –, bin ich in letzter Zeit zu dem Schluss gekommen, dass meine Arbeit ständig durch einen Weißen Blick gefiltert werden muss, sogar um Unterstützung oder Kritik zu bekommen – immer der Weiße Blick.

Selten treffe ich zuerst auf einen Schwarzen Blick, außer auf meinen eigenen, bevor ich filtern muss, um ihn dann nochmal zu wenden, in der Hoffnung, dass er andere Menschen erreicht.

Als ich das Archiv eingesehen habe, habe ich viel darüber nachgedacht, dass die Leben von Schwarzen Künstler·innen über die Generationen hinweg im Wesentlichen Variationen desselben Themas sind.

Es sind Kämpfe, die auch Paul und Eslanda durchgemacht haben und bei denen ich mir nicht sicher bin, ob ich in der Lage gewesen wäre, damit umzugehen.

Aber angesichts der Bösartigkeit des systematischen Rassismus und der Art und Weise, wie er in den meisten Institutionen immer noch an der Wurzel sitzt, ist die Betrachtung ihrer Arbeit eine Art Erinnerung daran, weiterzukämpfen. Sie haben es geschafft weiterzukämpfen!

Außerdem habe ich aus dem Archiv das Wissen mitgenommen, wie hart sie bis zum Schluss gearbeitet haben. Das lässt sich an den Briefen ablesen, die Eslanda Robeson noch vom Krankenhausbett aus schrieb. Oder wenn einem bewusst wird, wie viel Kraft Paul Robeson aufbringen musste.

Ich weiß nicht, wie sicher es – selbst heute noch! – ist, über die CIA zu sprechen, aber es geht auch um die Art, wie Paul und Eslanda Robeson in gewisser Weise, denke ich, und selbst wenn sie im Ausland waren, von ihrer eigenen Regierung gefoltert wurden.

Wenn ich also an Resonanzen denke, dann geht es um die Erinnerung an diese Kämpfe. Jedoch muss ich auch ein Gespür für die Ausmaße behalten. Denn es hat Zeiten gegeben, da bin ich aufgewacht und habe mir gedacht: Das wird nicht der beste Tag. Aber zumindest bin ich nicht auf einer Plantage und pflücke Baumwolle oder muss in einem großen Haus was auch immer tun, um eben zu überleben.

Das Archiv hat mich stark inspiriert, als Schwarze Künstlerin in der Welt zu bestehen, mich weiterhin durchzusetzen und meinen Kopf im Rahmen des Möglichen so hoch wie möglich zu halten, um eine Welt zu erschaffen, die ich sehen möchte.

world's relationship with Blackness. And what really comes out for me is a kind of creolized mosaic, a diaspora and identity for classical music. Now, in the essay, you wrote about Paul Robeson's 1960 performances in the German Democratic Republic: "Robeson's tour created the opportunity for East Germans to redress or affirm their own beliefs about Blacks, and musical aesthetics." And what I wanted to ask you was, Does the reception Paul Robeson had in the GDR reflect not only German constructions of race and African American identity but also Germany's own constructions of its own identity?

KT: That's a really great question. And I think the answer, at least in an East German context, is yes. Again, one of the reasons why I think Paul Robeson is held up, at least in part, is because he is so comfortably un-German as well, so in a way that allows Germans to celebrate him without necessarily having to wrestle with East German, anti-Black racism. So, maybe it's really interesting to ask ourselves the question, What does it mean that this archive, the Paul and Eslanda Robeson Archive, is perhaps the only, you know, official archive in Germany and German-speaking Europe dedicated to a person of African descent? And the Robesons were African American, not Black German. I think these are questions worth asking.

GL: Now, what I understood from you—and this takes me back to this idea of repetition—is this ongoing, repeated effort to deploy the Robeson story as a kind of epistemological "other," you know, in order to maintain a sense of continuity about the GDR. You quote all this reception in the press: he was a "Black giant, a Black prophet, a Black Jesus, a Black Saint Francis, their Black brother." Now, oh yeah, did I mention he was Black? I mean, what do you do, what are you gonna do with that! What I want to ask is, Was this a kind of dynamic limited to the GDR and its interpretation of socialism, or do we find similar resonances today?

KT: The thing that I find so interesting about Robeson's experience is just how neatly he was able to fit into a racial ideology and a Communist ideology in the ways he was able to fulfil so many wishes and desires. And I should say this,

---

GL: Kira, du hast kürzlich ein wunderbares Buch veröffentlicht, *Singing Like Germans: Black Musicians in the Land of Bach, Beethoven, and Brahms*. Du schilderst darin die Erfahrungen afro-diasporischer Performer·innen in Deutschland, die weit über ein Jahrhundert zurückreichen.

Außerdem bringst du auch verborgene Geschichten ans Licht, wie George Lipsitz sagen würde, die oft durch das Verhältnis der deutschsprachigen Welt mit dem Schwarzsein gezeichnet sind.

Für mich entsteht dabei eine Art kreolisiertes Mosaik: Diaspora und Identität in der klassischen Musik. In deinem Essay schreibst du über Paul Robesons Performances in der DDR im Jahr 1960: „Robesons Reise bot den Ostdeutschen die Möglichkeit, ihre Vorstellungen über Schwarze Menschen und musikalische Ästhetik zu korrigieren oder zu bestätigen."

Ich würde dich gerne fragen, ob die Rezeption von Paul Robeson in der DDR womöglich nicht nur die deutschen Konstruktionen von Race und afro-amerikanischer Identität widerspiegelt. Zeigte sie auch die Struktur von Deutschlands eigener Identitätskonstruktion?

KT: Das ist eine sehr gute Frage. Ich denke, die Antwort lautet ja, zumindest im ostdeutschen Kontext. Einer der Gründe dafür, dass Paul Robeson hochgehalten wird, ist meiner Meinung nach, dass er so komfortabel undeutsch ist. Man kann ihn feiern, ohne sich mit ostdeutschem, anti-Schwarzem Rassismus auseinandersetzen zu müssen.

Vielleicht ist es also wirklich interessant, sich diese Frage zu stellen: Ist das Paul- und Eslanda-Robeson-Archiv vielleicht das einzige offizielle Archiv in Deutschland und im deutschsprachigen Europa, das einer Person afrikanischer Abstammung gewidmet ist?

Zudem sind die Robesons Afro-Amerikaner, keine Afro-Deutschen. Ich denke, über diese Fragen sollte gesprochen werden.

GL: Nun, was ich durch dich begriffen habe – und damit komme ich noch mal zurück auf die Wiederholung –, sind die anhaltenden Bemühungen, die Geschichte der Robesons zu inszenieren, was etwas von einem epistemologischen „Anderen" hat, um damit eine gewisse Kontinuität der DDR zu erreichen. Du

because, by way of contrast, he had a friend and colleague in Berlin at the same time, an African American named Aubrey Pankey, who also has documents in the Akademie der Künste archives. And Pankey's experience in Germany was very different from Robeson's. Pankey fled, but Robeson pled for asylum in East Germany in 1955 and continued to live there until his death in 1971. So his whole career was spent in East Berlin, East Germany, Rostock, and other places; I think he also went to Halle, and he was a committed Marxist and socialist. Pankey was constantly pointing out to people that they were trying to put him in this box of authenticity, and he told them how he hated it. He expressed how he hated having these expectations put upon him. Did you know that he was a classically trained singer? He studied at Boston University, I think, and maybe also at the Juilliard School. But time and time again, nobody wanted to hear him sing German lieder. Nobody wanted to hear him give all different kinds of classical performances. They wanted him to play these roles of, you know, the African American preacher from a piece of music where his part was just spoken text.

This text is an edited version of the transcription of the panel "Resonating Struggles: Paul and Eslanda Robeson in East Berlin," which took place at the Akademie der Künste in Berlin on June 1, 2021.

zitierst all diese Pressemitteilungen. Da war er „Schwarzer Gigant, Schwarzer Prophet, Schwarzer Jesus, ein Schwarzer Heiliger Franziskus, ihr Schwarzer Bruder." Oh ja, genau, habe ich erwähnt, dass er Schwarz war?

Was macht man mit so etwas? Heute? War diese Dynamik auf die DDR und ihr Sozialismusverständnis beschränkt, oder zeigen sich heute ähnliche Resonanzen?

KT: Für mich passt die Erfahrung von Paul Robeson in vielerlei Hinsicht perfekt zu dem, was der ostdeutsche Staat von einer bestimmten Art von Schwarzem Aktivisten und einer bestimmten Art von Schwarzer Person erwartete und wollte.

An seiner Erfahrung wird deutlich, wie gut sich eine Rassenideologie in eine kommunistische Ideologie einfügen konnte. Paul Robeson musste so viele Wünsche und Sehnsüchte erfüllen!

Im Kontrast dazu hatte Robeson in dieser Zeit einen Freund und Kollegen in Berlin, Aubrey Pankey, ein afro-amerikanischer Musiker, von dem es ebenfalls Dokumente im Archiv der Akademie der Künste gibt.

Aubrey Pankey hat komplett andere Erfahrungen gemacht als Paul Robeson. Er ist geflohen, hat 1955 in Ostdeutschland Asyl beantragt und lebte dort bis zu seinem Tod 1971.

Er hat seine Berufsleben in Ost-Berlin, Rostock, Dresden, Halle und anderen Orten verbracht. Er war ein überzeugter Marxist und Sozialist.

Pankey wurde von der Presse und den Menschen ständig in diese Authentizitäts-Schublade gesteckt. Er hasste diese Erwartungen, die an ihn herangetragen wurden!

Er war klassisch ausgebildeter Sänger, der an der School of Music der Boston University studiert hatte. Aber in Deutschland wollte ihn niemand bei Konzerten klassischer Musik deutsche Lieder singen hören.

Sie wollten ihn für Rollen wie die eines afroamerikanischen Predigers, der nur den Text sprach.

Dieser Text ist eine bearbeitete Version eines Transkripts des Panels „Resonating Struggles: Paul und Eslanda Robeson in Ost-Berlin", das am 1. Juni 2021 in der Akademie der Künste Berlin stattfand.

CHARLES WHITE: AN AMERICAN ARTIST

Kathleen Reinhardt

CHARLES WHITE. EIN KÜNSTLER AMERIKAS

1. Charles White, Sidney Finkelstein, and Wolfgang Martini, *Charles White: Ein Künstler Amerikas* (VEB Verlag der Kunst, 1955), 5.

Charles White: Ein Künstler Amerikas is the title of a book that was published in 1955 by VEB Verlag der Kunst in Dresden. It was the first monograph on African American artist Charles White (1918–1979). According to the foreword, by the time the book came out, White had already "created a body of work that has a unique position in the art of the United States today."[1] White's relationship with the GDR can also be described as unique: he first visited the fledgling East German state in 1951 for the 3rd World Festival of Youth and Students; he became a corresponding member of the Akademie der Künste (East) in 1961, maintained friendly correspondence with the designer Klaus Wittkugel, and received numerous honors; his work was collected and exhibited by institutions.

White's focus was on the figurative depiction of Black life in the United States. He worked in the tradition of American realism with its critical take on society and taught at the Otis Art Institute, where major figures in contemporary American art such as Kerry James Marshall, Alonzo Davis, and David Hammons studied under him. Because of his teaching activities and his connections with the civil rights movement and its supporters in the entertainment industry, his life and work are an important nodal point in the current reappraisal of key Black positions, shedding light on facets of art history during the Cold War that have hitherto been disregarded. He had a wide-ranging friendship with Paul Robeson that included their close ties with the Communist Party USA, for which White illustrated flyers in the 1940s, their involvement in Wo-Chi-Ca, the legendary left-wing summer camp that took place each year in New Jersey, and their East German connections—White's works were reproduced in the GDR's exhibition brochure printed in honor of Robeson's seventieth birthday. Some of his works can be found in the Museum of Prints, Drawings and Photographs (Kupferstich-Kabinett) in Dresden: these include his 1965 lithograph *Harvest* and the profile view of a head in the portfolio *Internationale Grafik zum 30. Jahrestag der Befreiung vom Hitlerfaschismus* (International Works of Graphic Art on the Occasion of the 30th Anniversary of the Liberation from Hitler's Fascism). The scaling of this profile may seem unusual, but it is indicative of White's work as a mural artist: in 1943, as part of a major US-wide effort to boost the economy, he was given the opportunity to create one of his

Charles White. Ein Künstler Amerikas ist der Titel einer 1955 im Dresdner VEB Verlag der Kunst erschienenen Publikation. Das Buch war die erste Monografie über den afroamerikanischen Künstler Charles White (1918–1979). Dem Vorwort zufolge hatte White zu diesem Zeitpunkt bereits ein „Gesamtwerk geschaffen, das in der Kunst der Vereinigten Staaten von heute einzig dasteht".[1] Als einzigartig kann auch das Verhältnis von Charles White zur DDR beschrieben werden: Er besuchte den jungen Staat erstmals anlässlich der III. Weltfestspiele 1951, wurde 1961 korrespondierendes Mitglied der Akademie der Künste Ost, pflegte freundschaftlichen Briefkontakt mit dem Gestalter Klaus Wittkugel, erhielt zahlreiche Würdigungen und wurde institutionell gesammelt und ausgestellt.

Whites zentrales Thema war die figürliche Abbildung Schwarzen Lebens in den USA. Er arbeitete in der Tradition des sozialkritischen amerikanischen Realismus. Auch wegen seiner Lehrtätigkeit am Otis Art Institute, wo er bedeutende zeitgenössische amerikanische Künstler wie Kerry James Marshall, Alonzo Davis oder David Hammons unterrichtete, und seiner Verbindungen zur Bürgerrechtsbewegung und deren Unterstützer·innen im Entertainment-Bereich bilden seine Arbeit und sein Leben einen wichtigen Knotenpunkt in der momentan stattfindenden Aufarbeitung Schwarzer Schlüsselpositionen und erlauben es, bisher wenig beachtete Aspekte der Kunstgeschichten des Kalten Kriegs zu beleuchten. Einige seiner Arbeiten befinden sich im Kupferstich-Kabinett in Dresden wie die Lithografie *Harvest* von 1965 oder die Profilansicht eines Kopfes in der Grafikmappe *Internationale Grafik zum 30. Jahrestag der Befreiung vom Hitlerfaschismus*. Der damalige Direktor des Kupferstich-Kabinetts Werner Schmidt quittierte im April 1974 zudem die Entgegennahme von Whites Grafikmappe *Wanted*, welche ausgewählte Nachdrucke der großformatigen *Wanted*-Serie enthält, deren Motive auf Steckbriefen für entflohene Sklav*innen basieren. In Whites Werken sind Frauenfiguren oft zentral – die Kunsthistorikerin Kellie Jones beschreibt seine Arbeit als feministisches Engagement für ein Ende von „Sexismus, sexueller Ausbeutung und sexueller Unterdrückung".[2] Viele seiner Werke zeugen von der Ungeheuerlichkeit der Sklaverei als Basis des euro-amerikanischen Kapitalismus, jedoch auch von der Hoffnung auf eine bessere Zukunft durch Arbeit. Diesen Widerspruch versucht White durch sehr würdevolle Darstellungen von Schwarzen Arbeiter·innen aufzulösen, so etwa in *Harvest*. Das Haar der

1. Charles White, Sidney Finkelstein und Wolfgang Martini, *Charles White. Ein Künstler Amerikas*, Dresden: VEB Verlag der Kunst 1955, S. 5.

2. Kellie Jones, „Charles White, Feminist at Midcentury", in: Sarah Kelly Oehler und Esther Adler (Hg.), *Charles White: A Retrospective*, Ausst.-Kat. Art Institute of Chicago und Museum of Modern Art, New York, New Haven und London: Yale University Press 2018, S. 69–83, hier S. 69.

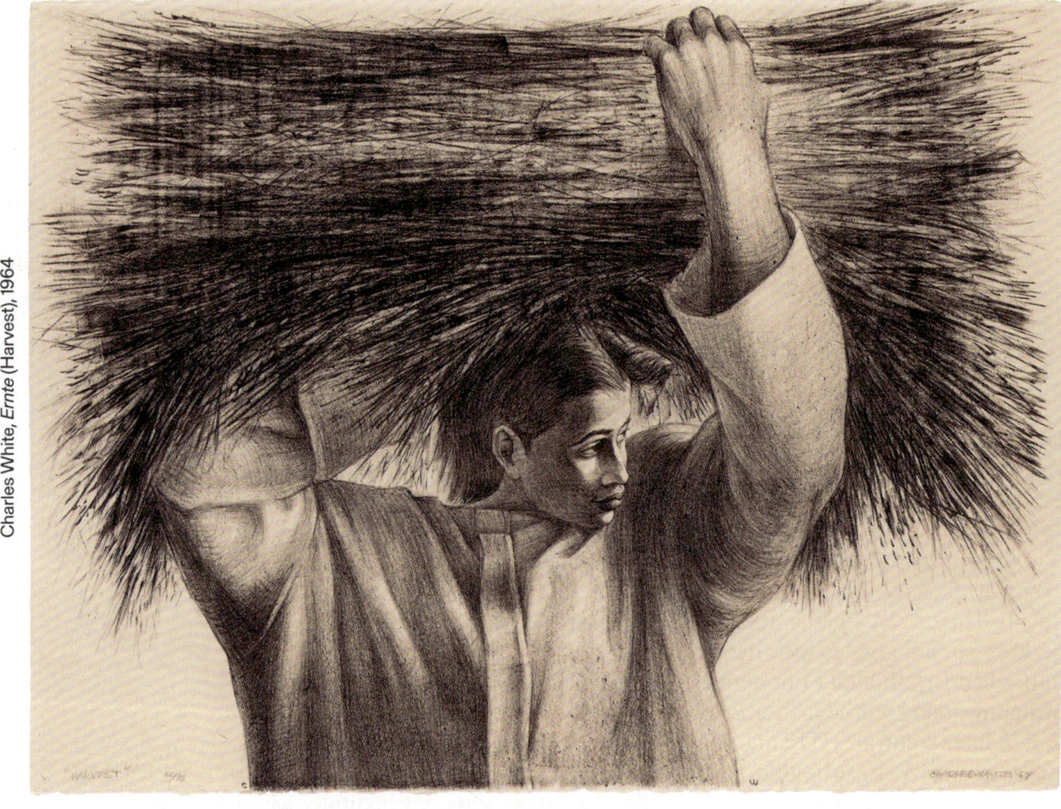

Charles White, *Ernte* (Harvest), 1964

Charles White, *Ernte*, 1964

2. Kellie Jones, "Charles White, Feminist at Midcentury," in *Charles White: A Retrospective*, ed. Sarah Kelly Oehler and Esther Adler, exh. cat. Art Institute of Chicago and Museum of Modern Art, New York (Yale University, 2018), 69–83, here: 69.

most famous works, the mural frieze *The Contribution of the Negro to American Democracy* at Hampton University, via the Works Progress Administration (WPA) program to support public art. Moreover, in April 1974, Werner Schmidt, the then director of the Kupferstich-Kabinett, acknowledged receipt of White's *Wanted* portfolio, which contains a selection of reprints of the large-format series of the same name, whose motifs are based on wanted posters for escaped slaves. Female figures often play a central role in White's work, which art historian Kellie Jones describes as a feminist commitment to ending "sexism, sexual exploitation and sexual oppression."[2] Many of his works stand testament to the monstrous nature of slavery as the basis of Euro-American capitalism, while also expressing hope for a better future achieved through work. White attempts to resolve this contradiction by depicting Black workers with tremendous dignity, as is the case in *Harvest*, for example. White blends the hair of the woman carrying a sheaf in the picture with the long, freshly harvested stalks she is supporting on her head, using fine strokes rendered with great skill to bring together the different textures of straw and hair. Her large, strong hand, emphasized by accent lighting—a typical feature of White's work—holds the bundle on her head, with the thumb in the brightest area of the picture disappearing into the straw and uniting with it, highlighting the corresponding condition and mutual dependence of harvester and harvested. The loose garment she wears has a timeless quality, betraying no discernible fashion, with no geographical positioning suggested by the background. With a few exceptions, White's oeuvre maps out an exclusively Black view of US history, ranging from slavery and the era of sharecropping and racial segregation to the tiring routine of life in the big city. The portraits he did late in his career have an almost transcendent character. Here, he often depicts the Black figure as a spiritual being detached from space and time, as is the case in his 1971 *Love Letter #1*, which became the motif of a campaign by the National United Committee to Free Angela Davis and All Political Prisoners. White's death in 1979 occurred as plans were being made for a solo exhibition at the Akademie der Künste in Berlin and the Kunsthalle Rostock, which ultimately came to nothing. The East German ambassador laid a wreath at the artist's funeral in Los Angeles bearing the words "For a great artist."

abgebildeten Bündelträgerin vermischt White optisch mit den frisch geernteten langen Halmen, die sie auf dem Kopf trägt, mit gekonnt feinen Strichen lässt er die Texturen von Stroh und Haar aufeinandertreffen. Ihre für White typische große, starke und durch Lichtakzente betonte Hand hält das Bündel auf dem Kopf, wobei der Daumen an der hellsten Stelle des Bildes im Stroh verschwindet und sich mit diesem vereint – die Betonung der gegenseitigen Bedingung und Abhängigkeit von Erntender und Geerntetem. Ihr weites Gewand entrückt sie der Zeit – keine Mode ist erkennbar, genauso wenig wie ein Hintergrund, der eine geografische Verortung ermöglichen würde. Bis auf wenige Ausnahmen entwirft White in seinem Gesamtwerk ein exklusiv Schwarzes Geschichtsbild der USA, welches von der Sklaverei über die Zeit des Sharecroppings und der Rassentrennung bis zum ermüdenden Großstadtleben reicht. Seine späten Porträts haben einen fast transzendenten Charakter. Hier stellt er die Schwarze Figur oft spirituell und losgelöst von Raum und Zeit dar. Whites Tod 1979 fiel mitten hinein in die Planung einer letztlich nie realisierten Einzelausstellung in der Akademie der Künste in Berlin und der Kunsthalle Rostock. Der Botschafter der DDR legte zur Beerdigung des Künstlers in Los Angeles einen Kranz nieder mit der Aufschrift „Für einen großen Künstler".

TIFFANY N. FLORVIL is an award-winning associate professor of twentieth-century European women's and gender history at the University of New Mexico, Albuquerque. She specializes in the histories of post-1945 Europe, Black Europe, the African/Black diaspora, Black internationalism, and queer and gender studies. Her work has appeared in *Signs*, *The German Quarterly*, and other journals. Florvil's publications include *Mobilizing Black Germany: Afro-German Women and the Making of a Transnational Movement* (University of Illinois Press, 2020) and its German translation, *Black Germany: Schwarz, deutsch, feministisch—die Geschichte einer Bewegung* (Ch. Links Verlag, 2023). Her 2020 book won various honors, including the Waterloo Centre for German Studies' First Book Prize in 2021. In 2023/24, she was the Joy Foundation Fellow at Harvard University's Radcliffe Institute for Advanced Study, where she worked on a biography of prominent Black German poet May Ayim.

AVERY F. GORDON is a writer, educator, and radio producer. With the focus of her work on radical thought and practice, she writes about captivity, enslavement, war, and other forms of dispossession and how to eliminate them. Her most recent volume is *The Hawthorn Archive: Letters from the Utopian Margins* (2017).

GEORGE E. LEWIS is the Edwin H. Case Professor of American Music and Area Chair in Composition and part of the historical musicology faculty at Columbia University. A fellow of the American Academy of Arts and Sciences and the American Academy of Arts and Letters, a corresponding fellow of the British Academy, and a member of the Akademie der Künste, Berlin, Lewis has had his music presented worldwide. He is regarded as a pioneer of interactive computer music, and his recent scholarship at the Akademie der Künste, Berlin, focuses on decolonization and creolization in new music.

FRANZ LOESER was born in Breslau (now Wrocław) and emigrated to Great Britain in 1938 as part of the Kindertransport. As a student in the US, he became affiliated with the Communist party and was subject to persecution by the McCarthy Committee. In 1951, he was expelled and moved to Great Britain, where he became general secretary of the Paul Robeson Committee. In 1956, he moved to the GDR and was made head of the Department of Ethics at the HU Institute of Philosophy. In 1983, he traveled to New York, where he applied for political asylum.

STEVE MCQUEEN was born in 1969 in London. Large-scale surveys of McQueen's work have been held at Pirelli HangarBicocca, Tate Modern, Schaulager, and the Art Institute of Chicago. Recent solo presentations include *Steve Mc Queen: Year 3* and exhibitions at the Institute of Contemporary Art in Boston, Massachusetts. He has been the recipient of numerous awards, including the Johannes Vermeer Prize, Harvard University's W. E. B. Du Bois Medal, and the Turner Prize. He is also the recipient of an OBE (2002) and a CBE (2011) and was knighted in 2020. McQueen has directed four feature films. He won the Caméra d'Or award at the Cannes Film Festival in 2008 and the Oscar for Best Motion Picture in 2014.

DOREEN MENDE is a curator, theorist, and professor of curatorial/politics in the Critical Curatorial Cybermedia curatorial and research practices program at HEAD – Genève, which is part of the University of Applied Sciences and Arts, Geneva, and since 2021, head of the research department at the Dresden State Art Collections (Staatliche Kunstsammlungen Dresden). Mende is a founding member of the Harun Farocki Institute in Berlin and the European Forum for Advanced Practices and principal investigator (PI) of the research project *Decolonizing Socialism: Entangled Internationalism* (2019–24), funded by the Swiss National Science Foundation.

KATHLEEN REINHARDT is director of the Georg Kolbe Museum in Berlin, where she curated the exhibitions *Lin May Saeed: The Snow Falls Softly in Paradise, A Dialogue with René Sintenis*, and *Noa Eshkol: No Time to Dance*. From 2016 to 2022, she was curator for contemporary art at the Albertinum (Dresden State Art Collections). Her projects for SKD include *1 Million Roses for Angela Davis, For Ruth, the Sky in Los Angeles* (both 2021) and *Revolutionary Romances?: Global Art Histories in the GDR* (2024). Reinhardt holds a PhD in African American art history, and her writing has appeared in numerous publications, including *Multiple Realities: Experimental Art in the Eastern Bloc 1960s–1980s* (Walker Art Center, 2023) and magazines like *Art Margins* and *Kaleidoscope*.

MATANA ROBERTS is an internationally known composer, bandleader, saxophonist, sound experimentalist, and mixed-media practitioner. Self-taught for the most part, Roberts works in many contexts and mediums, including improvisation, dance, poetry, and theater. Perhaps best known for the acclaimed "Coin Coin" project,

TIFFANY N. FLORVIL ist Associate Professor an der University of New Mexico in Albuquerque und wurde wiederholt für ihre Arbeit ausgezeichnet. Als Historikerin beschäftigt sie sich mit europäischer Frauen- und Geschlechtergeschichte des 20. Jahrhunderts, vor allem mit der Geschichte Europas seit dem Zweiten Weltkrieg, Schwarzem Leben in Europa, afrikanischer / Schwarzer Diaspora, Schwarzem Internationalismus und Queer und Gender Studies. Ihre Arbeiten sind in *Signs*, dem *German Quarterly* und anderen Zeitschriften erschienen. Ihr Buch *Mobilizing Black Germany: Afro-German Women and the Making of a Transnational Movement* (University of Illinois Press 2020) ist unter dem Titel *Black Germany. Schwarz, deutsch, feministisch – die Geschichte einer Bewegung* auch auf Deutsch erschienen (Ch. Links Verlag 2023). Für dieses Buch erhielt sie eine Reihe von Auszeichnungen, unter anderem den Preis des Waterloo Centre for German Studies für herausragende Debüts 2021. 2023/24 war sie Joy Foundation Fellow am Radcliffe Institute for Advanced Study der Harvard University, wo sie an einer Biografie der bekannten afrodeutschen Schriftstellerin May Ayim gearbeitet hat.

AVERY F. GORDON ist Schriftstellerin, Pädagogin und Radioproduzentin. In ihrer Arbeit geht es um radikales Denken und radikale Praxis. Sie schreibt über Gefangenschaft, Versklavung, Krieg und andere Formen der Enteignung und wie man diese beseitigen kann. Ihr jüngstes Buch ist *The Hawthorn Archive: Letters from the Utopian Margins* (2017).

GEORGE E. LEWIS ist Edwin H. Chase Professor für amerikanische Musik an der Columbia University, außerdem Fachbereichsleiter für Komposition und Mitglied der dortigen Fakultät für historische Musikwissenschaft. Er ist Fellow der American Academy of Arts and Sciences und der American Academy of Arts and Letters, Corresponding Fellow der British Academy und Mitglied der Akademie der Künste Berlin. Seine Musik wurde weltweit aufgeführt. Er gilt als Pionier der interaktiven Computermusik und befasst sich in seiner aktuellen Forschung mit Dekolonisierung und Kreolisierung in der Neuen Musik.

FRANZ LOESER wurde in Breslau geboren und emigrierte 1938 mit einem Kindertransport nach Großbritannien. Als Student in den USA schloss er sich der Kommunistischen Partei an und war daher der Verfolgung durch den McCarthy-Ausschuss ausgesetzt. 1951 wurde er ausgewiesen und siedelte nach Großbritannien um; dort wurde er Generalsekretär des Paul-Robeson-Komitees. 1956 siedelte er in die DDR über; dort war er Leiter der Abteilung für Ethik am Institut für Philosophie der HU. 1983 reiste er nach New York, wo er politisches Asyl beantragte.

STEVE MCQUEEN wurde 1969 in London geboren. Groß angelegte Ausstellungen von McQueens Werk wurden im Pirelli HangarBicocca, der Tate Modern, dem Schaulager und dem Art Institute of Chicago gezeigt. Zu den jüngsten Einzelpräsentationen gehören *Steve McQueen: Year 3* und Ausstellungen im Institute of Contemporary Art in Boston, Massachusetts. Er wurde mit zahlreichen Preisen ausgezeichnet, unter anderem dem Johannes Vermeer Prize, der W. E. B. Du Bois Medal der Harvard University und dem Turner Prize. Er ist Mitglied des Ordens des britischen Weltreichs (OBE 2002, CBE 2011) und wurde 2020 in den Ritterstand erhoben. McQueen hat bei vier Spielfilmen Regie geführt. Er gewann 2008 die Caméra d'Or bei den Filmfestspielen von Cannes und 2014 den Oscar für den besten Kinofilm.

DOREEN MENDE ist Kuratorin, Theoretikerin, Professorin für Curatorial / Politics im Programm „Critical Curatorial Cybernetic Research Practices" an der HEAD Genève, die zur Hochschule für angewandte Wissenschaften und Kunst gehört. Seit 2021 ist sie Leiterin des sammlungsübergreifenden Departments Forschung an den Staatlichen Kunstsammlungen Dresden. Mende ist Gründungsmitglied des Harun Farocki Instituts in Berlin und des European Forum for Advanced Practices sowie Principle Investigator des vom Schweizerischen Nationalfonds geförderten Forschungsprojekts *Decolonizing Socialism: Entangled Internationalism* (2019–2024).

KATHLEEN REINHARDT ist Direktorin des Georg Kolbe Museums in Berlin. Sie hat dort die Ausstellungen *Lin May Saeed: Im Paradies fällt der Schnee langsam. Im Dialog mit René Sintenis* und *Noa Eshkol: No Time to Dance* kuratiert. Von 2016 bis 2022 war sie Kuratorin für Gegenwartskunst am Albertinum der Staatlichen Kunstsammlungen Dresden. An der SKD hat sie Projekte wie *1 Million Rosen für Angela Davis; Für Ruth, der Himmel in Los Angeles* (beide 2021) und *Revolutionary Romances? Globale Kunstgeschichten in der DDR* (2024) realisiert. Reinholdt hat mit einer Arbeit im Bereich afroamerikanischer Kunstgeschichte promoviert. Texte von ihr sind unter anderem im Katalog *Multiple Realities: Experimental Art in the Eastern Bloc 1960s–1980s* (Walker Art Center, 2023) und in Zeitschriften wie *Art Margins* und *Kaleidoscope* erschienen.

MATANA ROBERTS ist ein·e international bekannte·r Komponist·in, Bandleader·in, Saxophonist·in, Klangexperimentator· in und Mixed-Media-Künstler·in. Matana Roberts arbeitet in verschiedenen Kontexten und Medien, darunter Improvisation, Tanz, Lyrik und Theater, größtenteils autodidaktisch. Am bekanntesten ist das vielgepriesene

a multi-chapter work of panoramic sound quilting, Roberts has been invited to teach, lecture, run workshops, and/or take up artistic residencies in a wide range of places and communities. In 2019, they were a fellow in the Artists-in-Berlin Program of the German Academic Exchange Service (DAAD).

ESLANDA GOODE ROBESON was a writer and activist. She attended Columbia University and the London School of Economics, where she earned, respectively, a degree in chemistry and a doctorate in anthropology. While a student at Columbia University, Goode married Paul Robeson. She focused her political activity on the colonized peoples of the world, cofounding the Council on African Affairs in 1941. When summoned to appear before the Committee on Un-American Activities (HUAC) in 1953 to defend her political affiliation, she refused to cooperate and was subject to retribution. After living abroad with her husband, Robeson returned to America when the Vietnam conflict broke out. She spoke out against involvement in the war and in favor of the 1960s peace movement. She died of cancer in 1965.

AARTI SUNDER works with the moving image, writing, and drawing. Her interest lies in technology and our relationship with it—in particular, the study of digital infrastructure. To date, she has focused on contemporary labor practices and the fictional margins of protest, myth, and digital-terrestrial play.

KIRA THURMAN is an assistant professor of Germanic languages and literatures and history at the University of Michigan. A classically trained pianist who grew up in Vienna, Austria, Thurman earned her PhD in history from the University of Rochester with a minor in musicology from the Eastman School of Music.

KATHARINA WARDA is a sociologist and literary scholar. In her work as a freelance author, her main topics are East Germany, marginalized identities, racism, classism, and punk. Her project "Dunkeldeutschland" (Dark Germany) explores the period of post-reunification from the social margins. Based on her own experiences as a Black East German woman, Ward sheds light on the blind spots in German—specifically East German—historiography after 1989/90.

„Coin Coin"-Projekt, ein mehrteiliges „panoramisches Klang-Quilten". Roberts hat an zahlreichen Orten und in einer Vielzahl von Kontexten gelehrt, Vorträge gehalten, Workshops veranstaltet und wurde zu Residencies eingeladen. 2019 war Roberts Stipendiat·in des Berliner Künstlerprogramms des DAAD.

ESLANDA GOODE ROBESON war Schriftstellerin und Aktivistin. Goode besuchte die Columbia University, wo sie einen Abschluss in Chemie machte, und die London School of Economics, wo sie in Anthropologie promovierte. Während ihres Studiums an der Columbia University, heiratete sie Paul Robeson. Goode Robeson konzentrierte ihr politisches Engagement auf die kolonisierten Völker der Welt und gehörte 1941 zu den Gründer·innen des Council on African Affairs. Als sie 1953 vor das Komitee für unamerikanische Umtriebe (HUAC) geladen wurde, um über ihre politische Position befragt zu werden, weigerte sie sich zu kooperieren und musste Repressalien hinnehmen. Nachdem sie mit ihrem Mann im Ausland gelebt hatte, kehrte Robeson nach Amerika zurück, als der Vietnamkonflikt ausbrach. Sie sprach sich gegen den Einstieg der USA in diesen Krieg und für die Friedensbewegung der 1960er Jahre aus. Eslanda Robeson starb 1965 an Krebs.

AARTI SUNDER arbeitet mit bewegten Bildern, sie schreibt und zeichnet. Ihr Interesse richtet sich auf die Technologie und unsere Beziehung zu ihr, vor allem auf die Untersuchung der digitalen Infrastruktur. Bislang hat sie sich auf zeitgenössische Arbeitspraktiken, fiktionale Ränder des Protests, Mythen und digital-terrestrische Spiele konzentriert.

KIRA THURMAN ist Associate Professor für German Studies und Geschichte an der University of Michigan. Die klassisch ausgebildete Pianistin, die in Wien aufgewachsen ist, promovierte an der University of Rochester in Geschichte. Im Nebenfach hat sie an der Eastman School of Music Musikwissenschaft studiert.

KATHARINA WARDA ist Soziologin und Literaturwissenschaftlerin. In ihrer Arbeit als freiberufliche Autorin beschäftigt sie sich vor allem mit Ostdeutschland, marginalisierten Identitäten, Rassismus, Klassismus und Punk. Ihr Projekt „Dunkeldeutschland" erforscht die Zeit nach der Wiedervereinigung von den gesellschaftlichen Rändern aus. Ausgehend von ihren eigenen Erfahrungen als schwarze ostdeutsche Frau beleuchtet Warda die blindenFlecken in der deutschen – insbesondere der ostdeutschen – Geschichtsschreibung nach 1989/90.

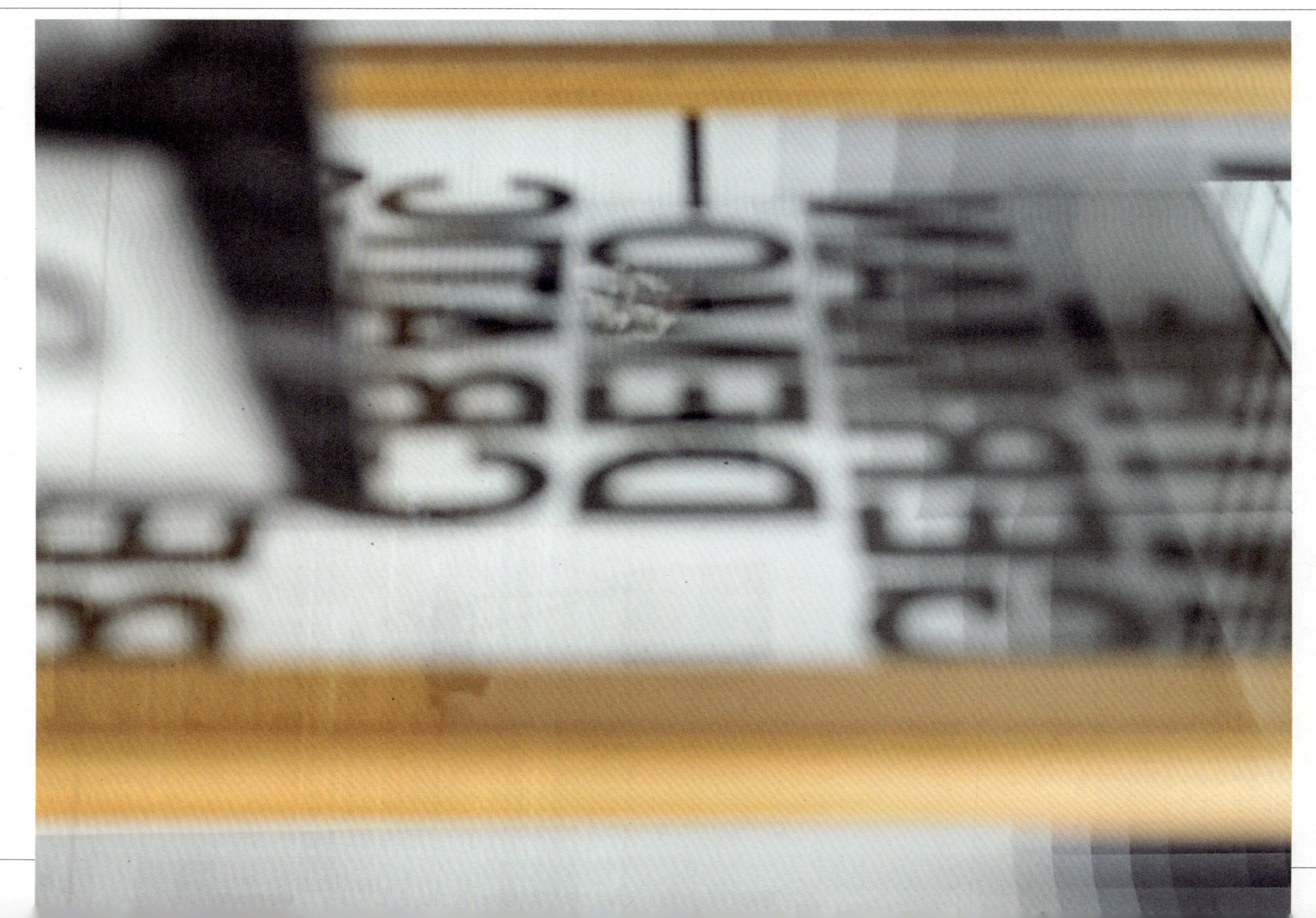

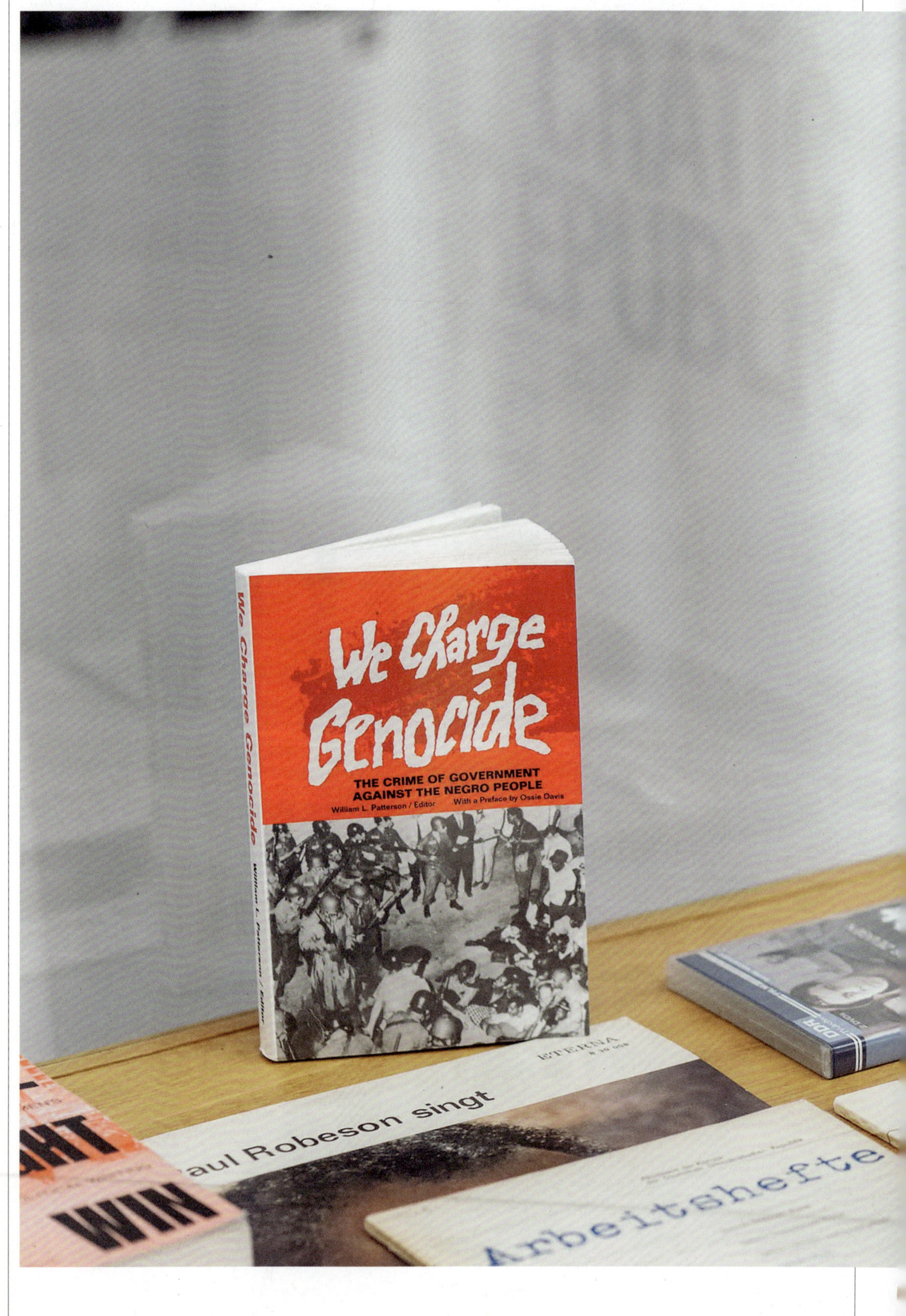
We Charge Genocide
THE CRIME OF GOVERNMENT
AGAINST THE NEGRO PEOPLE
William L. Patterson / Editor   With a Preface by Ossie Davis
We Charge Genocide
William L. Patterson / Editor
ETERNA
Paul Robeson singt
Arbeitshefte
FIGHT
WIN
DDR

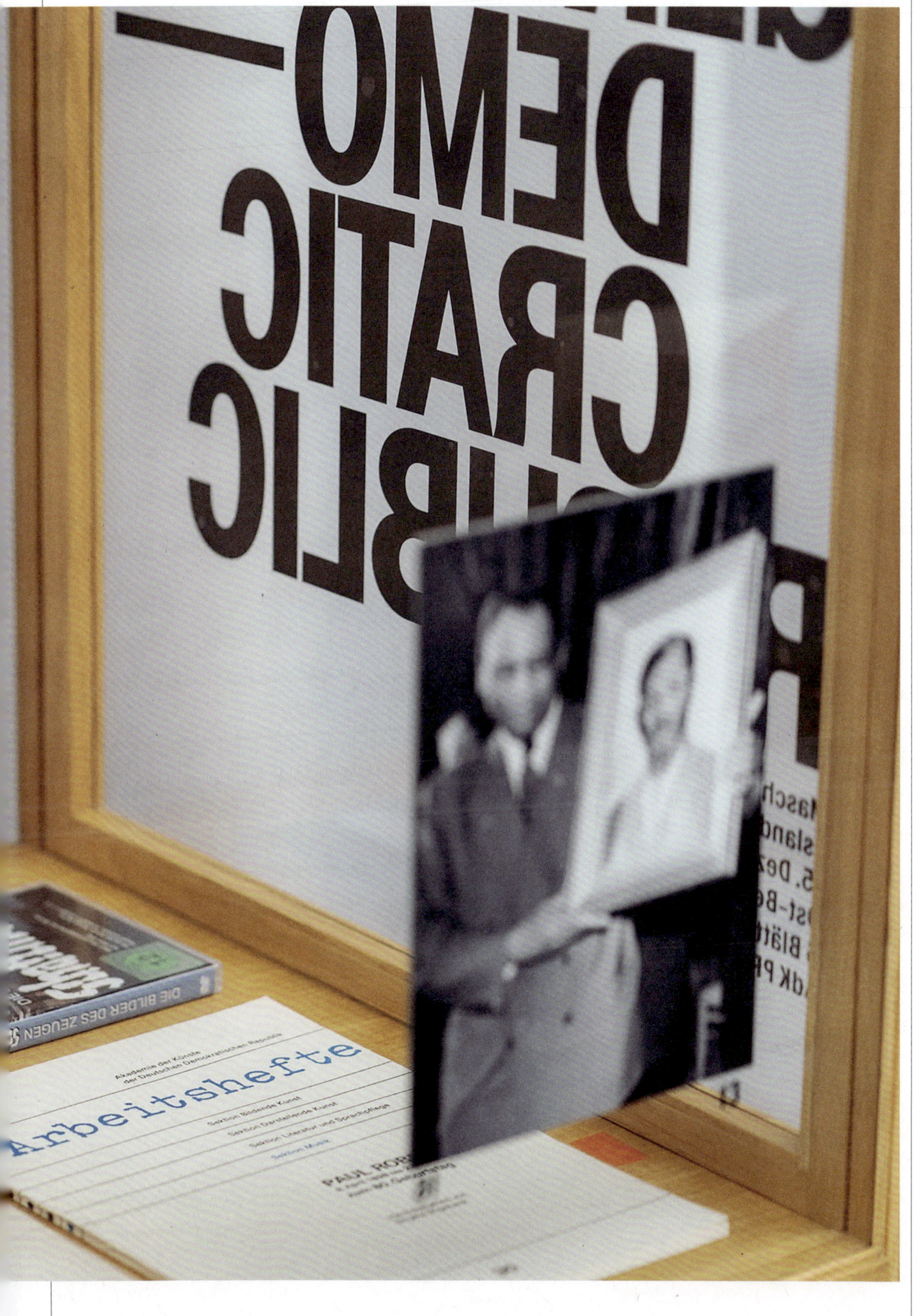

DEMO
CRATIC
UBLIC
Arbeitshefte
Akademie der Künste
der Deutschen Demokratischen Republik
Sektion Bildende Kunst
Sektion Darstellende Kunst
Sektion Literatur und Sprachpflege
Sektion Musik
DIE BILDER DES ZEUGEN

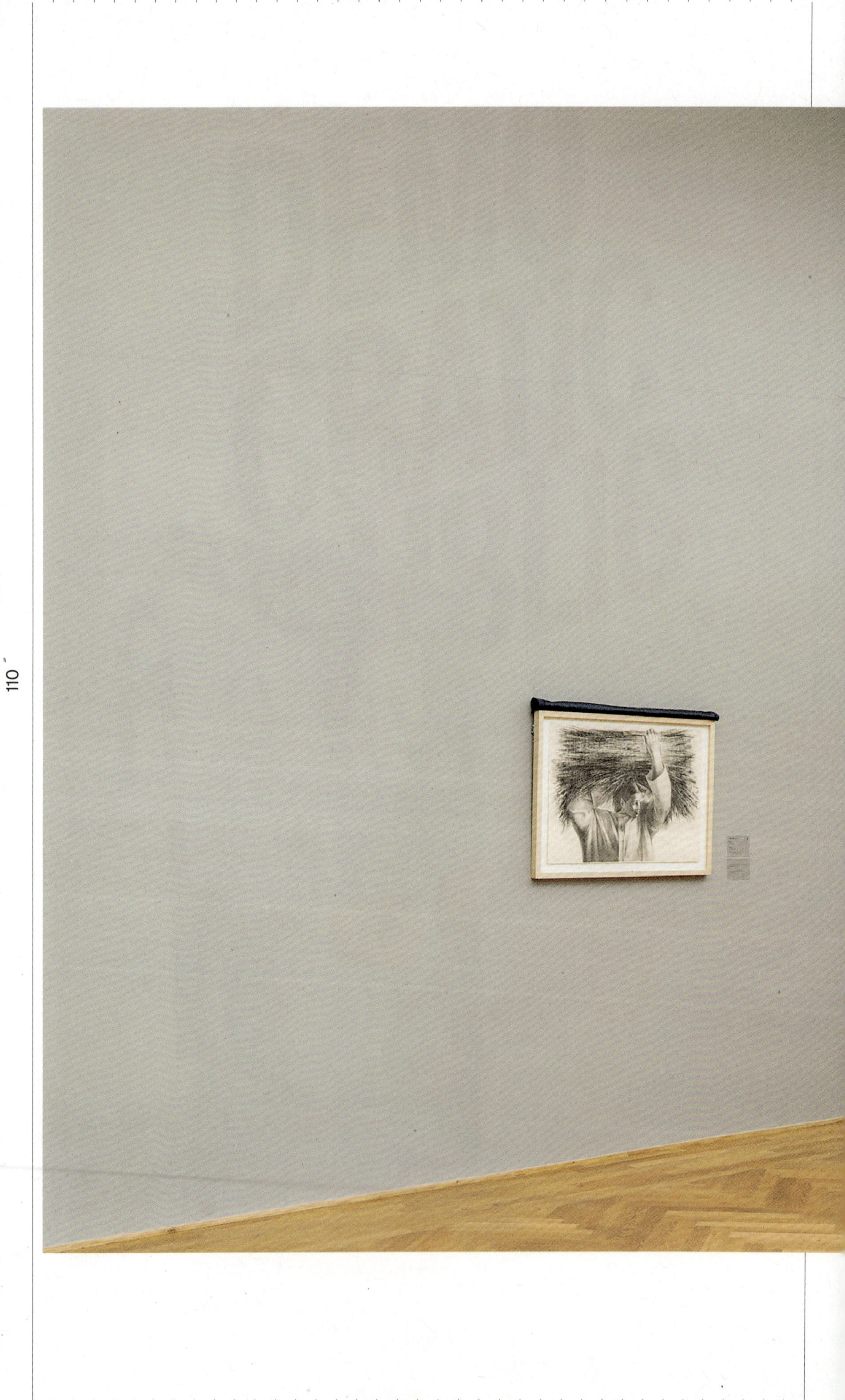

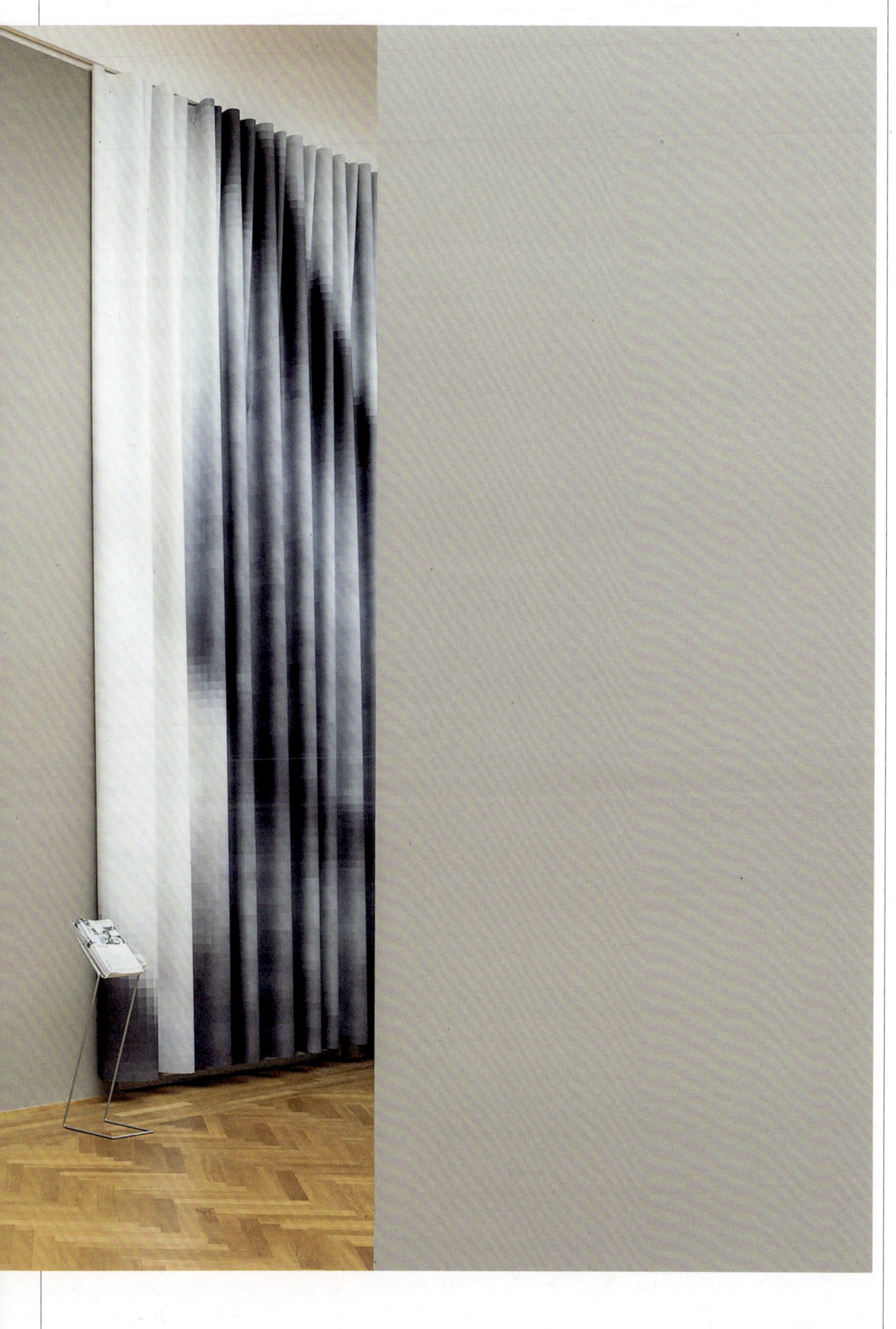

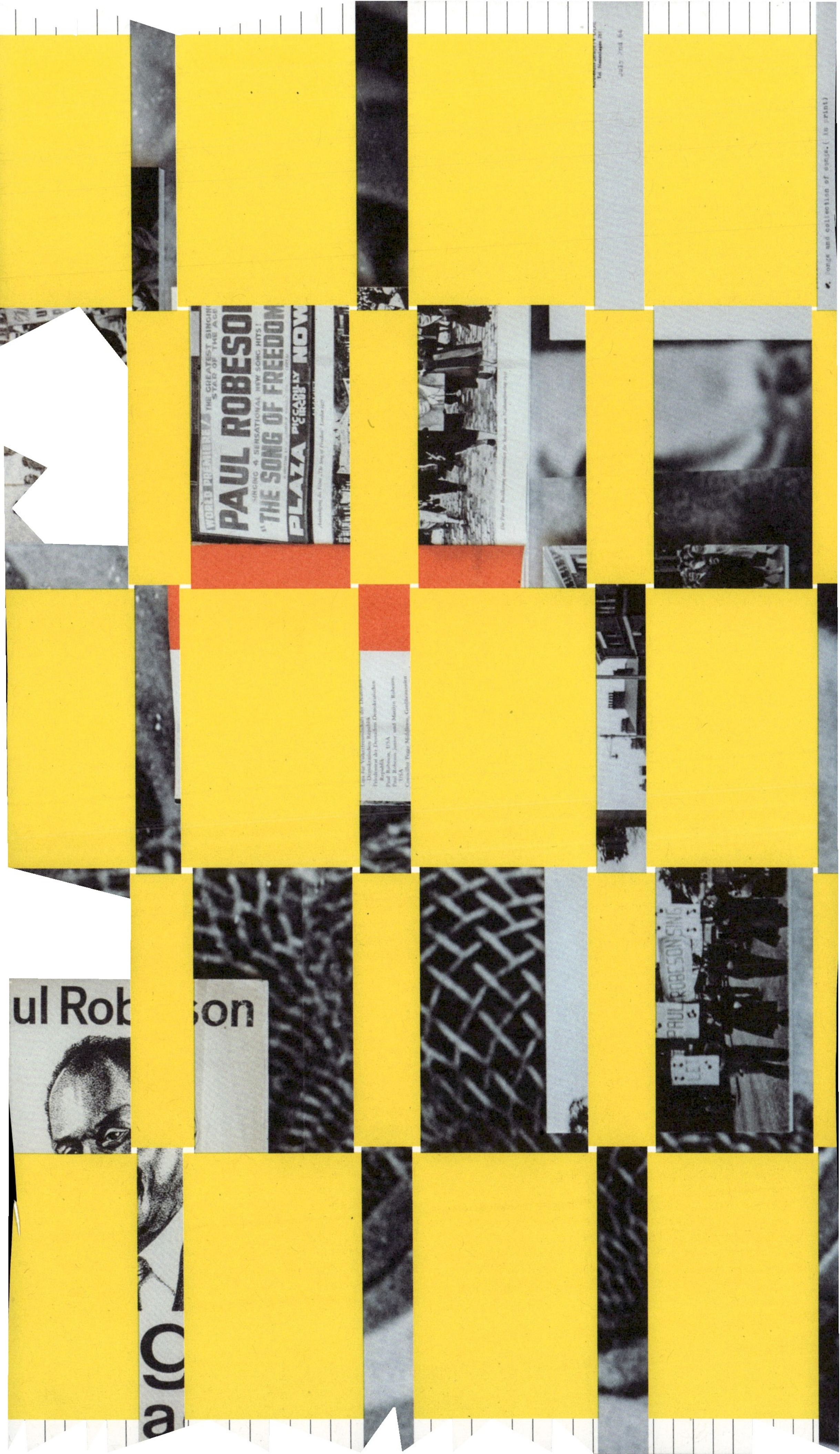

PAUL ROBESON
THE GREATEST SINGING STAR OF THE AGE
SINGING 4 SENSATIONAL NEW SONG HITS !
"THE SONG OF FREEDOM"
PLAZA
PICCADILLY CIRCUS
NOW
ul Rob   son
PAUL ROBESON SING
songs and collection of songs.(in print)

Entangled Internationalisms
Series editors: Staatliche Kunstsammlungen Dresden,
Doreen Mende,
with HEAD – Genève (HES-SO)

Till the Sun Rises, edited by vinit agarwal
Troubled Comradeship in the Arts, edited by Lea Marie
Nienhoff and Ambre Alfredo
The Missed Seminar, edited by Doreen Mende and
Avery F. Gordon
Reflexive Tema and Global Elsewheres …, edited by Kwasi
Ohene-Ayeh

The Missed Seminar
Edited by Doreen Mende and Avery F. Gordon
Editorial coordination: Christin Krause, Jan Wenzel
Production: Oliver Baurhenn (October 2024–December
2024), Jesi Khadivi (October–December 2024), Elisabeth
Schmidt (January–September 2024)
Translation: Philipp Albers (EN–DE), Elisa Barth (EN–DE),
Simon Cowper (DE–EN), Faith Ann Gibson (DE–EN),
Mandi Gomez (DE–EN), Lina Morawetz (EN–DE)
Copyediting English: Simon Cowper
Copyediting German: Jan-Frederik Bandel
Research coordination: Océane Vé-Réveillac (until
September 2024)
Design and concept: Malin Gewinner and Lyosha Kritsouk
Lithography: Aleksey Novikov
Printing and binding: Druckhaus Sportflieger, Berlin

The Missed Seminar. After Eslanda Robeson. In Conversation
with Steve McQueen's End Credits is part of HKW's project
The New Alphabet, supported by the Federal Government
Commissioner for Culture and the Media due to a ruling of
the German Bundestag, and realized in collaboration with the
Staatliche Kunstsammlungen Dresden (SKD).

The academic research for the case studies was made
possible by the project funded by the Swiss National
Science Foundation (#184864) *Decolonizing Socialism:
Entangled Internationalism* (2019–2024) at HEAD – Genève,
part of the University of Applied Sciences and Arts
(HES-SO), Geneva.

The production of the artistic research edition was funded
by the Federal Government Commissioner for Culture
and the Media as part of the project "Museums as Active
Places of Democracy" (MODemo).

Published by
Spector Books
Harkortstraße 10
04107 Leipzig
www.spectorbooks.com

Distribution:
Germany, Austria: GVA, Gemeinsame Verlagsauslieferung
Göttingen GmbH & Co. KG, www.gva-verlage.de
Switzerland: AVA Verlagsauslieferung AG, www.ava.ch
France, Belgium: Interart Paris, www.interart.fr
United Kingdom: Central Books Ltd, www.centralbooks.com
USA, Canada, Central and South America,
Africa: ARTBOOK/ D.A.P., www.artbook.com
South Korea: The Book Society, www.thebooksociety.org
Japan: twelvebooks, https://twelve-books.com
Australia, New Zealand: Perimeter Distribution,
www.perimeterdistribution.com

© 2024, Staatliche Kunstsammlungen Dresden,
Spector Books OHG, Leipzig, authors, artists
1st edition: 2024
Printed in Germany
ISBN 978-3-95905-879-7

funded by

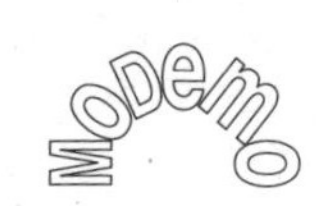

Staatliche
Kunstsammlungen
Dresden

 Federal Government Commissioner
for Culture and the Media

Verflochtene Internationalismen
Herausgeber der Reihe: Staatliche Kunstsammlungen
Dresden, Doreen Mende
mit HEAD – Genève der HES-SO

Bis zum Sonnenaufgang, hg. von vinit agarwal
Kameradschaft in den Künsten,
hg. von Lea Marie Nienhoff und Ambre Alfredo
Das versäumte Seminar,
hg. von Doreen Mende und Avery F. Gordon
Tema und seine globalen Widerspiegelungen …,
hg. von Kwasi Ohene-Ayeh

Das versäumte Seminar
Herausgegeben von: Doreen Mende und Avery F. Gordon
Editorische Koordination: Christin Krause, Jan Wenzel
Produktion: Oliver Baurhenn (Oktober bis Dezember 2024),
Jesi Khadivi (Oktober bis Dezember 2024), Elisabeth
Schmidt (Januar bis September 2024)
Übersetzung: Philipp Albers (EN–DE), Elisa Barth (EN–DE),
Simon Cowper (DE–EN), Faith Ann Gibson (DE–EN), Mandi
Gomez (DE–EN), Lina Morawetz (EN–DE)
Lektorat Englisch: Simon Cowper
Lektorat Deutsch: Jan-Frederik Bandel
Koordination der Forschung: Océane Vé-Réveillac
(bis September 2024)
Gestaltung und Konzept: Malin Gewinner und Lyosha Kritsouk
Bildbearbeitung: Aleksey Novikov
Druck und Bindung: Druckhaus Sportflieger, Berlin

The Missed Seminar. Nach Eslanda Robeson. Im Dialog mit
Steve McQueen's End Credits war Teil des HKW-Projekts
Das Neue Alphabet (2019–2022), das durch Die Beauftragte
der Bundesregierung für Kultur und Medien aufgrund eines
Beschlusses des Deutschen Bundestages gefördert und
in Zusammenarbeit mit den Staatlichen Kunstsammlungen
Dresden (SKD) realisiert wurde.

Die akademische Forschung für die Fallstudien wurde im
Rahmen des durch den Schweizerischen Nationalfonds
(#184864) finanzierten Projektes *Decolonizing Socialism.
Entangled Internationalism* (2019–2024) an der
HEAD – Genève der HES-SO ermöglicht.

Die Produktion der künstlerischen Forschungsedition
wurde im Rahmen des Projektes „Museen als aktive Orte
der Demokratie" (MODemo) von der Beauftragten
der Bundesregierung für Kultur und Medien gefördert.

Erschienen im Verlag
Spector Books
Harkortstraße 10
04107 Leipzig
www.spectorbooks.com

Vertrieb:
Deutschland, Österreich: GVA, Gemeinsame
Verlagsauslieferung Göttingen GmbH & Co. KG,
www.gva-verlage.de
Schweiz: AVA Verlagsauslieferung AG, www.ava.ch
Frankreich, Belgien: Interart Paris, www.interart.fr
Vereinigtes Königreich: Central Books Ltd,
www.centralbooks.com
USA, Kanada, Mittel- und Südamerika,
Afrika: ARTBOOK / D.A.P., www.artbook.com
Südkorea: The Book Society, www.thebooksociety.org
Japan: twelvebooks, https://twelve-books.com
Australien, Neuseeland: Perimeter Distribution,
www.perimeterdistribution.com

© 2024, Staatliche Kunstsammlungen Dresden,
Spector Books OHG, Leipzig, Autor•innen, Künstler•innen
1. Auflage: 2024
Printed in Germany
ISBN 978-3-95905-879-7

gefördert von

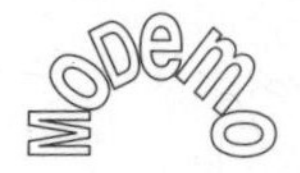

Staatliche
Kunstsammlungen
Dresden

Die Beauftragte der Bundesregierung
für Kultur und Medien

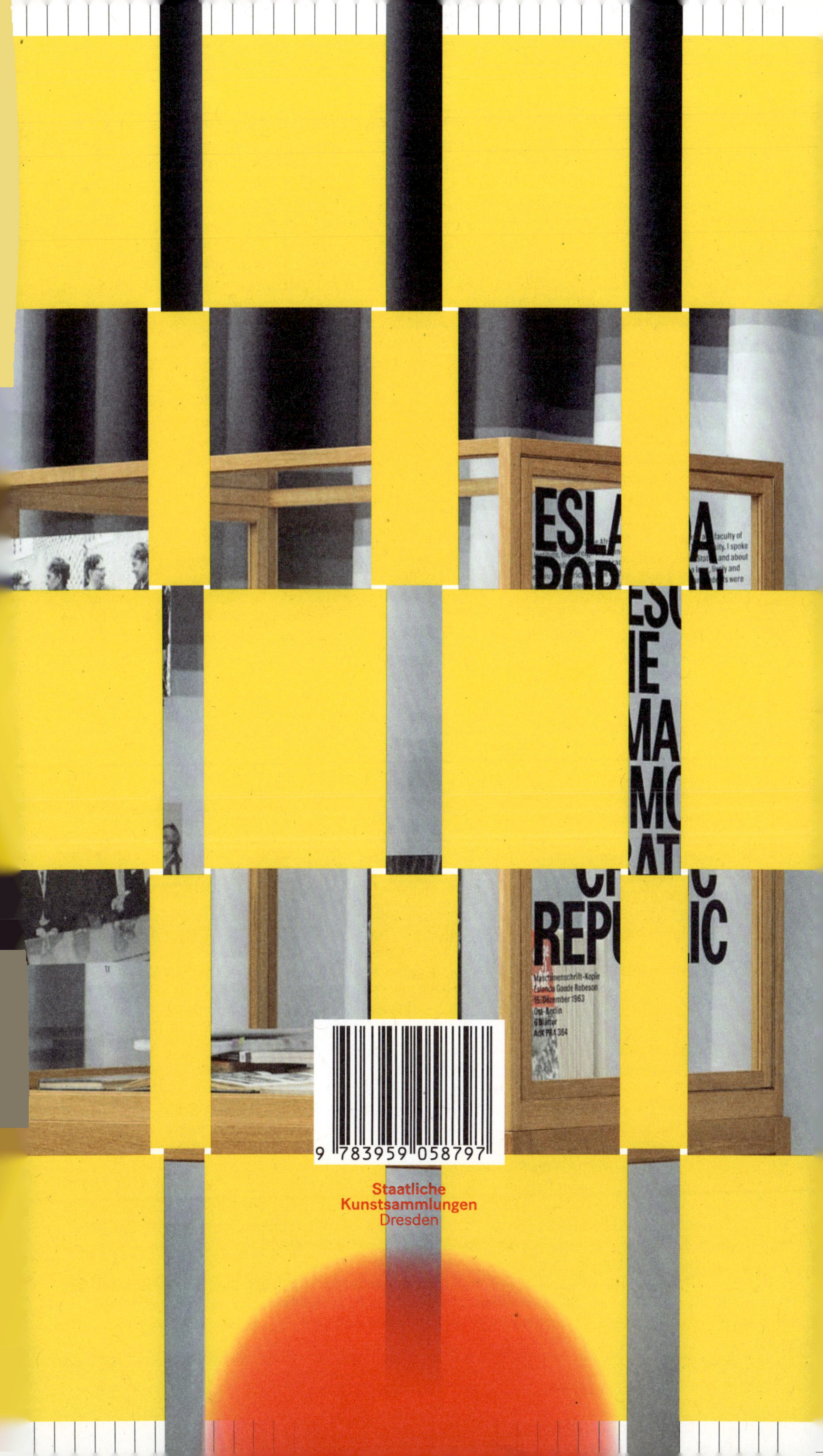

9 783959 058797

ACKNOWLEDGEMENTS

Without the trust, input, and support of numerous people, the realization of the artistic research edition as a series would not have been possible. At the Dresden State Art Collections (Staatliche Kunstsammlungen Dresden, SKD), my very special thanks go to Hilke Wagner and her team at the Albertinum, to Stephanie Buck and her team at the Museum of Prints, Drawings and Photographs (Kupferstich-Kabinett), to Kathi Loch and her team at the Puppet Theatre Collection, to Marius Winzeler and his team at the Green Vault (Grünes Gewölbe) and Dresden Armory (Rüstkammer), to Sylvia Karges and her team at the Coin Collection (Münzkabinett), to Léontine Meijer van Mensch and her team of the State Ethnographic Collections of Saxony (Staatliche Ethnographische Sammlungen Sachsen) in Dresden and Leipzig, to Vera Wobad of the inhouse archive of SKD, to Tanja Schomaker and Christine Gerbich from Outreach und Gesellschaft for managing the project "Museums as Active Places of Democracy" (MODemo), to Nina C. Illgen for fundraising, to Cindy Mehliß for budget management, and to my wonderful core research team, Oliver Baurhenn, Romy Jeschke, Michael Mäder, Anna-Lisa Reith, Thomas Rudert, and Elisabeth Schmidt. Last but not least, my sincerest thanks for their foresight to the SKD's Director General Marion Ackermann and Commercial Director Cornelia Rabeneck with her team, specifically Romy Kraut.

I would also like to thank my colleagues in Switzerland: the directors of HEAD – Genève (HES-SO) Jean-Pierre Greff and Lada Umstätter, as head of the Institut de recherche en art et en design (IRAD) and, above all, Christelle Granite-Noble for budget management at HEAD – Genève (HES-SO). I thank Ute Holl and Kenny Cupers of the University of Basel for their kindness and collaboration and Susanne Grossniklaus from the Swiss National Science Foundation for their unwavering support of the process.

Without the scientific/artistic coordination of the academic project *Decolonizing Socialism: Entangled Internationalism* (2019–2024) by vinit agarwal, Rada Leu, and Océane Vé-Réveillac, the process would not have come to fruition. Thank you very much—your work has been invaluable! I would like to sincerely thank the PhD researcher of the project, the historian and theater pedagogue Lea Marie Nienhoff, for her thoughtful contributions to the overall project.

My sincere thanks go to Jan Wenzel and Christin Krause from Spector Books for developing the concept of the research edition. I would also like to express my deep appreciation for the work put in by Jesi Khadivi, who joined the editorial process in its final phase. Malin Gewinner and Lyosha Kritsouk are responsible for the stunning design concept of the research edition!

Doreen Mende, December 2024

DANK

Ohne das Vertrauen, die Gespräche und die Unterstützung zahlreicher Menschen wäre die Umsetzung der künstlerischen Forschungsedition als Reihe nicht möglich gewesen. Im Kontext der Staatlichen Kunstsammlungen Dresden (SKD) gehen meine ganz besonderen Dankesgrüße an Hilke Wagner und ihr Team im Albertinum, an Stephanie Buck und ihr Team des Kupferstich-Kabinetts, an Kathi Loch und ihr Team der Puppentheatersammlung, an Marius Winzeler und seine Teams des Grünen Gewölbes und der Rüstkammer, an Sylvia Karges und ihr Team des Münzkabinetts an Léontine Meijer van Mensch und ihr Team der Staatlichen Ethnografischen Sammlungen Sachsen, an Vera Wobad vom Hausarchiv der SKD, an Tanja Schomaker und Christine Gerbich von Outreach und Gesellschaft für die Projektleitung „Museen als aktive Orte der Demokratie", an Nina C. Illgen für das Fundraising, an Cindy Mehliß für das Budget-Controlling und an mein wunderbares Kernteam in der Abteilung Forschung: Oliver Baurhenn, Romy Jeschke, Michael Mäder, Anna-Lisa Reith, Thomas Rudert und Elisabeth Schmidt. Nicht zuletzt mein aufrichtigster Dank für ihre Weitsicht an die Generaldirektorin der SKD Marion Ackermann sowie an die Kaufmännische Direktorin Cornelia Rabeneck mit ihrem Team, insbesondere Romy Kraut.

Ebenso möchte ich meinen Kolleg·innen in der Schweiz sehr herzlich danken: Jean-Pierre Greff (bis Dezember 2022) und Lada Umstätter (seit Januar 2023) als Rektor beziehungsweise Rektorin sowie Anthony Masure als Leiter des Institut de recherche en art et en design (IRAD) und vor allem Christelle Granite-Noble für das Budget-Management an der HEAD – Genève der HES-SO; für die Freundschaft und Zusammenarbeit danke ich Ute Holl und Kenny Cupers an der Universität Basel; Susanne Grossniklaus gilt mein Dank für die immer prozessorientierte Betreuung durch den Schweizerischen Nationalfonds.

Ohne die wissenschaftliche/künstlerische Koordination des akademischen Projkts *Decolonizing Socialism. Entangled Internationalism* (2019–2024) von vinit agarwal, Rada Leu und Océane Vé-Réveillac wäre der Prozess nicht umsetzbar gewesen, vielen Dank! Der Doktorandin in diesem Projekt, der Historikerin und Theaterpädagogin Lea Marie Nienhoff, danke ich aufrichtig für ihr mitdenkendes Mitgestalten des Gesamtprojektes.

Für die überaus freundschaftliche Zusammenarbeit gilt mein aufrichtiger Dank Jan Wenzel und Christin Krause von Spector Books. Malin Gewinner und Lyosha Kritsouk zeichnen für das umwerfende Designkonzept der Forschungsedition verantwortlich!

Doreen Mende, Dezember 2024